THE TRIBE

Also by Carlos Manuel Álvarez

The Fallen

THE TRIBE
Portraits of Cuba

Carlos Manuel Álvarez
Translated from the Spanish by Frank Wynne with Rahul Bery

Graywolf Press

English translation of "Offside," "Broken Doll," and "Fidel, the Butcher" copyright © 2022 by Rahul Bery. English translation of all other essays copyright © 2022 by Frank Wynne.

First published in Spanish with the title *La Tribu* in 2017 by Sexto Piso, Mexico City and Madrid. Originally published in English translation by Fitzcarraldo Editions in Great Britain in 2022. "Broken Doll" first appeared in the *Yale Review*. "Boarding Pass" first appeared in *Granta*.

The excerpt from *The Knight and Death* by Leonardo Sciascia that appears on page 296 was translated by Joseph Farrell (London: Granta Books, 2003).

This publication is made possible, in part, by the voters of Minnesota through a Minnesota State Arts Board Operating Support grant, thanks to a legislative appropriation from the arts and cultural heritage fund. Significant support has also been provided by the McKnight Foundation, the Lannan Foundation, the Amazon Literary Partnership, and other generous contributions from foundations, corporations, and individuals. To these organizations and individuals we offer our heartfelt thanks.

MINNESOTA
STATE ARTS BOARD

CLEAN
WATER
LAND &
LEGACY
AMENDMENT

Published by Graywolf Press
212 Third Avenue North, Suite 485
Minneapolis, Minnesota 55401

All rights reserved.

www.graywolfpress.org

Published in the United States of America

ISBN 978-1-64445-090-1 (paperback)
ISBN 978-1-64445-178-6 (ebook)

2 4 6 8 9 7 5 3 1
First Graywolf Printing, 2022

Library of Congress Control Number: 2021945922

Cover design: Kapo Ng

Cover photo: João Pina

For Carla, whom I love, and who loves me.

There is nothing more difficult than to be a stepson of the time.

—VASILY GROSSMAN, *LIFE AND FATE*,
TRANSLATED BY ROBERT CHANDLER

CONTENTS

THE TRIBE

POST-CASTRO CUBA, AN APPROXIMATION

I

It is December 17, 2014. Barack Obama and Raúl Castro are announcing to the world that, after fifty-three years of hostile rift, the United States and Cuba are restoring diplomatic relations. Needless to say, this news is not as momentous to Americans as it is to Cubans. Hence the fact that the announcement leaves no gringos bewildered, wondering what is happening and what will happen next.

Cubans, on the other hand—we who effortlessly make an epic of the everyday, who don't hesitate to declare the slightest skirmish or governmental whim a historic event—are instantly eaten up by questions, and frantically searching for some kind of clarity in our neighbors' opinions in a way we never have before.

In the meantime, something exists that should not. Something that, in its present form, is unsustainable. A state of mind, perhaps: indecision, inertia, amnesia. Or the run-of-the-mill commonplace: our Cold War mindset, our deeply ideological, sentimental education, a boundless bureaucracy, a ravaged social infrastructure. Beautiful, punch-drunk people that we are.

In an attempt to take no risks, Cuba took the greatest risk of all: it took none. As though the government has spent decades instilling in us the belief that the historical race we were running was a marathon, and to suddenly decide, with the beginnings of the thaw, that actually it wasn't. The distance was—and is—a hundred-meter sprint, and we were competing against a country guilty of doping.

The first great test of the schism that has just riven the Cuban people can be found in our psyche. Here was something that would not only change the course of our economic, cultural, and social realities, which in itself was more than enough, but that forced us to reinvent our language, the words we commonly used, the concepts to which we had adapted ourselves as a nation. Official policy abruptly changed, and with it the relationship and the discourse each of us had with that power, whatever the feelings it inspired in us: trust, love, hatred, disappointment, enthusiasm, revulsion. On *Mesa Redonda* (the televisual incarnation of official Cuban policy), the talking heads who, only a week earlier, were still referring to the United States as an "imperial force," now, with an equanimity verging on effrontery, used the word "neighbor."

And they were right after all. From then on, the United States was to be our neighbor. A notion that, if voiced by some reckless soul as recently as last night, would have earned them the shameful label "antipatriotic." The lines so routinely trotted out in history books—"Such-and-such a country went to bed capitalist and woke up communist," or "such-and-such a region went to bed feudal and woke up bourgeois"—were literally true in this case. Once upon a time, Cuba had cherished the magnificent dream of the Revolution, and our tragedy stemmed from the attempt to prolong that dream. After a long, protracted suspension spanning five decades, we woke to find the great ontological questions once again rattling around our brain: How are we going to contend with the United States? What will come of this struggle? Will our country be better or worse?

But there's a certain wariness to what's happening. As though the euphoria has been internalized, as though euphoria has left us anesthetized. We splutter. We babble clichés. Rapture is a rare and slightly irrational phenomenon for us, like an opiate ingested by the whole island, a collective drug smoked by everyone. And in a sense, our reaction seems reasonable. Having spent so many years marching for every triviality, waving banners and placards to celebrate as many anniversaries as possible, we now deserve to celebrate the other way, silence as a scream.

Today there was a prisoner swap in which three pro-Castro intelligence agents were returned in exchange for an American government contractor and an American intelligence officer of Cuban origin. Newspaper headlines trumpeted the return of the three agents—who, with two colleagues who had already returned, had been raised to the rank of heroes. The front pages showed them at home, reunited with their families. The three of them meeting with Raúl Castro. Their return to their districts. Their neighbors hugging them and and carrying them on their shoulders.

"Los cinco Cubanos"—the Cuban Five—were part of the *Red Avispa*—the Wasp Network. In 1998, they had been arrested by the FBI, charged with infiltrating an anti-Castro organization in Miami, and given sentences of varying lengths. In Cuba, no mention was made of them until June 2001: the date on which they were sentenced and the beginning of yet another movement of national liberation, one that—if what was said was to be believed—marked the latest epic crusade in the ongoing Revolution.

For sixteen years, Los Cinco have been a constant presence in our lives. They are mentioned on the radio in the context of the most unpredictable subjects. Danny Glover comments on their case. Naive hands daub portraits of their malnourished faces on city walls, school murals, and the doorways of job centers. High-ranking politicians weave the subject into their speeches. Medal-winning sportspeople offer them their gold, silver, or bronze. Absolutely everything is dedicated to Los Cinco.

——

A couple of days later, near the Estadio Latinoamericano, Silvio Rodríguez staged one of his free concerts in a poorer neighborhood. The Cuban Five were in attendance. At the end of the performance, one of them grabbed the microphone and shouted two slogans: "¡Viva Cuba libre!" and "¡Seguimos en combate!" Obsolete mottos, things no one says anymore. Slogans that date back eighteen years, to a time before Los Cinco's arrest. They are unaware of everything that has happened in the interim, a period they embody. And they are precisely what separates them from their country. The slogans we are familiar with are slogans that honor them. When the agent in question stepped up to the microphone, it was one slogan shouting another slogan.

What tone should we adopt when the speech patterns of fearless heroism have faded? Those same speech patterns that were the backbone of our education. An incantation unfit for purpose, one we long to shake off, yet one that conjures the affection of an old friend, that inspires nostalgia. With a flicker of dread, we are discovering that the good news is usurping our voice, because our whole vocabulary is based on confrontation, on warlike imagery. On December 17, Cubans are celebrating a possibility, something that may come to pass, but we are also suffering the heartache of a tribe laying its dialect to rest.

II

In early 2015, there are rumors circulating that Fidel Castro is dead, though for the time being, he is still alive—in fact, he will not die until the end of this book. Fears over his state of health are fueled by a specific detail. There have been no pictures—there will be none until early March—of the supreme leader of Cuba meeting with the three recently liberated agents.

January 6 sees the birth of Gema, daughter of Gerardo Hernández, the leader of *Red Avispa*—a gift from the Three Wise Men of socialism. The details are curious: when Gerardo returned to Cuba, his wife, Adriana Pérez, was already eight months pregnant. The insemination—we found out later—was the result of a high-level political agreement involving influential US senators and the highest echelons of the Cuban general staff.

It is likely that Gema is as much the daughter of Gerardo and Adriana as she is of the weariness between warring enemies. A pregnancy that lasted nine months, and also spanned fifty-three years. I don't know how Gema was delivered. But if it was by caesarean, it was a historic one. Press coverage of her birth veered between political thriller, romance novel, and socialist realism, penned by John Le Carré, Corín Tellado, and Boris Polevoy.

Gema showed us that when you mix Le Carré, Tellado, and Polevoy, the result is Orwell lite, tropical Orwell. A news story in the worst press in the world before she was even considered a person. A baby who, given all the things that had befallen her, already seemed very old.

The little girl who was born when Castro was dying.

———

From the outset, the Obama administration authorized an increase in the limit of annual money transfers that Cuban Americans could send to the island from $2,000 to $8,000. Obama also ended the requirement that those sending money have a special license and expanded commercial sales and exports from the United States of certain goods and services, seeking to "empower the nascent Cuban private sector."

Havana was quickly flooded with tourists. Hipsters from all over the world rushed to book their flights. All desperate to see the last retro corner of the Western world before it disappeared. With classic cars from the 1950s, no WhatsApp, no smartphones, a place where people did not stare at touchscreens as they headed to work, being too busy elbowing their way onto overcrowded buses.

If you were to tell a zealous revolutionary what these hipsters are thinking, that the old-world charm of Havana would never face down the onslaught of consumerism, the zealous revolutionary would think the hipsters were rabid capitalists, harbingers of evil who filed their teeth and dreamed only of the moment when socialism—this bargain-basement version—disappears.

Meanwhile, on calle Concordia in downtown Havana I stumbled across what I think must be the definitive image of the Revolution. On a street corner, two men sitting on upturned buckets, a board laid over their laps. Next to them, a plastic cup with a shot of rum. Their expressions utterly engrossed, so oblivious to the bustle all around them that you could only classify them as haughty. There is nothing about them that does not scream poverty, or even indigence.

Except that these men are not playing dominos. They're not playing dice. They're not playing *brisca*, or even poker. They're not playing any of the games such men usually play. They are playing chess. One of them reaches out and moves his bishop.

—

Around January 10 or 11, the rumors about Fidel Castro's death begin to fade. What could be killing him?

The knowledge that this new era has no place for him, that there is no way for him to play a leading role? Exasperation at the fact that an agreement has been reached with the United States and that, however good it might seem, he represents the polar opposite? Or the reverse: the joy of someone who has finally achieved his goal and now feels he can rest in peace?

On January 12, somewhere in the world, Maradona shows off a letter Fidel Castro has sent him, and the least important question is what is in the letter. If Fidel Castro wants to say something to Maradona, he doesn't have to send a letter; this isn't the nineteenth century. He could call him on his cell phone. Talk to him on Skype (assuming he has Skype, since no one else in Cuba does). Maradona is only the pretext. The true purpose of the letter is to shut people's mouths. Or open them wider, who knows?

To his defenders, the fact that Castro is still alive is a political victory; to his bitter enemies it is a defeat. The embodiment of the ideological struggle between Castroist and anti-Castroist forces is a little abstract. Logically, death is neither capitalist nor socialist. Death is the most democratic of dictators.

═══

On January 21, the first round of diplomatic negotiations begins in Havana. People are worried the talks will break down, that we will suddenly wake up and this whole thing will dissolve. Cuba as Sleeping Beauty who, after half a century, is waiting for a kiss. Cuba, so chaste, so stately, a snooty communist lady, who, with a single kiss, could be turned back into a simpering teenager.

The neo-Stalinists are the nation's father: they do not want their daughter to spread her legs. The pro-Yankees are the pimp, prepared to sell her on the first street corner. The ordinary people—the befuddled populace—are the meek, submissive mother who worries, who does not like to forbid, does not know whether it is better for her daughter to stay at home, date boys, go out on the town, or pack her bags and get the hell out. The government could be seen as the nation's grandfather, who firmly believes the people still hang on his every word, when in fact they politely pretend to listen while he rambles on.

Obviously, there are other terms—age-old terms—to frame the subject: sovereignty, independence, capitalism, equality, revolution, fatherland. But politics is also a love affair.

Exactly one week later, on the anniversary of José Martí's birth, Fidel Castro sends a message to the University Student Federation: "I do not trust the policy of the United States," it reads, "nor have I exchanged a word with them, but this is not, in any way, a rejection of a peaceful solution to conflicts and the dangers of war."

Everyone knows the message has come from him. First, because until now, the only people who have lied about the state of his health are those in the media who want him to die. Every time the official press has affirmed that he is alive, he has been alive. Second, because the message—which is significantly longer—bears the unmistakable stamp of his recent ruminations. A hodgepodge of the same topics: climate change, the extinction of life on earth, the squandering of natural resources, the danger of a global holocaust, the evils of capitalism, the inequality between rich and poor.

And, in between these topics, he would jump from one subject to another, whatever came to mind: Mao Zedong, the Big Bang Theory, Carl Sagan, the Bilderberg Group, memories of the Sierra Madre, Guayasamín, Kennedy, Reagan, Savimbi, Martí, Erich Honecker, ancient Greece, and so on, without pausing for breath, trying to link together things that seem—and indeed *are*—impossible to link. Gone—long gone—are the days of the unstoppable evangelist.

It is January 2015. And here we are, marathon runners with mud-spattered bodies, on the starting blocks of the one-hundred-meter sprint, trying to run it in ten seconds flat.

III

This is the portrait of the ending of a cycle: who are we, and in what conditions will we reach the end of the long trek that was the Revolution? We had faith and we have lost it; we have been maimed by impossible forces; we have run away; we have stood firm; we survived and we did not survive. What was this faith? Why did we lose it?

What do Cubans talk about when we talk about ourselves?

Throughout this book there is a parade of exiled sportspeople, major figures in conceptual art, internationalist physicians, celebrated musicians, and from the underworld, dissident poets, emigrants who trekked through Central America, fugitives from the FBI, homeless people and suicides, black marketeers, schizoid *balseros* who fled the country aboard makeshift rafts, and the drunkards, cops, and transvestites who teem in the riotous Havana nights.

The panorama created by these characters is as it is. I have not tried to unify them or set them apart, nor use them to prove some existing thesis, nor search in their stories for some new connecting thread, some registered trademark of what it means to be Cuban. This is the representation of a country.

This book also features the orthopedist Rodolfo Navarro, who deserves special mention because he is literally the last soldier of the Revolution.

In late afternoon on April 16, 2016, in his house in Puyo, the capital of Pastaza, in the Ecuadorian Amazon, Navarro feels a tremor that, at first, simply arouses his curiosity. On the other side of the country, a powerful earthquake measuring 7.8 on the Richter scale has just claimed the first victims of the hundreds of fatalities and thousands of injured that will be reported all along the Pacific coast of Ecuador in the following days.

Navarro immediately volunteers to help. He is fifty years old and his moral code is guided by the altruistic and militant example of Che Guevara. He packs a rucksack and when he presents himself at the Ministry of Health, he is firmly convinced that he is doing so because at some point the Revolution taught him it was the right thing to do. At the Ministry of Health he is told that he is not needed right now and that, in the event he is, they will come and find him. Frustrated, Navarro logs on to Facebook and publishes a post demanding that his skills be called on somewhere.

Since 2013 and the reform of emigration policy that made it possible for Cubans to travel abroad without governmental restriction, Ecuador has become a kind of obsession. It is one of the few countries that does not require Cubans to obtain visas. Tens of thousands go there, some to settle, others with the intention of traveling through Central America to the United States.

In September 2014, having returned to Cuba after a medical mission to Venezuela, Navarro signs up for a program called *Ecuador saludable*, which urged doctors to relocate, and in doing so became a living example of the Revolution fleeing the Revolution.

—

Medical internationalism, perhaps more than anything else, reflects the caricature to which Cuba has been reduced. The official media lionize clinicians and cardiologists as the foot soldiers of socialist altruism, mere pawns molded in the ideological furnace of the joyful everlasting solidarity factory that is the Revolution. They forget to mention that the doctors are paid a pittance for their contracts and are basically exploited. For their part, government opponents go so far as to equate these doctors with the totalitarian state, consumed by a fruitless attempt to discredit the program, despite the fact that in more than two thousand years of philosophy, no one has yet come up with a convincing argument that discredits the pure and simple work done by doctors and nurses.

What these doctors are actually doing is the least important factor to both sides. It is an insoluble paradox for militants, but one a nonmilitant might explain like this: Cuban doctors are saving lives in Africa and Latin America. Meanwhile these doctors and the lives they save are used by a regime with no civil liberties as calling cards, as political ambassadors, as cheap labor, as a smoke screen to hide the accelerating collapse of the public health service in the country, but Cuban doctors are saving lives.

———

Every time a Cuban doctor is interviewed, whether because he has just returned to the fatherland, or because he has abandoned his mission, it is with the intention of getting him to say what people want to hear. People like me. As the opposition, since he is not a defector. In the national political narrative, he is an outsider.

I was tempted to explore the idea of a doctor who no longer works for the government, yet continues to live according to the values that, as he acknowledges, were taught to him by that same government and how, simply because he is no longer working directly for it, the government does not hold him up as an example, or include a segment about him on the nightly news. And how, when it comes down to it, the Cuban government prizes subservience over the very values it purports to foster.

Solidarity is a sacrifice and consists of making other lives better by making your own worse. It is a logic that runs contrary to the logic of success, and even that of instinct, which is why it is in such short supply. In the end, Navarro managed to get to the city of Manta—the epitome of despair at that time—and to save the Ecuadorians who had been ravaged by the tragedy. He worked as a team leader in Tarqui, the area of Guayaquil worst hit by the earth-quake, and in Los Sauces, a neighborhood of fishermen. In the district of Los Ángeles, he worked with the disabled, with bedbound patients, and cured a nine-year-old girl with an infection in her knee.

Later, the girl brought him a gift. Navarro was surprised, knowing that the girl had nothing more than the clothes she stood up in, and he did not think it appropriate to accept her gift. She wore a pair of plastic flip-flops, a short-sleeved dress, and, in her hair, a string of daisies. Her gift was a bird that had fallen from the sky. And the little girl specifically wanted the doctor to put it back in its nest because, when all is said and done, that is what doctors do. Whether earthquakes or broken bones, they put things back in their place.

BLACK PITCHER, WHITE SOCKS

Señora Luz María is expecting a number of parcels from *up north*. Her brother Humberto, a bald, heavy-set black guy with a bushy mustache and eyes like open wounds, goes back out to the parking lot to fetch something from his gray Hyundai. Both are expecting packages—some clothes, a food mixer, a DVD player—that a delivery boy will bring out in the next few minutes.

Terminal 2 at José Martí Airport in Havana is horrible: the crowds are teeming, the seats uncomfortable, and there is little room to move. It is here that Cubans come and go from Miami. A cursory glance at the other terminals cannot help but make you think the cramped and claustrophobic Terminal 2 is some kind of implicit government payback.

The loudspeaker announces that the flight has landed. Luz María is waiting. Leaning against the trunk of the Hyundai 4x4, Humberto calmly smokes a cigarette and stares at the blue-and-yellow facade of the terminal building. He always comes here, always to receive packages. He has not seen his second-oldest brother in more than a decade other than in photos or videos, and has not heard his voice except on the telephone.

But now, an adolescent—fifteen years old at most—is telling his father to stop. The father pays no heed and the irritated teenager tells him that Contreras is on the plane that has just landed. Humberto turns pale. He listens intently, but what he is hearing seems to come in slow motion. Then Humberto bursts into tears and takes off at a run. And when he gives the news to Luz María, she too cries and starts running.

"Who?" asks the father, bewildered.

"Contreras," says the teenager. "The New York Yankees pitcher."

It is January 19, 2013. Five days earlier, a new immigration law easing previous regulations imposed by Raúl Castro's government came into effect. Among the new provisions, high-level athletes are now allowed to return to Cuba as long as they have been out of the country for a minimum of eight years.

Since 1959, any Cuban athlete who emigrated and launched—or attempted to launch—a professional career with any foreign league or championship had been denied the right to return home. Since 1959, as fans, we were denied any and all information about sporting idols who had later decided to emigrate, and to an extent this is still the case. Although these days they are allowed to come back, we still know nothing about their careers: no statistics, no records of their failures or their triumphs. And what little information we do have is smuggled in.

Contreras is the first of hundreds of athletes to come home, and he is instantly mobbed by everyone at the airport.

━━

Like so many others, Contreras was discovered by chance.

"It was an ordinary game on an ordinary day in 1990," says Jesús Guerra, the scout who spotted him. "He was playing third base for Las Martinas, in a cooperative tournament."

Guerra had been one of the great pitchers in the Series Nacionales. But he was also an outstanding coach, and a tenacious talent scout.

He scooped up Pedro Luis Lazo when he had been written off as a baseball player because he couldn't throw a fastball; later, in Santiago de Chile, he rescued Norge Luis Vera after some wise guy decided not to let him pitch.

Over the past twenty years, Jesús Guerra has single-handedly been responsible for spotting the three best pitchers in Cuban baseball. Not only did he find them; he also trained them, coached them, taught them to think on the pitcher's mound. And that is no mean feat. Saying "the three best Cuban pitchers" is like saying "the three best football players in Argentina," or "the three greatest mountaineers in Nepal." There are few arts in Cuba more important than pitching balls to home plate.

"What was it about Contreras that caught your eye?"

"His arm, obviously."

"What was it exactly?"

"In the last inning, the batter hit a ground ball to Contreras, who fumbled it. The ball was about a meter away from him, and from his position on one knee, he threw the batter out at first. And I thought 'Fuck, this kid's got one hell of an arm.' So I went down to the field and asked to talk to him."

"What did you talk about?"

"I suggested he sign up for the academy. Back then I was head of the Regional Pitching School in Pinar del Río."

"I don't like pitching," Contreras said. "I like third base better."

"A third baseman can play for fifteen years, or for as long as he likes," Guerra said, "and with your arm, I think you could become one of the great Cuban ballplayers one day."

He was talking about Omar Linares, the most perfect machine, the most brilliant third baseman ever to play in the Series Nacionales.

"So what did Contreras say?"

"He said he'd have to talk to his papa. This was Sunday, and by Wednesday I was standing on his doorstep."

He showed up, but there was no one there to welcome Coach Guerra, only women.

"I had to go out to the fields. I found them digging up sweet potatoes."

In the glare of the sun, from the abrupt gestures of the kid and the shimmer of his dark skin, Coach Guerra figured he had found himself a *cimarrón*—a wild man. He had no choice but to hang around, work for a couple of hours, and convince Florentino Contreras.

Eventually, he took his pupil away, and half a sack of sweet potatoes home. Contreras was twenty-one. Conventional wisdom would say he was too old to learn to pitch.

━━

Right in the middle of the Special Period (1991–92), José Ariel Contreras and Pedro Luis Lazo met at the academy.

For almost two years, they spent five days a week together. When they were on furlough, Coach Guerra would give them money to pay for transport. When they stayed at the academy, Guerra would walk for miles in search of food—a pig or maybe a chicken. And when he couldn't find anything, he bought them candy, anything to ease their hunger. It was a bleak period. Even so, it had its positive side. Not because starvation strengthened the pitching arms of Contreras and Lazo, but because of the ordeals they overcame. Guerra believes it made them mentally stronger.

"To pitch in a World Series, in the Olympics, in a Classic, you need to be more than a pitcher," he says. "That's where other things come into play."

He doesn't say which other things, but you can guess he means shrewdness, and *cojones*. Guerra's protégés did all of these things— pitched in a World Series, in the Olympics, in a Classic—and more.

Heads *and* tails. In 1995, both Lazo and Contreras were selected for the Cuban national squad for the first time, and won championships playing with Pinar del Rio and the National team. Lazo had an easygoing self-assurance whereas Contreras brimmed with an unpretentious shyness. Lazo would brazenly smoke tobacco in public, but Contreras only ever smoked in the company of friends. Lazo would joke on the benches, brag in the box, intimidate his opponents, barely stopping to catch his breath between pitches.

Contreras never opened his mouth, smiled rarely and awkwardly, and took much more time between pitches. He would watch, nod, and if he had something to say, he did so in a whisper, as though making confession in church. Contreras managed through hypnotism what Lazo did with defiance. Contreras waged a war of attrition, Lazo delivered a knockout blow. Contreras slowly strangled while Lazo swiftly stabbed. Lazo's weapon was a slider that curved like a scimitar; Contreras favored a forkball that landed like a grenade.

In November 2012, Pedro Luis Lazo was still proclaiming that the Cy Young Award was for others, that his country's glory was enough for him. Meanwhile, Contreras had deserted the Cuban national team. Some months later, wearing the legendary number 52 shirt, he made his debut in the Major League.

During his last season in Cuba, before he left for good, Contreras won thirteen games, struck out one hundred and forty batters, and had an earned run average under two for ninety games.

In the Baseball World Cup in Taipei in 2001, in the semifinal against Japan, he allowed only eleven hits and four walks. The following day, Cuba won the title, and during the ceremony to welcome the team home, Castro compared Contreras to Antonio Maceo and dubbed him the "Bronze Titan."

=

You know you are nearing Las Martinas when you see the countless hairpin bends on the road, the triangular huts, the teams of oxen hauling timber. And especially by the facial features of the people. They seem possessed of a grave solemnity. Their faces are etched with deep lines and furrows that look as though they have been chiseled.

At the entrance to the village—after a mind-numbing two-and-a-half-hour drive along the Carretera Panamericana—stands an unpainted church in a style that might be described as Gothic—or the basic notion most people have of Gothic. Next to the church are a bank, a café, and two skinny dogs, a couple of people standing in the doorways, and farther off, a deserted baseball field.

A couple of blocks past the church, we turn right, leave the paved road, and come to the Contreras family home. The ground is carpeted with a layer of dust so thick that people sink into it; they look as though their legs are cut off at the ankles. Coming from the city, you cannot help but wonder how anyone from here ended up pitching in Yankee Stadium. A throng of brothers, cousins, nephews, and neighbors are waiting for the homecoming of the prodigal son. Also waiting for him is a *lechona*—a fifteen-pound suckling pig—transformed by the carver's art to create *perniles*, *masas*, *higado*, *rabo*, *cabeza*, pork stew, and a mountain of crispy *chicharrones*.

It is a modest house still. A television with a forty-inch screen, a tiled kitchen, furnishings that, for want of a better word, are comfortable, but something fills this space, binds it with an invisible cement that no millions, something that no dazzlingly successful son can cancel out: the conformity of humility.

"This is where I'm from," Contreras will say. "This is my land, this is the house my father built. The only things I'm good at are pitching and planting sweet potatoes. When I can't pitch, I come back here to plant sweet potatoes."

Some five hundred meters farther on are meadows, the land on which the house where he was born once stood, and the concrete foundations that are all that remain. "Huevo," a local farmer and a friend of Contreras since childhood, takes the role of guide.

"I was really excited to meet up with this ugly black guy again. 'Cause he's one ugly black guy. A lot of people wouldn't want to meet up with him, because they think he struts around like a millionaire."

He points to the stunted ceiba tree where, as boys, the two of them played ball.

"Maybe afterward I'll have to fess up that he's a black guy turned white. But I don't think so. Back when he was on the Cuban national team and he was already famous, he still came here. He was still happy to ride a horse or drive a cart, no problem."

He nods toward the well where Contreras went to fetch water, again and again, every day of his childhood. These days, it is just a black hole surrounded by bricks and weeds, half-covered by a sheet of metal.

=

It is now three in the afternoon on January 30. Contreras will not make an appearance before six o'clock. Eleven tumultuous days have passed since his arrival. After landing in Havana, he climbed into a gray Hyundai with Humberto and Luz María and headed straight for Salvador Allende Hospital, some ten kilometers from the airport.

In the National Institute of Angiology, a dilapidated four-story building, Contreras's mother, Modesta Camejo, now seventy-seven, is having surgery. Her left leg is severely necrotic and needs to be amputated before the toxins spread to the rest of her body. The operation is a success. And, all things considered, Contreras is happy.

Within forty-eight hours, the patient is discharged, but this will not be an ordinary convalescence. The family is torn between these conflicting circumstances: José Ariel's homecoming and Modesta's ill health. When they leave the hospital, they do not head to Las

Martinas but to Guanabo. They rent three villas overlooking El Megano, one of the most popular beaches east of Havana, where they stay for a week.

Contreras's sister María, a skinny, charming black woman with a shaved head, once drank sixty-four beers in a single night. Contreras, on the other hand, spends his time training. He runs on the beach, gives interviews to NBC, signs autographs for local kids, and throws between fifty and seventy pitches every other day, while Coach Guerra watches how he swings his arm, how he delivers the pitch. All of this comes after a severe injury in June 2012 in which he tore the tendon in his right elbow and was benched by the Philadelphia Phillies for the remainder of the season.

And so it is only today, eleven days after coming back, after visiting the Parque Central in Havana and the major towns in Pinar del Rio, after going out to a night café with Lazo, that Contreras arrives home.

The gray Hyundai rounds the corner. The neighbors come from their houses, they watch from their doorways, they gather by the roadside, in a tumult of whoops and tears of happiness.

——

In 2010, the government granted Modesta Camejo permission to travel to the United States for one or two months every year and return to Cuba. During one of those trips, the problems with her circulation worsened.

When Modesta landed in Philadelphia, Contreras took her to the Phillies stadium. Suddenly, this woman who had never set foot outside her little town found herself sitting on the bleachers in Citizens Bank Park. She had never been to Capitán San Luis Stadium or to the Latinoamericano because Pinar Del Rio and Havana were a long way from where she lived; now, in a twinkling, she was at the home of the MLB champions, a stadium that could hold more than the entire population of Las Martinas.

As a closer, Contreras played only two games that week. He managed a 97-mph cutter, brought his earned run average down to 0.93, and Modesta burst into tears. Not because of her son's achievements, which she did not understand, but because it was not she who should be sitting in the bleachers, but his father, Florentino Contreras. An upstanding man, a former baseball player who, in 2002, when rumors began to spread that Contreras had defected, sat out on the stoop of his house and declared that he refused to believe it, that he would wait until the Cuban team came home and his son did not come around the corner. And he waited.

"I left because I was ambitious," Contreras explains. "I wanted to prove myself in Major League Baseball, I wanted to try. It came at a cost, but I wanted to prove myself."

"The old man locked himself in his room and refused to come out," says Francisco, Florentino's son by his first marriage. "He was a communist, a militant, he was deeply committed."

Francisco cries almost without shedding a tear; he looks like a gnarled branch.

Florentino kept to his bed for days. Eventually he got up and told anyone who would listen to let Contreras know that, whatever happened, he would always be his son.

Francisco explains: "They talked on the phone a couple of times, but a little while later, the old man died."

"How much later?"

"About two years, maybe."

"In 2004?"

"Yes, in 2004."

"What did he die of?"

"An obstructed bowel."

"Not a broken heart?"

Francisco says nothing. Then he shakes his head, a vehement no, and says that the old man had been ill for some time. But in his eyes, a flicker of doubt makes it clear that he, and everyone else, has considered the idea.

——

No one was expecting his defection, not even those closest to him. The first person to find out was his sister, Francisca, the eldest of the family, who lives in La Víbora in Havana.

"There was a cyclone in Cuba," she says, "and I thought they were phoning to check in on us. But no. I was the one who had to tell papá."

"What did Florentino say?"

"He said why didn't he have the balls to tell me himself. But we never mention that. People said he was influenced by Miguelito Valdés. That's a lie. José himself told me that when he showed up at the meeting point and saw Miguelito, he thought he had been ratted out."

Miguel Valdés was head coach of the Cuban national team, a distinguished man with more than thirty years' experience. People speculated—not unreasonably—that Valdés had been the brains behind the defection, and that it was he who had managed to persuade Contreras.

"I was in Las Tunas coaching the provincial team when I heard the news on the television," says Guerra. "There had never been a news flash in Cuba about an athlete defecting. They were talking about Contreras like he was a hero who had died on the battlefield. I couldn't listen. I stormed out of my room and I fought with everything."

"What do you mean 'everything'?"

"You don't want to know."

It would take years before the two men were in touch again. In fact, Guerra let it be known that if Contreras ever did come back one day, he could come looking for him in the cemetery in Guane, that he'd be waiting.

Initially, they talked about technical issues. Contreras would ask Guerra for advice, but perhaps beyond his questions about using a forkball in the Major Leagues, he was simply looking for a little paternal affection. With Lazo, on the other hand, there was never a time when the two were not in touch.

"After I left," says Contreras, "I didn't want to talk to him. I didn't want to cause him any trouble, but he sent me his phone number and told me I had to call him. I kept asking for advice. He would watch the games and talk to me about arm angles, technical stuff. And now, since I've been back, he's come to find me, to see me."

When Lazo inflicted humiliating defeats on Venezuela and the Dominican Republic during the first World Baseball Classic, Contreras, who was in a bar in Arizona, leaped up onto his table.

"I shouted and screamed. How could I not?"

Obviously, the fact that they held one or another role was pure chance.

———

The winter of 2002 was bitter and brutal. Contreras holed up in a hotel in Managua while he waited for confirmation that he was a free agent in the Major League. A Nicaraguan journalist who interviewed him during his stay said he had never seen anyone with such sad eyes, and ran the piece with a headline worthy of Darío: "A Melancholy Millionaire." Even so, the stay had its moments of grace. The great archrivals of MLB—the New York Yankees and the Boston Red Sox—were fighting to the death to sign him up.

Theo Epstein, general manager of the Red Sox, flew to Nicaragua

and rented out every room in the hotel where Contreras was staying so that none of the rival teams could talk to Contreras or to
Jaime Torre, the legendary agent of Cuban baseball players who im-
migrate to the United States. Contreras signed a four-year contract
with the Yankees for $32 million, an exorbitant sum for a man who
had never pitched a ball professionally, who was not a guaranteed
success, who had not even proved himself in the Minor Leagues.

From the start, Contreras broke rules, but he is, and has always
been, a very private man, someone who needs to be among friends,
not the typical city guy who likes to go it alone. There is proof.
Contreras had notable upticks in his career in the Majors when he
felt supported by friends and family: when his first wife brought his
daughters to Miami, or when Modesta came to Philadelphia. This
is completely understandable to anyone—except the Yankees. New
York, as everyone knows, believes only in destiny.

Contreras made his debut on March 31, 2003, against the Toronto
Blue Jays, taking over from the legendary Roger Clemens, but he
never truly managed to find his footing in a high-pressure city, or
win over the "Bleacher Creatures," an arrogant, supercilious fanbase
that was accustomed to success, with a few select heroes and numerous retired numbers. It is not as though Contreras's stats with the
Yankees were always bad, at least not in the second half of his first
year. But he committed a number of mortal sins, trivial misdemean-
ors that would have gone unnoticed anywhere else, but that enhance
the mysticism of historic organizations.

In the 2003 playoffs, he fell twice, and, when the Yankees played
against the Florida Marlins in the World Series, he barely put his
head above the parapet. To make matters worse, he never managed
to beat the Boston Red Sox. As a result, by midseason, the Yankees
had decided to trade him to the White Sox for Esteban Loaiza,
another average pitcher—a nobody for a nobody, one of the routine

trades people barely notice since they happen every summer, which is a busy MLB trading period.

The last months of 2004 and the first half of 2005 were not much different. Run-of-the-mill stats with a couple of respectable strike-outs in the odd game. He seemed more like an impetuous pitcher with lots of energy and little talent barely hanging on in the Major Leagues than the decisive, volcanic pitcher he would later become. Don Cooper, Contreras's new coach, realized that, despite his 95-mph fastball and his "forkball from hell," this inexperienced kid from Las Martinas was tipping his pitches to the batters.

By eliminating this tell, with the support of the charismatic White Sox manager, Ozzie Guillén, and Contreras's customary dedi-cation in training, Cooper eventually managed to light the fire and—long story short—later declared, "The other teams didn't beat him; he beat himself. He shot himself in the foot. He had some demons he had to overcome, and he's overcome them."

In the long story, there were other protagonists. Orlando "El Duque" Hernández—who had left Cuba in 1996 and quit the Yankees in 2003 with three World Series rings in his pocket—was the one who took on the task of finding out why a talented pitcher like Contreras couldn't seem to find his top form. He offered advice, pushed him, became his mentor, and posed a key question: Why had he stopped pitching sidearm sinkers? Why had he stopped releasing the ball at multiple angles?—key characteristics typical of Cuban pitchers that give them a crucial advantage. This is what El Duque did for his countryman.

After that, Contreras started against the Yankees in August 2005, beginning one of the longest series of consecutive wins for a pitcher in the Major Leagues: seventeen. But this, which seems like a lot, is actually very little. Contreras led his team into the League post-season when he defeated the reigning champion Boston Red Sox in the Division Series, lost his first game against the LA Angels in the American League Championship Series, but rallied and took the next four to lead the White Sox into their first World Series since 1959.

The White Sox hadn't made it through October since Fidel Castro marched into Havana, and hadn't won a World Series since 1917, when Woodrow Wilson was president, the period of notorious game rigging and the Black Sox scandal. Since the time when Babe Ruth was batting for the Red Sox and Hemingway was a reporter for the *Toronto Star*.

Contreras started in the final game of the series against Roger Clemens, then batting for the Houston Astros. It was not his greatest performance, but he hung on until the eighth inning and cleared the path that led to the symbolic World Series ring, this one a gold signet ring set with clear stones and emblazoned with the team logo. He is still wearing it today, in Las Martinas, almost eight years later. On his hand, it shimmers like a jewel in dark earth.

"I was out in the street with the fans," Contreras says, "and Ozzie asked me to say something. There were two thousand people. I didn't speak much English—I still don't—but people wanted me to say something. I gave a shout-out to Cuba, to Pinar del Rio, and to Chicago."

In 2006, Contreras was scheduled to start for the American League All-Star team in the Midsummer Classic when he suffered an injury, one of many. The forkball, a weapon as lethal as it is wearing, had probably weakened his throwing arm. Later, he was named Latino of the Week; he staged spectacular comebacks, but also suffered disastrous losses and several assignments to the Minors. He stayed in Chicago until 2009, then moved to Colorado and from there to Philadelphia.

During this period, his skill and determination earned him much-deserved fame. So much so that Will González at ESPN told Yoenis Céspedes, an outfielder hired by Oakland in early 2012, that

he could learn a lot from Contreras about how to deal with the difficult transition from Cuban exile to Major League star.

―――

A little more than ten years have passed between the day he left and
today, January 30, 2013. Someone asks what difference there is between the pitcher who left and the one who has just come home, and
Contreras simply says: experience. What about the man who left and
the man who has just come home? "Ten years, spent far from here,
without my fans and my people, everything else is the same."

But there are a couple of differences. Anyone looking at the living room in his house would notice. On the back wall is a team portrait of the New York Yankees with Contreras next to Jeff Weaver,
Roger Clemens, and Andy Pettitte. Opposite hangs a Pinar del Rio
poster in which Contreras is sitting on the bench, holding a baseball
glove, staring far beyond the camera lens. Whether or not it is para-
doxical, the Contreras of the Yankees is courageous and cheerful;
the smile is put on, as smiles in publicity posters always are, while
the Cuban Contreras is nostalgic and contemplative.

The Yankees Contreras is an absolute marvel, a figure carved from
a single piece of ebony, a body with no visible joints: a thick bull
neck, arms like the branches of a guava tree, legs like trunks of cedar.
He looks like a concrete tree. Looking at the Cuban Contreras, on
the other hand, the constituent parts are evident, he is like a rag
doll. Powerful, yes, but still a work in progress. He lacks the glow,
the glamour, the weight. You can see the joint between shoulders
and arms, forearms and wrists, fingers and nails, the stitching and
the fabric.

The Yankees Contreras—according to the expedient sense of
market and brevity common to North Americans—is, simply, José
Contreras. The more disheveled Cuban Contreras is José Ariel

Contreras. And today, sitting on a rocking chair on his porch in Las Martinas, he is just Jose. No emphasis, no accent.

"Right now, I get up and I just stand there and I think, 'Wow! I'm back.'"

His eyes blaze with pleasure; on his chin, a short, elegant goatee; around his neck, a long chain with a medallion and, emblazoned on the medallion, the number 52. His right arm is limp, dangling over the armrest, his fingers holding a cold beer. Someone calls to him. He drains the last dregs and crushes the can. He gets to his feet. He makes to throw the can. Slips into the sinuous windup.

Until the last minute, it's impossible to know whether Contreras will throw a splitter or a forkball.

WANTED

It is late at night on November 8, 1971, in Albuquerque, New Mexico, and State Policeman Robert Rosenbloom is about to die. He's a twenty-eight-year-old US Army vet. At 11:00 p.m., several miles to the west of the city, a 1962 Ford Galaxie is hurtling down I-40 from Oakland when Rosenbloom decides to stop it. Traveling in the Ford, which is loaded with three military rifles, a 12-gauge shotgun, political pamphlets, bomb-making materials and grenades, are three members of the Republic of New Afrika: Masheo Sundiata, Antar Ra, and Fela Olatunji.

The RNA is a political organization basically attempting to establish an African American nation in five states of the American south: Louisiana, Mississippi, Alabama, Georgia, and South Carolina. Rosenbloom is probably attempting something less ambitious: to make a successful arrest.

All around is desert: here and there a scrawny shrub, here and there a shadow. The three men, who are on the run, get out of the car. Rosenbloom asks them to pop the trunk and Olatunji says that they will only open it at the police station. Rosenbloom tells them to follow him. But, obviously, no one will be following. Someone pulls a .45, someone pulls the trigger, and the fatal bullet pierces the state policeman's throat. Olatunji steps closer, looks at the patrolman's elegant hat lying on the ground, watches as the viscous pool of blood spreads. He checks for a pulse. There is none.

Rosenbloom has two children: Tammy, three, and Robert, who has just turned two.

====

"They'd be in their forties now."

"Yeah, the other day I was thinking about the son. But if he didn't come in a ranger's uniform to kill me at twenty or thirty, he's not likely to do it now."

When he talks, Charles Hill has a strange accent.* He muddles up the gender of Spanish nouns and adjectives, twists words as though his tongue were a vice mangling the language.

"Maybe he won't be the one to do it."

"Maybe not. Awhile back, when they raised the bounty on Assata, I read a bunch of messages between bounty hunters talking about possibly tracking her down."

"How were you able to read the messages?"

"No. No."

"Are you in touch with Assata?"

"I don't want to be in touch with her."

"Can you tell me how you were able to read the messages between the bounty hunters?"

"No, because I can't tell you who forwarded them to me."

"Have you ever had suspicions about anyone in particular?"

---

* Charles Hill is still living in Cuba as a refugee while the issue of fugitives from justice is the subject of the ongoing negotiations between Washington and Havana. Since April 2015, Charles has been represented, pro bono, by Jason Flores Williams, an attorney from Santa Fe, New Mexico. One of his first suggestions to his client was that he stop giving press interviews.

"Yeah, it would have been back in '93 or '94. A man came up to me in the Parque Central and gave me the phone number of the Hotel Ambos Mundos. I wasn't sure what I was supposed to do. Initially, I figured I wouldn't go, but curiosity got the better of me. It was a couple of journalists from Albuquerque who said they wanted an interview, but then I found out they didn't have press visas, so I reported them to the Security Services. That afternoon, as I was heading home, I saw them filming outside my house, and I hadn't given them my address."

"So, what happened?"

"They were told to leave the country. At that point, I told the authorities that I wanted to make a deal, that I was scared. They said I had nothing to be scared of. Back then, I was still doing work for the government, translations for a fishing magazine and for the Cuban Book Institute—does the Book Institute still exist?"

"Yeah, it's still there."

"Wow, really? I haven't seen anything published by it, but . . ."

"Did you feel isolated, vulnerable?"

"Oh yeah, of course I did."

"In what way?'

"Have you ever kicked off the blankets while you're asleep?"

"Yeah."

"That's how I felt. Permanently naked. Permanently cold."

=====

It is early 2014, Havana, and both the Cuban and American governments are still looking for a head on a spike.

In his apartment there is little more than a small fridge, a kerosene stove, a broken bed, and a dressing table with a tarnished mirror. Piled up in a corner behind the door are coins, a coconut husk, a hatchet, and a carved wooden effigy of the face of Eleguá: symbols of

Santería. In the living room, there is an armchair, and rocking back and forth in the armchair is Charles.

He is wearing black moccasins, rumpled white socks, and a pair of threadbare jeans cut down into fringed shorts. His calves and his thighs are crisscrossed by thick, bulging veins. A deep black scar runs down his right arm. His hair is beginning to turn gray; his skin is brown and glossy, like the skin of certain timorous reptiles. These days, he needs bifocal glasses, but his athletic body does not seem to have aged.

He is frequently visited by his Cuban daughter, who is twenty-nine. His seven-year-old son, Antar, lives a couple of blocks away. Antar is the most important thing in Charles's life. He has no friends, though once upon a time, he had two: Ralph Goodwin and Michael Finney. Goodwin was drowned in 1973 off one of the beaches east of Havana, and Finney finally lost his battle with lung cancer in 2004.

This left Charles Hill alone. Right now, he is talking about a dream he had a long time ago. A dream that has never left him, one that turned out to be a premonition.

═══

"Do you remember having suspicions about anyone else?"

"Sure, thousands of times. You see so many people. A couple of Americans had come over to meet me. Students, professors from the University of California, representatives from Pastors for Peace . . ."

"Do you think about it much?"

"The thoughts come pretty frequently. There's nothing I can do to stop them. They're the hard drive, and every now and then they pop up so I never forget the danger. This thing, this feeling."

"What's it like, this feeling?"

"Like I'm fighting a whole crowd of people at once."

═══

It is 1956 or 1957, we are in Olney, a city in Richland County, Illinois, and Charles Hill is seven, perhaps eight years old. He is plagued by a dream, a dream he does not yet realize will one day turn out to be a premonition. His paternal great-grandfather was a fugitive slave who lived in the mountains with the Cherokee. His father is a master stone-mason. His mother is a housewife. There are fifteen siblings in the family. There is no shortage of food. Charles plays basketball and baseball. He hunts deer and pheasant. He fishes. It is a happy childhood. He does not understand why he has the dream he has, but he does.

Later, like many other black families, the Hills are forced by the technological revolution of the '50s to move north, to Michigan, to Ohio, then New York. Later, they travel south, to Albuquerque. Now a teenager, Charles works in Los Alamos, where scientists are conducting experiments. In 1967, Charles dodged military service and enlisted in the army. He studied shorthand in Germany. He drafted reports and communiqués about the Six-Day War. But in the revolutionary year of 1968 he was finally posted to Vietnam as a sergeant with the "Screaming Eagles"—the glorious 101st Airborne Division.

Charles does not see much action. He asks to quit and is reduced in rank. He is confined to a psychiatric clinic for six months where—for no reason—he is pumped full of chlorpromazine, a liquid medication that blocks certain chemical reactions in the brain and is used to treat schizophrenia and bipolar disorder. As a result, he suffers from recurring mental problems and hallucinations. He cuts a deal with the army. He signs his discharge papers and gives up any claim for compensation. Two weeks later, he flies back to the United States.

By now, his parents are divorced. Charles is not yet twenty, and all recent memories have been wiped out. A powerful drug is causing chemical reactions in his brain. He suffers dizzy spells. Sometimes he passes out.

——

"Talk to me about your son, Antar."

"He's a good boy, though his mother sometimes beats him. I don't like the idea of hitting kids, it doesn't teach them anything. The other day the school called for me to pick him up because he hit a little girl."

"And what did you say?"

"He respects me. I did the angry tough guy act and he started crying. But he's a little shit. A few minutes later he was asking for money for candy."

"And did you give it to him?"

"Of course, how could I not?"

"Is it mostly about your son, this fear you feel?"

"It's like when you're at war. Fear doesn't matter. It's too late to feel scared. I cry, but for my son, not for me—or for my daughter. She's a grown-up now."

"Do you sleep with a weapon to hand?"

"What? You mean a machete?"

"Whatever."

"What would be the point? If they did come for me, the only thing to do would be to take the machete and hack my own head off. I was in the army. There's nothing I can do to save myself. If they're going to kill me, let them, I'm not going to try and stop them. There's only one thing I want."

"What's that?"

"That Antar isn't there when they come for me."

===

At 11:11 p.m. on November 8, 1971, Rosenbloom's body is discovered by a motorcyclist named Dennis Arnold, from Greeley, Colorado. At 11:30 p.m., State Police Sergeant C. A. Hawkins launches a search for the Ford Galaxie. Half an hour later, the car is spotted and a high-speed chase ensues, with vehicles traveling at 75 mph but then, at the intersection between Coors Boulevard and Gun Club Road, the Ford Galaxie vanishes. The longest manhunt in the history of New Mexico lasted eighteen days. Everywhere, there are posters, TV bulletins, offers of rewards, while the area is swamped by 250 officers from federal, state, and local law enforcement agencies trying in vain to track down the fugitives.

The fugitives ditch the car and manage to get as far as the home of Olatunji's mother. Later, they move to a friend's house on the same street. In the meantime, the only prints found in the Ford are those of Masheo and Antar. They get inside information from a police informant. An RNA contact brings food and water.

On November 26, the FBI confirms that it has also found Olatunji's prints. After talking to his informant, Olatunji thinks the best thing to do is run. Masheo and Antar refuse. Olatunji wishes them good luck and leaves. Later, Masheo and Antar decide to follow suit. Which is just as well since, within hours, the house is surrounded by a SWAT team, but by now the three fugitives have made it as far as the desert, to a rubbish heap near the airport.

Olatunji keeps out of the sun, and at night he uses a beat-up sofa to shelter from the cold. On the night of the twenty-seventh, he walks to a nearby gas station, where he calls for a tow truck. When it arrives, Olatunji puts a gun to the driver's head and tells him to cooperate, says that he doesn't want to kill him; the driver says he won't need to.

Olatunji picks up his friends and takes the airport road. They already know that, at 11:55 p.m., a Boeing 737 is scheduled to take off for Chicago. Slowly, they drive the truck onto the tarmac. Olatunji tells his friends to go on ahead while he covers them, and when they reach the steps, he will follow, and they can cover him. Masheo and Antar take off at a run. A flight attendant gestures for them to show their boarding passes. Thinking the man is signaling to someone,

Olatunji prepares to fire. In the end, he does not fire, but gets out of the tow truck and keeps his gun cocked. The flight attendant gets down on his knees. Olatunji boards the plane. He goes into the cockpit, and from there, he issues orders. Police are deployed, but in vain. Masheo and Antar keep an eye on the hostage crew while Olatunji diverts the plane to Tampa, Florida. There, they demand that the plane be refueled, and only then do they allow the hostages to disembark through one of the rear doors. On November 28, shortly before midday, the Boeing 737 lands at Havana's Rancho Boyeros airport. It was not until 1973 that Fidel Castro and Richard Nixon signed an antihijacking agreement, with each side agreeing to prosecute or repatriate hijackers violating Cuban-US airspace. But in the 1960s and early 1970s, hijacking a plane to get from one country to another to seek asylum was little more than a formality.

"Antar" is actually Ralph Goodwin, a former physics professor at UC Berkeley. "Masheo" is Michael Finney, a former police officer from the same city. And Fela Olatunji had a dream that turned out to be a premonition.

———

"Do you regret it?"

"I don't regret it. I was a revolutionary. Rosenbloom's death was regrettable, but there are a lot of other deaths just as regrettable, a lot of black men who were hanged, a lot of black men who were lynched. There are a lot of unwarranted deaths in those parts."

———

It is August 1969, and Charles, paranoid and mentally unbalanced, is trying to track down his maternal uncle in Oakland. When his uncle dies, Charles and his cousin inherit equal shares in his construction company with a staff of ten or twenty laborers. They sell off the equipment and head for Alaska, where they can earn more money. There, Charles and his cousin spend their nights working on an oil pipeline. There, also at night, and also with his cousin, Charles reads the works of Malcolm X, Frantz Fanon, and Che Guevara.

Sometime later, they move back to Oakland, and in June 1971, Charles joins the RNA. He adopts a nom de guerre. He, Masheo, and Antar rob shops, plan bank raids, abduct guards. He favors a 9mm pistol and Browning sawed-off shotgun. This is how he gets by, with no clear plan, until an incident at the RNA headquarters in Jackson, Mississippi, in which a police officer is killed and an FBI official and agent are wounded. The Oakland cell of the RNA is disbanded, and Charles takes off for Louisiana in a 1962 Ford Galaxie.

——

"You had two kids before you turned twenty-two?"

"A daughter, Caroline, and a son I've never met. My wife was pregnant when I came to Cuba."

"What became of them?"

"The boy died. He was shot, I don't know why. I'm still in touch with Caroline from time to time."

"Do you ever talk about this stuff?"

"Only once. She asked why I did it."

"So what did you say?"

"Because of the way things were. To liberate our people. But I don't think she got it. I understand that. She has no reason to get it. She's not Antar. She's only my daughter because we've got the same blood in our veins. We're like an engaged couple who've never met and will never meet, but they're still engaged."

——

In actual fact, the most recent communication from his daughter Caroline, informing him of the death of a relative or something like that, dates back to 2011 or 2012. Charles is a *babalawo* (the Yoruba word means "father of the mysteries")—a sort of priest in the Yoruba religion Santería, a child of Shango and Oshun—whose only regular communication is with the dead. He probably has more regular contact with Rosenbloom, or with Finney and Goodwin than he has with Caroline.

When he first arrives in Cuba, Charles sees it as springboard to carry on the fight in Africa. He spends the first six weeks in custody, being investigated, and afterward he is found a house in Siboney, a district that houses other refugees. In the 1970s, a lot of famous African American leaders spent time in Havana: Huey Newton, Eldridge Cleaver, Angela Davis.

"Cuba was really impressive," he says. "There were people here from all over the world, particularly Africa. Young students. You could feel the fire, the fervor of the Revolution. Police officers wore guns in their belts. The whole place was intense, it was electrifying."

There were other details, just as typical of the times, and Charles mentions them. In Cuba in 1973, cigarettes cannot not be sold openly, and food is rationed. No alcohol is sold in shops. Religious worship is forbidden. If you have family abroad, you're a pariah. Charles wears sports clothes and people call him a faggot. He is allowed to read the foreign magazines sent to him and his friends, but is not allowed to show them to Cubans.

There is a moment, as much for Cuba as for Charles, when it feels as though the Revolution is trickling away. There is a crack in Charles's reality, one that feels ridiculous and absurd, but also murky and strange, where facts become disjointed and reconnected to a different reality.

He cuts sugarcane, sows pangola grass for fodder, and in 1975 he starts to study history. In 1979, he is found guilty of forging currency exchange receipts. He serves fourteen months of his four-year sentence. In 1986, he is imprisoned for eight months for possession of marijuana. On one occasion, he is thought to have died. His then wife is called in to identify the body, but the feet of the corpse are not those of her husband. Eventually, Charles shows up again. No one knows where he has been. Later, he starts to do private translations from English, mostly of religious manuals and, encouraged by necessity, trades Marxism for Santería.

He is still on the FBI list of wanted fugitives known to be living in Cuba, together with JoAnne Chesimard (aka Assata Shakur, the infamous leader of the Harlem chapter of the Black Panthers, who currently has a bounty of $2 million on her head) and William Morales (the pro-independence Puerto Rican activist accused of planting bombs in New York in the 1970s).

The difference is that Assata—who was found guilty of the first-degree murder of a New Jersey state trooper in 1977 and sentenced to life imprisonment, escaped from the Clinton Correctional Facility for Women, a maximum security prison in Hunterdon County, New Jersey, in 1979, and sought asylum in Havana in 1984—has received public support from Fidel Castro himself, while Charles seems like a burden, an inconvenient relic of a different era, someone who stirs little interest, so much so that, in 2014, he fears that one day, if US-Cuban relations improve, he will be used as a bargaining chip.

———

"When did you guys decide to shoot Rosenbloom?"

"It wasn't a decision. It was foregone conclusion. It's not like we could talk to him. He had already drawn his service revolver. He wanted to play the hero, like John Wayne. Another racist cop. We didn't murder him."

"What about his widow? She says you're a coward. She says it was murder."

"That's her right."

———

It is early 2015 and Charles's whole world has suddenly been turned upside down by a twist of fate bordering on cruelty. The first black president of his country, Barack Obama, may turn out to be the president who succeeds in negotiating his extradition and his conviction.

"Sometimes, I get depressed and I just throw myself on my bed, and I toss and turn, or I read a book. But I can't let depression get the better of me."

In 1996, Bill Richardson, a New Mexico congressman, visited Havana to request Charles's extradition. But that was 1996, when tensions between the Clinton administration and the Castro regime were at their height.

Now, with the advent of diplomatic conversations between the countries after a break of fifty-three years, the extradition request made by Susana Martinez, the governor of New Mexico, does not seem futile, it seems well timed. The ongoing presence of fugitives in Cuba is the chief justification that the White House has used (as it did until mid-2015) to keep Cuba on its list of "state sponsors of terrorism."

According to a recent announcement by the US State Department, Washington and Havana finally plan to sit down and discuss the cases of Assata and Morales. There is no reason not to think that their next discussion will be about Charles Hill.

But today—on this quiet, overcast morning—Charles has already knocked back two glasses of rum, deliberately shrugging off what may be going on outside his door. He is as garrulous and charming as always, and agrees to talk about recent months and his incredible reversal of fortune.

On December 17, he tells me, he was staying in the house of some nephew or other in Cárdenas. It was here that he heard Obama's speech via a Miami TV channel. On his return to Havana, someone paid him a visit to tell him that nothing was going to happen and to ask that he please keep a low profile for a while.

For Charles, keeping a low profile means not wandering through Havana old town, which is what he does to earn a living. He finds tourists in need of a guide. He shows them the major sights of the old quarter: the hotel that was home to Hemingway, the famous restaurants, the leafy parks, the monuments to the Republic.

"I have *aché*, a powerful spiritual energy," he says.

He has put up with a lot, he says, but he can't put up with any more. You've got to come out fighting. Because a man can't live on a 250-pesos pension; he needs to buy shoes for his son and rum for himself.

"Whatever happens, happens. If I run into a US senator, I'll just give him a guided tour."

He has the accent of a refugee, but the sentiment couldn't be more Cuban. I ask him again about Assata Shakur; he tells me that she's a master of disguise, that he saw her on the street a couple of months ago and she gave him a conspiratorial little wave.

"If I were in her shoes, if someone was sending me $200 or $250 a month, I'd be able to live the good life."

But Charles can't live the good life. He has the most powerful government in the world on his heels. And up ahead, nothing but Cuban poverty. Since he needs to survive, he has no time for fear. And because he is afraid—because there are things he fears—he can't spend time fretting about survival. He has been spotted so often, in so many strange places, that now, at the age of sixty-five, his fears, which, though few, are not insignificant, are smaller than his apathy. Next to his tablet of Ifá lies a book by Noam Chomsky and another about the FBI secrets and the war on the Black Panthers called *Agents of Repression*. There's also laundry drying, a can he is using as an ashtray, and one of José Martí's notebooks.

===

"You said justice was hammering on your door."

"I said justice was chasing me down."

"Do you owe a debt to justice?"

"No."

"How do you explain that?"

"This is why I have a cat, because my Sign of Ifá says that, in order to keep justice at bay, I must knock on the door three times, open and close it three times, spray it with alcohol three times, or keep a black cat to frighten it away."

"Tell me about this dream, the premonition that never gives you a moment's peace. What is it?"

"I was a kid, and I dreamed people were chasing me with a spear, that I was being hunted by a lot of people. And I felt alone. My father wasn't there with me, or my brothers. I had nobody. There was a hole through the middle of the spear, and I just stood, frozen, waiting for someone to rescue me. I was just a kid, and they threw the spear and I saw the spear hurtling toward me."

DEATH OF THE TRAIN DRIVER

A soundless requiem is taking place in the lobby of the Sala Avellaneda, at the Teatro Nacional de Cuba. Hanging from the second-floor balconies, or laid upon the ground with funereal reverence, wreaths of flowers bear the names of various institutions, schools, celebrities, jazz combos, and *timba* groups. To either side of the casket, on twin stands and tied with ribbons, two resolutely somber martial bouquets from Fidel and Raúl Castro. The former, a spray of the white roses favored by José Martí; the latter, a bouquet of tender red roses.

To the right of the small wooden casket stands a '50s-style radio microphone. To the left, propped up on a chair, is a double bass so pristine and pure it seems sacred, the exemplary silence of the dead. Inside the casket, hidden from view, as though they were not the very reason for this outpouring of grief, are the ashes of Juan Formell. The idea of a human being reduced to ashes remains too unsettling if it lingers too long in the mind.

It is 4:00 p.m.; the blazing sun looks as though it might melt the window panes. People file past the casket, bow their heads, privately pay their respects. They are paying tribute to the leader of Los Van Van, the most important Cuban orchestra of the past half century. A father, carrying his baby son, pauses before the casket and bows his head. There is an *azabache*—a black onyx amulet—pinned to the baby's clothes, to ward off the evil eye.

The baby doesn't yet know what dance is. He doesn't know what music is. He knows nothing. But he has just been baptized.

===

In the early '50s, before his father moved from the central neighborhood of Cayo Hueso to the district of Lisa in the suburbs of Havana, before the music lessons when he learned to play the bass, little Juan Formell had already memorized passages of rumba, and the jam sessions of Ángel Díaz and César Portillo de la Luz and their pioneering movement "*el feeling.*"

"Although my father knew I was drawn to music," Formell said in January 2005, "he didn't want me or my brother to grow up to be musicians . . . My father was right to try and steer me away from music, because the uncertainties of the profession mean that musicians often lack basic necessities."

Formell knew it only too well, having started out playing in nightclubs for nickels and dimes. In 1959, aged seventeen, he made his debut playing for the military band attached to the newly founded National Revolutionary Police. Later, he played with the legendary "Charanga Rubalcaba" and with Peruchín, and, on the guitar, played accompaniment for some of the greatest vocalists, including Elena Burke and Omara Portuondo.

While playing as a bassist for the Hotel Habana Libre orchestra, he began to explore arrangement and composition. In 1967, his predilection for jazz led him to join the Revé Orchestra, which favored a *charanga* lineup: piano, double bass, violins, timbales, and five-key flutes. It was hardly an obscure orchestra, nor was it top-of-the-line. Meanwhile, Formell had been listening to Radio Kramer, where he heard Elvis Presley, Little Richard, and the Everly Brothers, and after a while, his desperation to shine led him to break drastically: he left the Revé Orchestra, taking César "Pupy" Pedroso with him, and started searching for a third musician, the crucial third head of the troika.

On December 4, 1969, with the blessing of Saint Barbara, he created Los Van Van: electric bass that was more rhythmic than melodic, keyboards, a standard flute replacing the five-key flute, electric guitar, three vocalists, and a percussion section that quickly became the backbone of the group, with José Luis Quintana (known as "Changuito") as percussionist and strategist.

The double bass laid down the groove. Pupy's keyboard playing, with its distinctive arpeggios, defined the style. But the crucial part of *songo*, what defined songo, was the percussion: timbales, drums, cowbells, cymbals. Changuito transposed the feel of leather into the plasticity of drums. He decanted an ancient liquid into a modern vessel.

━━

Today is May 2, 2014, and as people file past Formell's ashes in the lobby of the National Theater, a mixed-race woman with tattooed eyebrows and a pink dress is sobbing inconsolably.

"Can you imagine?" she says to anyone who is listening. "I learned to dance from Juan Formell when I was seven years old, and I'm forty-one now. I've spent my whole life dancing to Los Van Van."

She takes a handkerchief from her cleavage and dabs at her tears.

Four days ago, Juan Formell was admitted to the CIMEQ Hospital with a recurring liver condition. Yesterday, on May 1, while the whole country was celebrating International Workers' Day, Juan Formell's liver started to bleed. He was rushed to surgery, but there was nothing to be done.

"I've just come from a concert in Cienfuegos, singing the same songs I used to sing with Los Van Van," says Pedro Calvo, the orchestra's former lead singer. "And the crowd was singing along like they'd been written yesterday. They called my cell to give me the news. It was like a gut punch, a terrible pain in my chest."

To a greater or lesser degree, most Cubans would have felt similarly distraught when Formell's death was announced on the eight o'clock news. Beatriz Márquez, who recently recorded "That Love That Dies" with Formell, puts it succinctly: "Cuba's heart is broken."

From behind the perimeter in the lobby of the Sala Avellaneda, the mourners call out to Pedro Calvo, and Pedro Calvo—with his scarf, his wide-brimmed hat, his bushy mustache, his twinkling eyes, and his lothario charm—goes over to greet them. He shakes hands with a black woman who is clearly an initiate of Santería and another black woman wearing a red ribbon who appears to be Calvo's daughter. He shakes hands with a man cradling his baby son. He shakes hands with a disheveled, painfully thin white woman. He shakes the hand of a distracted redhead who has not even proffered hers, and a blond woman who elbows her way in front of a twentysomething mixed-race woman, one of the new generation of fans of Los Van Van. Wedged between them is a dumpy woman in her fifties who cannot reach Pedro Calvo's hand and feels a fleeting sadness.

A voice pipes up and the crowd start to chant "Marilú."

"My mother's name was Marilú," says Telmary, Cuba's foremost female rapper. "Formell used to tell me little stories about her, because I was really young when she died."

Together with "Yuya Martínez" and "La bola de humo," "Marilú" was one of the first songs Los Van Van managed to inject into the heart of Cuban rhythm. The early seventies, when Los Van Van started to develop the style known as Rueda de Casino, melding rock and roll with string arrangements, were remarkable.

Formell simultaneously worked across various genres, including *guaguancó*, *danzón*, and *changüí*, penned *boleros* like "Tal Vez," which would be included in any self-respecting greatest hits compilation, and wrote a number of songs for the Cuban diva Mirtha Medina, his wife from 1977 until the mideighties. (He had three children from his earlier marriage to the dancer Natalia Alonso, and called on one of them, Samuel, to reinvigorate the orchestra.)

In this early period, the dominance of Los Van Van was almost absolute. Dance bands like Ritmo Oriental and Karachi could not keep up. More than that, Los Van Van triggered a sartorial revolution. Members of the group sported sideburns and mustaches. Popular singers like Israel Cantor and Armandito Cuervo were eager to hang out with Pedro Calvo, and in doing so, set the fashion. They partied all night. They drank. Women of all races came and went.

At the time, Formell did not break boundaries, or if so, only the healthy boundaries that his group was determined to break. He had a peculiar mustache, wore caramel-tinted glasses, spoke in a slow drawl, as was always his custom; more than anything, he seemed determined to work out what it was the public wanted.

In the seventies, what the public wanted was *guararey*.

———

Ten years after its founding, the band was celebrated for its hugely successful style of dance music, but Formell torpedoed it with what he claimed was the most daring step ever taken by Los Van Van.

The circumstances were not exactly propitious. Irakere had begun to dabble in popular music. The flautist José Luis Cortés ("el Tosco") had left the group to join the Chucho Valdés all-star big band. In 1980, Los Van Van released *Cuéntame*, an album featuring classic songs from the repertoire such as "De la Habana a Matanzas" or "La rumba no está completa." But it sank almost without trace. So Formell introduced trombones—the trombones so crucial to contorting the waists of *casinero* dancers—and began to include synthesizers.

In 1982, after recording César Pedroso's classic "Seis semanas," Formell came up with another harebrained idea.

"As soon as he'd got people up and dancing, Juan would slow things down," says Pupy. "And it bombed! It hit the dancer where it hurt. That's what happened with 'El buey cansao.' When we started rehearsing the song, we gave him a lot of shit, we told him he was mad."

"So what did he say?"

"He said, 'Okay, then, leave me to my madness.'"

More than thirty years later, "El buey cansao" feels like Formell at his most outrageous, an extraordinary display of virtuosity, courage, and dazzling intuition. There is a secondary theme in the song that rises and fades. It does not fit into any genre. It owes nothing to anyone. Los Van Van would still be Los Van Van without "El buey cansao," but "El buey cansao" is the icing on the cake, the irrefutable proof of genius. An exercise in style into which Formell pours everything he has: music, lyrics, dance. A preposterously emasculated country shrugged its shoulders, began to move to the rhythm, and everyone was happy.

The year 1983 saw the release of *Por encima del nivel*, the album and its title track. In the original mixdown, between the trombones and the effortless, overflowing grace we call *sandunguera*, Formell—doubtless knowing exactly what he was doing—wrote solos for his two cohorts that now seem prescient, even transcendent. César Pedroso astonishes on the piano, before Chango, "el Misterioso," smashes it on the timbales.

In later arrangements, "Por encima del nivel" opens with a dominant violin figure. Formell never truly abandoned the sort of symphonic string arrangement typical of charanga, allowing it to evolve without leading it astray.

The '80s were a crowning achievement. Los Van Van released a huge number of powerful songs, all based on a single simple principle: forget the music, embrace the social.

As Formell said, "To me, the most important thing is the story I'm telling. I can't write a note until I find that story, a story I've found somewhere. I've never stopped being part of the lives of ordinary people, not for nothing, but because I like to live among ordinary people. I like standing in line, listening to their conversations. Queuing for bread is ideal."

Once he found his story, he would start looking for the chorus or the *montuno*—the horn section.

"It's the refrain or the horn section that makes or breaks a dance number. So, I work in reverse, I look for a *montuno* that electrifies the dancer. Inspiration is a mysterious thing. One day it just comes to you—I've no idea from where—and you start writing the number. One example of inspiration was the song 'La titimanía.' Obviously, I'd come across the phrase before, but then one day, I'm driving in my car, and I see a middle-aged man drive up. He stops next to a pretty young girl and opens the door, and I think, 'He's got a bad case of *titimanía*' and right then, I started writing the song."

It should be said that Formell was not quite telling the whole truth: there was no other driver.

It was 1985. Diana Margarita Delgado was a twenty-one-year-old member of the Cuban synchronized swimming team. Formell had recently broken up with Mirtha Medina. He wasn't isolated by his fame. In 1980s Cuba, fame didn't come with a velvet rope. Formell got to travel abroad (not as much as he later would, but he did travel), and the government and cultural institutions recognized his importance, but Formell's daily routine remained much the same as other Cubans.

"He was driving past in his Lada, he stopped the car, offered me a lift, and that's where 'La titimanía' came from," says Diana. "Later, he'd invite me to his shows, he'd take me out dancing, although he never danced himself—who would have imagined?"

On January 26, 1986, Juan and Diana were married. In September 1989, they had a daughter, Paloma. The marriage lasted twenty-two years, until June 2008, and is crucial in understanding the strange twists Formell's life would later take.

——

It wasn't until the nineties that Los Van Van, like Cuba itself, began to break boundaries, to expand into international shows and tours. It became legal for Cuban citizens to have US dollars. There was an influx of foreign investment. Havana was overrun by tourists and, with them, the *jineteras*—the prostitutes who serviced them. As the whole country sank into poverty, having no income of any kind, the nightlife, the hotels, and the cabarets offered the orgiastic debauchery that follows every diplomatic thaw.

Stepping into the ring came Dan Den, "the Charanga Habanera," and Paulo FG, "the Salsa Doctor." Adalberto Álvarez polished his sound. La Original de Manzanillo were regaining popularity. Then NG La Banda burst onto the scene with a raw, kamikaze sound. The whole scene exploded to the sound of timba.

As Formell puts it, "Timba is a raw, aggressive sound, it's hardcore, the instruments drive hard, the lyrics don't really matter."

We all know where *hard core* leads. There are some people who believe a monument should be erected to the *salseros* and the *jineteras*—the dancers and the prostitutes—who, being the only reliable sources of foreign currency, saved 1990s Cuba from utter disaster. Tickets for a salsero event could go for $100. The average monthly wage in Cuba at the time was five bucks. The salseros rose to the status of mob bosses. They ruled Havana. It was Formell who led the bureaucratic battle for career, prestige, reliability. To some extent, it's thanks to

Formell that Cuban musicians were granted certain privileges. They were allowed to buy cars, and to charge fees in US dollars.

After years of hermetic confinement, the sudden freedoms offered by the 1990s led many people astray, to such an extent that, on one occasion, the Ministry of the Interior summoned a number of the major musicians to the Hotel Comodoro for a blood test. Formell, by then an addict, was among those who protested loudly. At the last minute, Abel Prieto, then minister of culture, interceded to stop any further investigation. It was a providential intervention.

Musically, during this period, Los Van Van's greatest talent was its ability to adapt, because by now rhythm and tempo were being set by NG la Banda. The man who truly knew how to put the pedal to the metal was José Luis Cortés: the prodigal son, a flute player with a *heavy* sound. In adopting the prevailing tempo, Formell accentuated the sound of the trombones, allowing the string arrangements to fade into the background. These tweaks simply confirmed what everyone already knew: things may change, but what distinguished Los Van Van, what made them untouchable, was the percussion.

But then, in 1993, Changuito left Los Van Van, and Samuel Formell took over on drums. This was another perilous transition, one Formell addressed by doing what he did best. He penned the song "Pura vestimenta" for Ángel Bonne, and "¡Qué sorpresa! (Tu foto en la prensa)" for Mario (Mayito) Rivera. He didn't write anything specific for Pedro Calvo because Pedro didn't need anyone to write for him, but even so, with Los Van Van at the height of their powers, and before recording "El negro está cocinando," his last big hit, Pedro Calvo sang the hits of the period, like "Que le den candela."

The prosperous Cuba of the '80s that Pedro Calvo epitomized better than anyone—the social chronicle, the veneer of tradition, the cheerful, lighthearted tone—all but disappeared in the '90s. It was replaced, as in any financial crisis, by a renewed feeling of mysticism and faith. There was a rising interest in the Afro-Cuban religions, in Yoruba beliefs, in babalawos, santeros, and paleros: themes that a band as astute as Los Van Van inevitably found a way to weave into their songs. Looking back, it is clear that this was the point at which Pedro Calvo gave center stage to Bonne and Mayito, who sang the majority of the great songs of the period—"Disco Azúcar," "Un socio."

In the mid-'90s, Formell began to spread himself too thin. One of his definitions of timba offers a key to understanding what happened: "The thing about timba is that the woman dances alone, something rare in our culture. The woman dances, sways her hips in a way that is sexual and provocative, what we called '*despelote*'—a frenzy. I don't know why they have to shake their hips so fast, anyone watching would get a headache. . . . Maybe I find it surprising because I don't know how to dance, because I can't express myself physically."

This is the crux: Formell could not dance but he wanted to keep up with the rhythm. He was constantly using booze and hard drugs. True, every song he had ever made was written while he was drinking, but this nosedive seemed irreversible.

He no longer sported a mustache. He looked like shit. He was in his early fifties, his wife in her thirties. In 2011, when the singer-songwriter Amaury Pérez asked him about his wives, Formell said, "My second wife, Diana, well, she was crazy, everyone has their . . ."

"Divine," said Pérez.

"Everyone has their strengths and weaknesses, but to a lot of people, she was an amazing woman, she was cool, and well . . ."

Two inconclusive sentences. Formell's ellipses allow us to suppose that his ex-wife was unstoppable.

"That's the heart and soul of timba. The dancer, particularly the woman, demands a great deal of musical power and aggressiveness . . . and if she doesn't get it, she won't dance. It's like she's asking, Why did you bother showing up with the band?"

Los Van Van were in crisis. Their popularity and the quality of their music were slipping.

"It was the period we were living through," says Diana. "We had this amazing lifestyle, and we started to stay up into the early hours. There were parties, friends. But I don't think the drugs and alcohol were to blame, because Juan was always completely honest. He never hid his addiction from the band members, and he never missed a rehearsal."

Paradoxically, in 1999 the group embarked on a twenty-six-city tour of the United States. The *Los Angeles Times* called them "the undisputed king of Cuban dance orchestras and one of the most influential forces ever in Afro-Cuban music." The *New York Times* dubbed them "the Rolling Stones of salsa."

We understood this nomenclature. Those of us brought up listening to Los Van Van—and this isn't a paean to nationalism—ended up feeling as though there was something insipid about salsa, too much treble, maybe, and not enough bass. As though salsa slams on the brakes just where Los Van Van pumps the accelerator. If New York salsa charged the atmosphere with booze and cigarette smoke, Los Van Van upped the ante with dry ice and marijuana.

———

In 2000, the band finally won a Grammy Award for *Van Van Is Here*, in the Best Salsa Album category. When Formell finally received the long-awaited certificate judging him worthy of the award, he launched into a funny and revealing explanation: "There's a wax seal on it and when you take it off, look, here, it says we won . . . shit— we won a fucking Grammy."

The fact that the album won a Grammy says less about its quality than it does about effective international distribution. They put out much better albums in the 1990s, including *Ay dios Ampáreme* or *Disco Azúcar*. The Recording Academy, belatedly, was dazzled by a Van Van album that Cubans knew was not their best. Another clue: the three best songs on *Van Van Is Here*—"La bomba soy yo," "Temba, Tumba, Timba," and "El negro está cocinando"—are all by Pupy.

At this point, Formell was in failing health and handed over the musical direction of the group to his son. Although the close friendship between them has meant that César Pedroso has never discussed the subject, everyone knows his reasons for quitting Los Van Van are related to Formell's decision.

Diana confides: "We'd just gotten back from a European tour, and Pedrito gave him a letter explaining why he didn't want to carry on. Pupy's letter was much the same, but Juan was more hurt, he was really hurt, because he loved Pupy both as a man and as a musician. Personally, I think—though it's only an impression—that bringing in a number of young musicians, and not just Samuel, made the old guard feel insecure. I don't know."

In the documentary *Eso que anda*, Pupy says, "I didn't want it to be that way. I wanted them to come to me and say, 'Look, let's talk about this.' But it never happened."

He falls silent, and the camera stays on Pupy as he bows his head, steeling his whole body to choke back his tears.

"We all quit," Pedro Calvo says in the same documentary, "but Los Van Van carried on. Doesn't matter if the group quits. As long as Formell's still there, Los Van Van will still be Los Van Van. Fuck it."

That seems to be the real problem. Formell miraculously recovered from his various addictions. When he was diagnosed with cirrhosis of the liver, he decided to call it a day. But even Formell can't make a comeback from death. Only now can we begin to judge whether his role with Los Van Van over the past decade was superfluous or, as many of us believe, utterly crucial. Perhaps Los Van

Van should do what their leader always did in times of trouble: write more songs. Although, as everyone knows, it's tough to reinvent a formula without its creator.

After Pedro Calvo leaves the group, Formell brings in Abdel Rasalps, known as "El Lele." To stifle the comparisons between El Lele and Pedro Calvo, he takes a chance and brings in Yeni Valdés (the first and, over time, the most successful female member of Los Van Van), a move that would put the spotlight on her.

Yeni has a more powerful voice than El Lele, who can take on a song and come out the winner, but never quite delivers a KO.

In 2013, the Latin Recording Academy presented Formell with a Special Award for Musical Excellence. The citation reads, "Juan Formell is the very definition of a musical innovator."

Between their two Grammys, Los Van Van released *Chapeando*, *Arrasando*, and *La Maquinaria*, records that were more coherent but that, while more innovative, more frenetic than anything being recorded by their peers in Cuba, were not quite up to the standard they had set.

These days, Los Van Van resort to playing '70s and '80s arrangements of their songs, and various repetitive, self-referential tracks that are a reminder of their long history, a reminder of how consistent and how brilliant they can be, of how many years they've managed to capture the popular imagination. The worst thing is that they do so not because they're complacent but because they seem to have run out of ideas.

It hardly matters. No other group could have contributed so many of the individual styles of *casino*, or more fiercely defended the variants of each style. From the elegant, sensual, traditional casino of the '70s, with dancers in two-tone shoes, Bolshevik hats, a loose-fitting *guayabera* shirt, and razor-pleated trousers, to the style of "Agua," one of Los Van Van's most recent hits. A number so wild that it would be a real challenge for the band to play live if they decided to pull out all the stops.

—

The watchword today is trauma.

"This is our first day without Formell, and I don't think we've truly realized what that means," says Ian Padrón, director of the documentary *Eso que anda* and all of the audiovisual material Los Van Van has produced in recent years. "In time, we'll realize how unlikely it is that we will even come upon another Formell, someone of the stature of Pérez Prado or Benny Moré."

Although we might assume its editors are also shocked and saddened, the May 2 issue of *Granma*, the official newspaper of the Cuban Communist Party, cannot seem to come to terms with the magnitude of Formell's death. Of the newspaper's sixteen pages, pages 2, 3, 4, 5, 6, 7, 8, and 9 are devoted to coverage of the May 1 International Workers' Day parades taking place across the country, the speeches, the impressions, the medals, and the atmosphere. The huge photograph of the Undefeated People thronging the Plaza de Revolución on the front page takes up more space than the third of a page afforded to the Cuban Institute of Music's article about Formell's death on page 14.

"National Music Prize Winner Juan Formell Dies" reads the ill-worded headline. Juan Formell was so much more than a National Music Prize winner; it wasn't the National Music Prize that gave Formell his status, but the reverse. Just once it would have been nice to see a more honest, less officious headline, one that did not try to use the death of an artist in the service of militaristic nationalism.

But the lobby of the National Theater is a fitting place for this last farewell. In September 2009, a stone's throw away, on the Plaza de la Revolución, the Peace without Borders concert organized by

Colombian singer Juanes ended with Los Van Van giving one of the finest performances anyone in Cuba can remember, and one of the most representative of the group.

"When I stepped onto the stage and saw the huge crowd of people, I nearly dropped dead," Formell later told Amaury Pérez. "I thought, I can't do this, this is something that's never . . . never happened to us."

After a day of sweltering sunshine, after four hours of music, after months of tensions and pressure from political groups in Miami not to stage the concert, in this heady, intoxicating atmosphere, Los Van Van walked out onto the stage and played, even when the sound system failed. And the people danced.

Today, in the lobby of the National Theater, everyone is dealing with their own grief. Some are visibly shocked, huddling together in the midst of the commotion, erecting a wall of silence. Ian Padrón and the salsa singer Alain Daniel seem to be pacing in their respective rooms, stunned and solitary. César Pedroso struggles to speak, his self-consciousness an indication that he has just lost someone without whom he cannot express himself.

There are actors, troubadours, jazz musicians, rumberos, film directors, cultural attachés, people from all walks of life and, as if to confirm the link between the Havana baseball team Los Industriales and Los Van Van, a long line of famous baseball players.

Needless to say, there are occasional moments of comic pathos. Singers Jacob Forever and Juan Guillermo (aka "JG"), two hip young guys, hug each other fiercely and exchange phones numbers or something using their bulky cell phones. As Jacob Forever walks around, he is trailed by two mestiza women taking pictures or filming a video of him, whispering, "OMG, he's so cute! OMG, he's so handsome!"

It is not yet five o'clock. The ashes will remain on display until seven, but the pace of events will remain the same.

El Lele says, "Just now some said you have to be strong. Maybe I just don't know how, maybe that's why I'm crying."

Robertón, another singer with Los Van Van, says, "Formell is sheer joy. I am grateful to him for more than ninety percent of my life."

Together, the contrasting feelings evoked by these two sentences lay bare the contradiction faced by those who have come to the vigil: how to express grief at the death of someone they remember as the epitome of joy, as having built an empire of joy.

As an example, at the Peace without Borders concert in Havana (one that, we now know, was the end of a cycle), Formell held a million people spellbound and achieved the impossible: he had had a crowd of perfect strangers dancing casino with one another. Los Van Van improvised over Compay Segundo's "Chan Chan" and Martí's "Versos Sencillos." Mario Rivera sang in his husky, almost hoarse *sonero* voice. A bewildered Juanes applauded. Alexander Abreu gave an improvised trumpet solo. Olga Tañón cried. Miguel Bosé cried. People danced in their own individual casino style—whether '70s, '80s, or '90s. And that moment was a photo.

Formell played bass, bent slightly forward. On one hand, on the arch between his thumb and forefinger, he had a tattoo of a clover leaf.

TIGHT-LIPPED

Reynaldo Villafranca, "Coqui," should have died ten years ago, on the main drag of Los Palacios, when some neurotic homophobe stabbed him in the stomach. Minutes earlier, in the town's only nightclub, Coqui had played a little joke on his murderer—flirted with him, maybe, or gave him a slightly smutty compliment—nothing particularly malicious.

"My son was always like that," says Justa Antigua, twirling her hands in the air, then letting them go limp. "Always joking around."

For weeks, Coqui was kept in intensive care, technically dead.

"They put plastic guts in him and saved his life," says Alicia Cordero, a slight, stooped woman. "But later we got worried, because Coqui needed to fart, and he couldn't. And we all wanted him to fart to see whether the operation had been successful. Then, finally he let one rip. We had a party."

It is a petty story, but if Coqui had died at that time, rather than now, in January 2015, death would have had its advantages. He could have been buried in the town cemetery, a few blocks from his home, surrounded by the dead he knew, rather than the foreign dead who surround him now and make everything even more inhospitable for Villafranca.

On the other hand, dying as a result of the stabbing would have had its disadvantages. It wouldn't have been an international news story and would have elicited the same reaction as any death in a small town: a little morbid curiosity—perhaps more than a little in Coqui's case, since it would have been murder—a little rowdy nostalgia, and then a tedious interlude until the next death came along.

It is January 28, 2015. Reynaldo Villafranca died ten days ago, from malaria with cerebral complications. He had just turned forty-three. He was a nurse and one of the 165 members of the Henry Reeve International Medical Brigade sent by the Cuban government to Sierra Leone to combat the Ebola virus in October 2014. He is the second member of the brigade to die, and the first of the health professionals.

This is why I'm sitting in the living room of Alicia Cordero at 19a, calle 28, where Villafranca also rehearsed, lip-synching to English songs—Cindy Lauper, Whitney Houston—in front of the television, and later would dress up in drag and perform at the nightly activities organized by the municipal authorities at the Ranchón de Los Palacios.

"All completely legal," clarifies Nereida Hernández, the district head.

And this is why I now cross the street, walk through a front garden, knock on the front door of number 16a, ask for permission to enter, and wander through the rooms: the living room—broken dolls, a Santería altar in the corner; the bedrooms—dark and foul-smelling; the kitchen—crudely painted a cloudy blue; and out into the backyard—a dripping hose, hanging laundry, a rusty cistern. I reach the little shed where Villafranca slept, far from the rest of his family: a miserable wooden shack.

"I told you," Nereida whispers. "It's a dump."

For the first time, Justa breaks down and weeps inconsolably. She pleads to have her son back. Though it is a logical reaction, it leaves me stunned. Justa has just spent the afternoon telling me that we must accept what God ordains. That if Coqui survived more terrible brushes with death only to die now, suddenly, it is because this is what was written. To me her neat little equation—the untimely death of a child, the will of the Almighty, human resignation—seemed to conceal a lot of cruelty and very little love. But now, as I watch her weeping, her cataleptic sobs so characteristic of mothers, it occurs to me that in the face of what happened, of what happens every day, this woman justifies remaining impassive or even calm in the face of death, at least on the surface.

I try to comfort her and, as I do so, I glance around to get a sense of the place. There is a cast-iron table with a flower-print tablecloth, an electric stove, another stove that is rusted and useless, a saucepan caked with frijoles, a greasy dishcloth, a coffee pot with no lid, plastic bottles of various sizes, an empty beer bottle, scraps of orange peel, and clumps of rice on the tablecloth. On another, smaller table stands a Russian television, which seems to be broken.

"Remember that, to many people, your son was a symbol," I say. Anything to comfort her.

"That's what I've been telling you," says Nereida.

The transcendence of death, which always seems like an insult when compared to death itself, seems to calm her a little.

I go into the bedroom. A couple of broken fans and some old clothes: a folded baseball cap, a pair of rolled-up trousers. In the wardrobe, a pile of tangled clothes, as though it was a dog's kennel. There are wooden boxes, crates, suitcases, a sink that has never been plumbed in, a dusty bed, a tatty shutter covered with Major League Baseball stickers. And in the bathroom, a broken cup.

To all of the above, which, though untidy, is not particularly alarming, let us add one, perhaps even two layers of crud. Let us add a thick crust, bare patches of soil, grease stains to the clothes, the fans, the curtains, the tablecloths. Lots of neglect, lots of grayness, lots of poverty.

Though the shack has probably deteriorated during the past ten days of mourning, it must not look much different from how it was when Villafranca was alive. Maybe in the belief that the fight against

Ebola is not, in itself, a sufficiently humanitarian endeavor, official reports neglect to mention how much members of the brigade were paid, and talk only of altruism, solidarity, selflessness, greatness of spirit. It is crystal clear to everyone. There are lots of ways to make money without exposing yourself to the Ebola virus. But if you are paid to do so, that's completely legitimate.

At this point, Justa Antigua mentions something that no one has dared to say, something fundamental: "He went to Africa so he'd be able to buy a little house and get out of this place. I wanted both of us to get out. He liked that idea. But he wouldn't be swayed, and he was so close to coming home."

This is not true. He was not nearly finished. He had half the mission still to go.

===

The stabbing outside the nightclub was not the first tragedy that Villafranca experienced in his life. His mother, a *santera* with a curious way of calling on God, has spent her life styling and straightening hair. At age five, Villafranca drinks some of the defrizzing liquid his mother has left lying around and suffers chemical burns to his throat. He has to be fitted with a plastic oesophagus.

Villafranca has five brothers and sisters. All but him by the same father. All except him grew up to be career criminals and ex-cons. So it's hardly surprising that, from a very young age, he crosses the street to seek refuge in Alicia Cordero's house. He carries on visiting her for more than thirty years—until he leaves for Sierra Leone—to confess his sins and to eat whatever Alicia might have in a saucepan or in the fridge: chicken, some croquettes, a *batido*, a glass of fruit juice. And it is he—no one else—who in time becomes Alicia's masseur, her private nurse, the person who takes her blood pressure, the one who rubs her back.

"The real grief over his death took place here," Nereida says, standing in the courtyard of number 19a.

"The only thing he didn't do at my house was sleep," says Alicia.

After high school, Villafranca decides not to carry on with his studies. His mother makes no objection.

"He was always very independent," Justa says, "and I supported him, because he always knew what he was doing."

And apparently, he did know. He goes to university to study for a bachelor's degree, and completes it. Afterward he works as a farm laborer for a cotton factory in Los Palacios. Later he becomes a dockhand for an agricultural company. Then, around 1997, through a series of state-sponsored courses, he begins to study nursing, the profession he really loves. After he graduates, he specializes in intensive care nursing: treating foot ulcers for diabetics, performing CPR, and so on. For a year, he works in the intensive therapy room of Abel Santamaría provincial hospital in Pinar del Río. After this, he is transferred to the polyclinic in San Diego—about twenty kilometers from Los Palacios—and there he stays.

He continues to take courses in health sciences and in English, improving himself, as they say. He also tends to neighbors on his block (a common practice among Cuban doctors and nurses, working outside working hours). He has a fondness for elderly patients. Colostomies, cancer. And, according to everyone who remembers him, he is invariably cheerful, funny, and has a silver tongue. He never hides his homosexuality. He gossips and jokes with the neighbors. He is open, perhaps too open for such a small town. It seems likely that Villafranca was an exquisite bird of night. One of the friends he parties with, Hanói, is HIV positive.

"But Coqui was always looking for condoms," says Alicia. Nereida nods.

From time to time, Villafranca cries his heart out. A curt psychological sketch might suggest that he laughs and jokes to blot out the violence at home, and cruises the streets to dispel the ghosts that haunt him.

"A little while ago," says Alicia, "he showed up with a gash across his head, dripping blood like an animal." The wound required four stitches.

The wound was simply the culmination of an argument with one of his brothers.

Alicia starts to list the countless times Villafranca was robbed by members of his family. The washing machine and the bathroom suite that was stolen from him; the clothes, the perfume, and the slippers that were filched; the missing turkey of which nothing was left but feathers; the little piglet he had before he left for Africa, which was sold as soon as he stepped onto the plane.

Alicia doesn't have to work hard to be convincing—just take a cursory glance at where some of the Villafranca brothers are today.

Tomás Zayas was deported from the United States for various crimes. Manteca, the oldest of the siblings, was recently released from prison and placed under house arrest because he had terminal cancer, and in a few short hours had robbed two of his other brothers and disappeared; no one knows where he is. Mayeya, one of his sisters, is behind bars because during visits to her son she slipped trihexyphenidyl, a drug for treating Parkinson's, into his food. Her son, for his part, is serving a sentence for murdering two people in Los Palacios.

Needless to say, none of them has any respect for Justa Antigua. Justa Antigua has no respect for them. The only thing Villafranca had left was his mother. And the only person who cared about Justa, now seventy-nine, was Villafranca. Justa's youngest son was her last real chance to get out of the hellhole where she lives.

But that possibility is gone now. Stolen from her by malaria.

═══

In the photo—possibly a passport photograph—taken of the members of the brigade before they flew to Sierra Leone, Villafranca projects an imposing gravity. He is bald, with an oval face, noble eyes, his skin black and glossy, his full lips pursed. Everything seems contained and about to explode, as though Villafranca is trying to say to the photographer, "Come on, *chico*, get it over with."

In town, there are rumors that Villafranca was scared before he left on the mission. But Nereida, Justa, and Alicia cannot confirm this. In this, it should be said, none of them can really be trusted. They may think that if Villafranca felt fear, that would detract from his virtues. They are accustomed to hearing that all those who die on Cuban missions face death fearlessly, unwaveringly, as steadfast and unbowed as a rock. So they are unwilling to let Coqui be thought of as the only coward.

On the other hand, Villafranca, appearing in some of the television footage shot before the volunteers set off on their mission, seems to be his usually cheerful self.

"Have you ever heard the roar when Pinar del Río hits a home run? Well, that was the roar that went up all over town when he appeared on the news: 'Look, it's Coqui! Look, it's Coqui!'" Nereida says, distraught, dabbing at her tears.

Villafranca's excellent communication skills, and his ability to speak English and even some Portuguese, meant that he spent days in the Kerry Town Ebola Treatment Centre, away from those suffering from the disease, focused on procedure and other issues. This, obviously, didn't mean he wasn't at risk.

On the morning of January 17, he begins to suffer from diarrhea, and by the afternoon his temperature has spiked to 38°C. He is tested for malaria. The test proves positive. He is given oral antimalarial medications. His temperature continues to soar. He loses all sense of time and space. Doctors transfer him to the British Army hospital, where he is admitted. A second test for malaria is positive, while a test for Ebola proves negative. He is given the latest IV anti-malarial treatment.

Through the night and into the early hours, Villafranca's condition worsens. He is now suffering from breathing difficulties and seizures. Doctors put him on a ventilator, but he does not respond to treatment and some hours later, he dies.

"I was doing a defrizz," Justa says, "when I see these people in white coats, a stream of people coming in, and my heart stops."

The people are from the municipal and provincial public health authorities. Justa knows she can't just stop in the middle of the defrizzing treatment without risking burning the hair. Even so, the straightening iron slips from her fingers and she faints. No one from the public health authority has ever come to her house. The news doesn't need to be stated. The very presence of the messenger says it all. While Justa finishes straightening the woman's hair, one of the officials tells her what she already knows.

The following day, a posthumous tribute to Villafranca takes place at the Galería del Arte in Los Palacios. People stand vigil next to a photo of him, his passport photo. Those in attendance include deputy ministers from the public health service, city and provincial officials, coworkers, health-care workers, people who knew Villafranca and people who didn't know him but want to show their solidarity.

At the last minute, Nereida manages to persuade Justa to go to the vigil. One person who does not attend is Hanói, Villafranca's wingman in their nocturnal escapades. When he comes to the door, Hanói says, "I'm sorry, but I'm in no fit state to talk. I've got nothing to say. I carry him in here." He lays a hand over his heart. "He'll always be with me. That's all."

=

It is more than three years before Villafranca's body, or more likely his ashes, are repatriated. The salary for the mission will be paid, though no one yet knows who Villafranca named as his next of kin. No one dares discuss it openly. Alicia says she's heard rumors that she might be the beneficiary. But she says it as though it were a bad thing.

"It would have been a shitty thing for him to do. I don't even want to think about it. Just look what happened about his phone."

One of Villafranca's nieces is demanding the phone be assigned to her uncle as a member of the brigade. But Villafranca had insisted that the phone be installed in Alicia's house.

"A phone costs more than $500," says Nereida. "If the family get their hands on it, they'll sell it."

Death inevitably brings with it material issues that create a ticking time bomb. It is a problem that worries Alicia, but she doesn't want her worry to indicate a lack of love. At the end of the day, Alicia has spent decades caring for Villafranca, so she has every right to worry or fret about whatever she likes, even practical problems, even a telephone.

The last time she talked to her boy, she was sitting in the living room of her home. It was December 30. Villafranca called to wish her a happy new year. Alicia says he was in good spirits because they had managed to save three children, that he laughed with unadulterated joy, in that camp, affected manner of his.

DANCING IN THE DARK

I. The Dancers

A year ago, before it was overgrown by weeds, before the stench gave way to the metallic smell of silence, a savage rain was falling around the garbage dump and they were huddled like sick animals in Luz María's *quimbo*—her shack—a putrid hovel.

Chen was saying something about climate change. Luz María was picking fleas off her hairless dog. And Yorgelis was still expending most of his energy maintaining the lifeless rictus smile that adorned his face in all circumstances and made him look miserable.

They stayed inside out of sheer habit. Motionless. Bristling. There was nothing to suggest they were any less wet than they would be outside. Fat raindrops fell from the ceiling with a splash. Until, providentially, the rain stopped, they stretched themselves out, and the trance was broken and replaced by a righteous sun that put everything in its place.

Yorgelis headed out to sell two large bags of plastic bottles he'd collected. Luz María picked up the bottle of pungent moonshine. And Chen went back to his quimbo, to sleep, he said. But there was still an hour to go before dark, so Chen decided to go to the garbage dump. He had worked out what time the trucks from the airport and the army base would show up. The military trucks would

often throw out whole pig's trotters and heads, gallons of marma-
lade, bread that had been baked earlier in the day. Chen preferred
the army trucks.

Meanwhile, Luz María was talking to herself as she stirred the
pot of frijoles.

"How long does it take for them to soften?"

"You just keep putting more wood on until they're soft."

She seemed anxious and constantly glanced toward the bridge.
She paced around, then stopped, crouched down, and started pulling up weeds. She didn't stop drinking. And still she kept clanking
around, watching for something.

"How did your mother seem?"

Three or four days earlier, her mother and her stepfather had
come to visit. Luz María's stepfather, a fortysomething Asian man,
had previously been her partner. And it was Luz María who had
fixed him up with her mother, a sixty-year-old woman who talked
little and scuttled around from place to place, doing chores no one
asked her to do out of sheer maternal obligation, and who, during
one such outing, to drown out her daughter's voice, tossed a muddy
bottle full of gasoline into the campfire and the flames flared so high
they singed her right eyelid.

Nobody seemed particularly concerned. Not even the woman
herself.

"She's better," Luz María said. "She had another black eye, but
I warned her about him."

A few feral chickens pecked through the dust. The dog prowled
around the big tree, an ancient varicose cedar. In the soot-blackened
pot, the beans simmered over a low heat. Soaking in a basin of murky
water were a pair of trousers and foul-smelling stockings; this was
what they called "doing the laundry." The last traces of rain faded.
Just as the silence threatened to become absolute, a figure appeared
at the other side of the bridge, heading toward the quimbo.

"Here comes Huevo," called Luz María.

And she started to bellow. She went over to the dog. She told the dog to guard her. She took another swig of hooch and pleaded with the dog to protect her, for God's sake. She bellowed again, sinking into despair, as though knowing that no one could protect her. Yet even so, her voice now barely a whisper, she went on pleading for someone to protect her, Mother of God, for someone, no, not again, for someone, anyone to protect her.

II. The Garbage Dump

The Bote de Cien is the largest landfill in Cuba: 104 hectares, taking 80 percent of Havana's garbage—about 1,650 tons a day—and with a total capacity of 7.8 million cubic meters. Since it first opened in 1976, it has been dubbed an "environmental hazard" and a "major source of pollution."

It is, or was intended to be, a sanitary landfill. As organic waste rots, it produces methane; the gas accumulates in the spaces in the garbage and ignites. For decades, fires have raged over the garbage dump, and the fetid cloud of smoke has spread to the surrounding areas, as far as residential neighborhoods like Marianao and even to the CUJAE, the Technological University of Havana José Antonio Echeverría, the largest technological university in the country.

To avoid this, the garbage should be crushed as soon as it is dumped into the landfill's cells and valleys. It should be compacted over and over, then covered with a layer of soil, to create a "sandwich." In fact, this sandwich method is what defines a sanitary landfill.

The bote de Cien, which started out as a lake, and is now four or five stories high, has gone through good and bad periods—or bad and less bad. With very little equipment, sometimes none at all, no bulldozers, no compactors, none of the equipment necessary to treat toxic gases, garbage has continued to accumulate, spilling out until it is almost on the doorsteps of the nearby shacks. To continue calling the bote a sanitary landfill is a euphemistic technicality. With no controls in place, a landfill quickly becomes a garbage dump.

The situation deteriorated during the Special Period. Later, Comunales, the government service tasked with collecting and managing waste, became self-financing. But after the economic centralization in 2005 and the reallocation of government funds, Comunales found it had to compete for funds with more critical public sector facilities—transportation, housing, education, and health services—and as a result, between January 2005 and June 2006, it didn't receive a centavo.

Needless to say, the sanitary landfill project collapsed and has never fully recovered. They managed to build roads and embankments, and there were unsuccessful attempts to negotiate mixed investments between the Cuban government and European companies.

As the recycling industry knows all too well, garbage is not garbage—it's money. On a smaller scale, as a means of survival, ordinary people know this too. The most valuable raw materials are aluminium and other metals. Then glass, plastics, and, for some people, clothing and food scraps. Metals are sold to recycling companies; plastics are often sold to illegal soft drink companies; clothes not intended for personal use are traded with others.

In the savage subculture of the Bote de Cien, there are various types of "divers," or garbage collectors, all of whom are hunted by the authorities. If caught, they're accused of spreading epidemics, but they are quickly released and come back only to be arrested again, then others are arrested and they too come back, and if they don't come back, it makes no difference. There are always new people joining the garbage business.

In this vicious circle, the forces of law and order have the upper hand. First, because those prepared to trawl through a garbage dump in order to survive have already lost everything. They don't care what happens to them. And second, because the only real solution would be to make all or most laboring jobs more profitable than collecting garbage for resale. In a country where the average monthly wage is about twenty-five dollars—the equivalent of a couple of days spent digging through the garbage dump—this seems little short of impossible.

There are dozens of them. There are those who travel from Havana every day to the spot where trucks unload the garbage. There are those who stay for two or three or four days at a time, sleeping on-site, embarking on collection marathons before taking a break and coming back later. There are nomads like Yorgelis, who come from other provinces and stay for two or three months until they have amassed a reasonable amount of money. And then there are those who live next to the dump full-time: Luz María and Chen.

III. The Outskirts

From the outskirts, the garbage dump looked like a papier-mâché volcano: a solid wall of garbage soaring diagonally toward some point of convergence. And inside, the lava. It was not particularly difficult to find. Head through Boyeros, then, seven or eight blocks past Avenida 100, turn right, and at the end of the dirt track, cross the bridge.

Amid a dense undergrowth that offers camouflage, protection, and shade, ringed by a fetid ditch that floods during heavy downpours, the barren peak harbored smells of the greatest chemical simplicity. It was not simply the stench; the molecules that created the stench clung to every nostril hair, creating sensory overload. Over time, your olfactory receptors, your nose, even your mind seemed to stink.

In order to cope with the rank air, the cavernous hunger, the nightly visits of mosquitoes, and the unrelenting heat, Luz María, Chen, and anyone who spent time there were forced to numb themselves with booze. There was so much alcohol that they no longer got drunk. Drunkenness and its effects were the norm.

"I told her to change her hair," Chen said. "I don't like it that way."

"Well, I like it," Luz María said, picking at her toenails with a toothpick.

"The way she had her hair yesterday was more classic, more natural."

"So, what does it look like now?"

"It's overdone, it puffed up, it's not her," Chen said.

"Yeah sure," said Luz María, the bangs falling over her face and the blue scarf covering her head giving her the appearance of a Romani gypsy.

"Yeah sure what?" Chen said.

"Yeah sure," Luz María said and got up to go look for her dog.

"I only say it so she'll look pretty, but she never listens to me," Chen said.

Later Luz María would come back and say that the food Chen liked best was the food she cooked.

"And you like the food I cook," Chen said.

"The meals we make ourselves are the ones we like best," Luz María said.

They talked offhandedly about food, but the most protein-rich delicacy to pass through their shack was the dark shapeless mass of meat—chicken, they claimed—simmered in boiling water after four days spent rotting.

"We cook it both ways," Chen said.

Spicy and extraspicy.

It sounded slightly sleazy.

"Are you guys together? Do you like each other?"

But that was not how things worked in the quimbos. There were no partners, no preferences. Only instincts.

"A little flea," Luz María said as she stroked the bald back of her starving, mange-riddled dog.

"Friends. Friends who love each other very much," Chen said, pretending things worked that way in the quimbos.

Forgetfulness weighs like an anvil. Much of the past had to be forgotten in this hard, unforgiving present. The law of the landfill—lives that were precarious, but uninhibited—imposed a form of freedom very much like slavery.

IV. Luz María

A slip of a woman. A thirty-nine-year-old wizened stump who looked sixty and who had already endured more than any life could bear.

All her teeth were missing, except for the two canine teeth. Parts of her right ear were missing. Her breasts were two dry dugs. Her bones protruded so severely it looked like they might break through her skin. The hardened flecks of spittle at the corners of her mouth formed a permanent white paste. When she cried, she shed no tears. When forced to remember some detail of her former life, she recounted it like a fairy tale, or something that had happened to someone else, someone close to her, but not her.

She had come to Havana from eastern Cuba in the '90s. She had worked as a dancer in Varadero and later in Tropicana. She brought her mother and her grandmother to live in Havana. When her grandmother became ill, she was forced to stop working. By the time she went back, she had lost her job.

At some point, she met her husband, who introduced her to the garbage dump. But her husband had been arrested twice for garbage diving, and now she was alone with a pile of letters in which her husband told her that he loved her and asked her to wait for him. She sent him cartons of cigarettes in jail. When her husband came back, everything would go back to normal.

"I'm exhausted from working all the time," she said. "I've got painful hernias, and my knees are shot."

Her quimbo is built from cardboard boxes, sacks, plastic garbage can lids, Styrofoam, scraps of all manner of materials.

"This is where I wash," she said, pointing to a dark corner. "Nobody can see me." A piece of board divided the bathroom from what was supposed to be the living room. Every object, every ornament came from the dump: the glasses she drank water from, the basin she used to wash dishes, the porcelain dolls, the bottles of deodorant, the rags piled up in corners.

There was no order, no method. Nothing but a desperate urge to accumulate garbage.

"I sometimes entertain myself with the television over there." A screen, on a table.

There were plastic flowers, pamphlets about Pope John Paul II and the Kama Sutra, DVDs of series such as *Addicted to Love*, fashion magazines with the blank face of some sexy blond smiling on the glossy pink cover.

"I also like to knit—I knitted this myself." She takes down a plastic factory-made doll.

Luz María didn't even know what year it was. This was reason enough to believe every word that came out of the dark, terrifying, cavernous maw that was her mouth. Every man who passed through ended up having sex—or whatever—with her. It was the closest she came to being a woman. Not that they raped her. They fucked.

Her swollen belly was like taut leather, so caked in dirt it looked as though she had a second skin. Her belly button protruded like a dial of misery. And always, using a very pale pencil, she would paint the trembling outline of her lips and the rough bags beneath her brows.

V. Chen

He was sixty-four, prominent ribs down to his sternum, a look of stony cynicism or terrible indifference, and a scar that ran from his navel to his groin. He had been a bricklayer in Varadero, where he had worked to build hotels like the Sol Palmeras, which "architecturally, seen from above, looks like a rose."

He was the doyen of the bote. For the past eight months he has been living in a new quimbo. The authorities had torn down several previous shacks, and for about a year and a half he had lived outside, in all weather. According to him, it was best to be on his side, because no one messed with him. "Here comes broken-ass Chen," "Hey, look, it's Chen the faggot," people said when he showed up, but only as a joke. Huevo, the delinquent feared by many of the residents, was Chen's godson, so Chen could do whatever he liked at the garbage dump and no one could touch him. Even the cops didn't mess with Chen, though this wasn't out of respect, but sheer apathy. Chen knew that. There was no point in arresting him.

"If they move me on from here, I go elsewhere. And if they move me on from there, I come back here. It's not a crime."

"What if they shut down the landfill?"

"I'll go wherever they build the new dump. Because that's where we belong. Our class."

"What class is that?"

"The underclass. Not because we're criminals. The class I really belong to, the honest underclass. The millionaire belongs to one class, the semimillionaire to another, and I belong at the bote. I could show you where I slept last night—and I slept like a president. And d'you know why I slept like a president? Because I've got no one dragging me down, I don't need people around me. I have a little drink, I smoke a cigarette, and I think."

On more than one occasion, Chen has been committed to La Colonia, an asylum for the homeless and the mentally ill located relatively close to the dump. But he always runs away.

"They shit themselves in that place. So, maybe I stink because I live in the dump, but they stink a lot worse than me."

"The lunatics used to claw at me," says Luz María, who has also been institutionalized.

Chen leaned back against the roots of the varicose cedar, took the grocer's pencil from behind his ear, and like a shaman, tried to decipher a riddle.

"What is born on land and dies in the sea?" he read. They all thought about it.

"A turtle," said Yorgelis.

"Could be," said Chen. "Or a plane. Planes get lost at sea."

"A river," said Yorgelis.

"River is good," said Chen. "River is 71 and last night I threw a 76. Mary is the mother of Jesus and the first mother, and I threw it on Mother's Day."

Then he took out another piece of paper and started.

"What lives only when it flies? Clue: the wind."

"Don't know," said Yorgelis.

"A kite, which is 74," said Chen. "That's it, 71 and 74."

He always wore khaki trousers. A Mickey Mouse doll hung from the ceiling of his quimbo.

VI. Yorgelis

He hailed from El Cristo, a town on the outskirts of Santiago de Cuba. He worked as a farm laborer and lived with his mother. A friend had tipped him off about the garbage dump.

These days, he collected old plastic bottles and sold them to a soft drinks company in Alquízar. When he decided he'd collected enough, he would go home, give the money to his mother, then come back to Havana. Luz María and Chen had taken him in. He wasn't the only person who lived part-time in the quimbos. He was the duty "diver." He said little and kept to the shade.

He was twenty-four years old and could always be found reading something—books, magazines, whatever.

A few days earlier, he'd been arrested and taken to the police station by cops who mistook him for a burglar. He informed them that, even though he hadn't gone to college, he knew his rights, and they had to tell him why they had arrested him and what he was charged with.

"If the woman who'd called the cops hadn't shown up and told them I was innocent, I'd be there still."

"So, were you scared?"

"No," Chen interrupted. "If you're scared at the police station you might as well go down to the cemetery and dig your own grave."

"No, I wasn't scared," said Yorgelis.

Perhaps the most painful and the most striking things about him were his cheekbones and his nose. His face was disfigured by virulent red acne pustules that festered from the filth of the garbage dump and turned him into a clown without an audience. Calloused boils, congealed pus, small crimson golf balls that, had they been outside the skin rather than inside, would have come loose and fallen off.

VII. The Dancers

Huevo didn't wait to get to the quimbos before getting drunk. He showed up drunk. He was no taller than five foot eleven. He was skinny and loudmouthed. There were so many stories about him, so many rumors, that he might as well have been a fictional character. He kept a knife tucked into the back of his trousers. The handle poked through his sweater.

He asked Luz María what there was to eat and when she said "frijoles," he flew into a rage.

"Just frijoles?"

"Just frijoles."

Chen emerged from his quimbo. He was incapable of sympathy for anyone. He was greedy.

"Go get the rice," said Huevo. "I know you've got some."

"I haven't got any rice," said Luz María.

"Do I have to get it myself?" said Huevo.

"Get the rice, Luz María," said Chen.

"Do I have to get it myself?" Huevo said again.

He tripped over his tongue. His eyes were jaundiced, shot full of booze and pride.

"I haven't got any rice," said Luz María like the animal she was. "Ask anyone, I haven't got any rice."

Huevo headed toward the quimbo and Luz María ran after him.

"Don't you go in there, you faggot," she said. "You've no business going in there."

Huevo pushed her aside and Luz María fell to the ground. Chen watched from a corner.

"She knows what he's like," he said.

Huevo emerged triumphantly brandishing a bag of rice. Then he poured the rice onto the ground and said, "So, this is the rice you haven't got?"

Luz María howled. Huevo strode over to her and asked why she was fucking with him. He grabbed her shoulders and shook her. He squeezed her mouth, bit it, placed his hand on what would have been Luz María's vagina, her rags. He led her into the quimbo, and Luz María allowed herself to be led, while Chen turned his back and wandered off down the track.

He walked for a while until he came to the scales where the trucks are weighed before being unloaded, then climbed onto the first truck to arrive. License plate: HUF 943.

Feral dogs teemed in this lunar landscape. The dusty white cliffs, the gaping cells, the compacted mounds of garbage, the scant natural light. All around, the lights of the city twinkled like a staircase hovering in midair.

When the driver of HUF 943 reached the unloading area, raucous bodies emerged from the ground, gradually getting to their feet, clutching spikes, torches, flashlights, and surrounded the churning machine.

As the putrid mass of garbage spilled out, the divers deftly began their assault. They wore boots, long-sleeved shirts, bandanas over their ears, some wore miners' helmets. Using their spikes, they rummaged around until they found something plastic or metal. They rooted through the acid. Black liquid spread like drool. All the waste discarded by Havana had its final inspection here.

The trucks continued arriving. It was a peaceful day, there was no violence. There were stories of machetes and stabbings at the bote, and one or two dead bodies had been found there. But, in general, the divers helped each other. If someone found something he couldn't sell, he gave it to someone else.

When Chen decided to head back, at about 10:00 p.m., Huevo was already sprawled and snoring in a corner, letting out loud snorts. Near the campfire, Luz María was dancing by herself. She took Chen's hand and asked him to dance with her, to sing the old Álvaro Torres song he sang so well. At first, Chen refused.

In that moment, they had no inkling of what would happen. A year later, Luz María would die of a vaginal infection, Chen would disappear, and the quimbo would be swallowed up by the dense undergrowth. In that moment, unaware, they danced in the midst of this desolation.

"Give me a kiss," said Luz María.

"Shut up," said Chen.

"You haven't washed in a month."

"I wash every day."

"Yeah, I believe you."

"You should believe me."

"Go on, then, give me a kiss."

And then Chen, feigning reluctance, grabbed Luz María around the waist. She puckered her lips.

"It's like I always say," he said at length. "Two good people always find each other."

THE MALECÓN: THE ORGY OF FORMS

At ten to midnight, the Italian, still scratching his ankle, said that even communists wanted a good life now. I couldn't work out why he said it, nor to which of the three other members of the group he was speaking, but his tone was authoritative.

Poverty is a sign that communists allow others to hang on them, one they hang on themselves. To the communist, poverty is a synonym for dignity, so when the communist tries to prosper, the anticommunist reminds him that prosperity is unacceptable to communists. At which point, the communist agrees and in time he ends up believing it, perhaps because it suits him.

A girl—the color of burned sugar, about twenty, her movements wary—attempts to contradict the Italian, but the Italian quickly shuts her down. He gives a contemptuous wave of his hand.

As if to say: Bah!

As if to say: You think you can tell me something, darling? A man who's been to the Sistine Chapel, the Piazza Spagna, the foot-hills of the Alps? A man who's seen the Opera dei Pupi?

The girl falls silent and the conversation carries on. The Italian is the only foreigner. It looks as though the girl is on her way to becoming his partner, but she is not there yet. The other two are clearly a couple. She is wearing a Brazilian football shirt, he is sporting a baseball cap, both are clearly friends of the girl. Every now and then they kiss, or stroke each other's hands or thighs.

The four are sitting on the wall along the Malecón, opposite the gas station on Avenida Paseo, not far from the Hotel Cohíba and the Hotel Riviera. I am two meters away, also sitting, one ear cocked, pretending to be preoccupied. I stare out at the sea. Tiny lights teem amid the darkness that, when they set out from the shore, were full-sized fishing boats. Two buskers are playing something by Roberto Carlos. The moon on the water is misshapen. Before crashing against the cliffs, the crests of the waves reflect flittering silver sequins.

———

It is summer, the end of August, and I've come down to the Malecón prepared to do battle with an age-old canard: the syrupy, sentimental claptrap that third-rate poets, hack journalists, and miserable minstrels have poured over the long wall that girdles the city's entrails.

Over the years, I have spent enough time looking at or strolling along the Malecón to go from adulation to contempt. I arrived in Havana in 2008 and I was given a room on the twenty-second floor of Fy3ra, the university dorms for those coming up from the provinces. All I had at the time were dairy products for breakfast, trays of calamari for lunch, and a vast stretch of sea; a vast stretch of the Malecón.

Whenever I felt life was being too hard on me, I'd go down to the Malecón. When I felt I hadn't suffered enough, I'd go down to the Malecón. And what could be more salutary than watching and observing and writing down what was happening at the Malecón than watching and observing and writing down what was happening to me, which, in cold, hard terms, was nothing. Studying, watching, and observing, I came to the facile conclusion that the Malecón was a version of Dante's *Inferno*, circles within circles, and the only thing to be done was to trace them all.

Seventeen thousand tons of Portland cement, 22,000 cubic meters of sand, 45,000 of aggregate, 35,000 of ballast, 4,200 tons of rebar, 295 of steel girders, and a million feet of wood that daily supports the frustrations, the apathy, the nostalgia, and all the other passions the people of Havana come to resolve by the sea, as if to confirm that no ritual, no tradition can endure unless there is a delicate piece of engineering work to support it.

It's now midnight. The Italian and his bullshit are beginning to get on my nerves. A woman comes up to me and asks if I want to buy something.

===

Her name is Ileana. She looks to be at least fifty—she looks Indian, wrinkled skin, lowered head, long skirt, something extinguished in her eyes. She's one of the women who sell candy, popcorn, chocolate cookies, and bags of sweet potato chips and walks God knows how many kilometers a day.

"I get here around ten o'clock and leave at four, sometimes five o'clock in the morning," she tells me.

She's not one for conversation. She lives out in Arroyo Naranjo. She lives with her shoulders permanently stooped. She has spent four years working along the Malecón. When Ileana retired—she had no choice: she has grandchildren—she took up the suggestion offered by the government.

"Weekends are better," she says. "I make more sales."

There is nothing unusual, nothing particularly arduous about what Ileana does, but there is something obviously not right. The world should not be a place where destitute women on the verge of old age have to spend six or seven hours every night hawking things to make four measly pesos. They sleep for a few hours, tidy the house, then start all over again. Ileana isn't my grandmother, but if she were, I'd feel very uncomfortable.

I'm currently in what I've decided to call the "white zone" of the Malecón. To the east—Havana old town and the city center—the streetlights are yellow, and life is more or less diurnal. Gangs of young boys diving off the Malecón into the sea, desperate taxi drivers touting for fares, hawkers flogging cheap jewelry and candy, and legions of ragged, crippled beggars trying to cadge a couple of dollars from the passing tourists. Here, in the west—Vedado, from La Chorrera to Avenida 23—the streetlights are white LED bulbs, and life is nocturnal.

I set off walking eastward. Two women are swigging a bottle of rum. To judge by her hysterical giggles, one of them smoked a little weed earlier. They are eating *chicharritas*. Around them are five sleeping children. It's impossible to tell whether the children belong to one or the other, or a mixture of both. The kids are sleeping soundly, as though they got drunk earlier and now it is their mothers' turn. As though all of them, neighboring families, had decided to up and leave home, their respective fathers and husbands, for good.

Two other women—one in yellow Lycra, one in booty-hugging denim shorts—both overweight, with rolls of fat spilling out of the figure-hugging outfits, cheap hookers, ask me for money without bothering to stop—they know I'm not going to give them any.

It is not a balmy night. The mawkish strains of someone butchering a José Luis Perales song come drifting on the air. By and large, behind every bad song badly sung is someone trying to make a living.

A few men—three, in fact—are playing dominoes. An old guy—white shirt, blue trousers, probably a driver—hurries past, and another, hugging a bucket filled with bits and pieces, runs to catch up with him.

A group of twentysomethings are playing a video game—their disheveled heads reflected in the touch screen—while another group is listening to disco on a Bluetooth speaker and trying to breakdance. A woman is screaming into her cell phone, "Yeah, yeah, I know her husband, he's a waste of space."

Someone is talking about Cuban baseball players in the Major Leagues: how José Dariel Abreu is faring with the Chicago White Sox, or Yasiel Puig with the LA Dodgers, and what the pundits are saying about them.

This running commentary is larded with the usual dose of hero worship and fantasy I know only too well. Cubans whose only knowledge of the Major Leagues comes secondhand—from someone with (terrible) internet connection at work, or someone who works as a waiter or a busboy at a hotel and tunes in to ESPN or Fox Sports—but who persuasively manage to pass themselves off as firsthand spectators.

An exercise in mythmaking. They repeat what they've heard, adding a little detail that makes the story sound more impressive and makes them feel like the bearers of fresh and exciting news. In this way, long after they disappear from the pages of Cuban newspapers and the usual sports programs, Cuban baseball players in the Major Leagues end up becoming—at least to Cuban fans living in Cuba— the most amazing, the most talented, the most spectacular, the most superhuman of anyone playing in the Major Leagues.

To be number one, you don't need to rack up player stats. You just need to be the seed for someone else's dream.

———

I'll never know the fisherman's name. I've never known how to talk to a fisherman. Fishing has always seemed to me to be more a metaphysical than practical occupation: the hobby for the privileged, a banal pretext that masks profound philosophical meditation. The fisherman does not come to catch fish. A couple of tilapia, a sea bass, or whatever is a poor reason for spending four or five hours standing holding a fishing rod. The fisherman pretends to catch fish, but actually, he comes for a much more important reason, one I haven't worked out yet.

The fisherman is wearing leather sandals, a blue sweater, and checked shorts. His frizzy hair—a tangle of weeds—sticks out from under his cap. He must be about forty. He has a glass of rum within reach and is surrounded by other fishermen. One of them, an older man, is wearing a torn T-shirt. Another, who is younger, is dealing with the bait: chunks of squirrelfish.

After a while, I ask him if the fish are biting. He says yes, a couple of red snappers, sometimes a tilapia. He gives me a half smile.

"Don't you find it boring?" I say.

"No. It's my only hobby."

"You come every day?"

"As much as I can."

"And how much is that?"

"As much as I can."

"So, you stay here all night?"

"Sometimes I stay until dawn, sometimes I leave earlier."

"Based on what? On whether the fish are biting?"

"I don't know. I can spend a whole night here and not catch a thing. It depends."

At this point, we both trail off, the fisherman offers me a swig of rum, I politely shake my head, then the fisherman says, "I come here to clear my head, to switch off from work. That's how I manage to put up with things."

I'm not sure I understand what he means by "things." Whether life in general, the situation in this country, the passing years, or some very specific personal dilemma. Nor does he explain. When all's said and done, he's a fisherman, the kind of man who talks in parables.

"Take my word for it. Without this, without some way of clearing your head, nobody would be able to put up with it."

———

Ten meters farther along, four young people are chatting. From the look of them and the way they talk, they seem like typical university students who like to spend hours unpicking a subject—preferably political—so they can go home happy, confident in the notion that this—what they're experiencing, what they're suffering, what they're discussing right now—this and nothing else is what they will later remember of their time at university.

I don't hear the whole conversation, but I manage to jot down a lot of what they are saying in a notebook that I hide as best I can.

"First and foremost, we have to start with the needs of the human animal," explains a very voluble girl, with the energy of a senator.

"I wanted to go to the Louvre," says a short white guy whose curly hair spills over his shoulders.

Later, he says, "With as little as ten million, you could sort out the whole of Havana, no sweat."

"I'm passionate about and saddened by Havana," says the girl.

"Me too," says the guy. "But passion and sorrow are the same thing, aren't they?"

"The people don't know their own city," says the girl. "They don't know the history. They know nothing about the city they live in."

"Ours is a lost generation," says the guy, who has probably not turned twenty, an age at which no one has any sense of what a generation is.

"You know what they should do? Read Ciro Bianchi," says the girl, and at this point I choke on my saliva and can't help making a guttural sound, a sort of hiccup that makes everyone turn to look at me and, caught in flagrante, I try to seem invisible.

I pick up a pebble and toss it into the water. I tie my shoelace. I scratch my right earlobe and yawn. A chubby woman in a polka-dot blouse is crossing the street. I'm so busy worrying they'll find out I've been listening to them that I lose the thread of their conversation.

"I think it's important to have an open mind," says the guy.

"I'm open-minded," says the girl.

"You say that," a third student interrupts, pushing his glasses up his nose, "but you can't actually know that. Everybody thinks they're open-minded."

"Here in Cuba, prostitutes don't think of themselves as inferior," says the girl, "because they know that later they'll be able to integrate into society."

"Here, people prostitute themselves because they've got to eat," the fourth student says finally, joining the conversation. He hasn't said a word until now, or if he has, I didn't hear him.

"That's not quite how it works," the girl says.

"How does it work, then?" asks the third student.

"In this matter, in particular, I feel totally defeated," says the guy with the curly hair.

"There are prostitutes here, but not that many, and they're mostly university students," says the girl.

"This place is filled with human misery," says the fourth student.

"They have human misery in other countries, too," says the girl.

"In other countries, the human misery is material," the fourth guy says, "but here, human misery is written on the flesh."

Nobody understands what the fourth guy is trying to say, and they all fall silent. Then they start talking about the possibility of leaving Cuba. Then they talk about what would have happened if

Cuba—and I don't know what historical twist leads them to this doorway—if Cuba, like Korea, had been divided in half.

Then someone says, But that doesn't mean I identify with imperialism.

Then someone adds, Latin Americanism.

Then someone tries to ease the tension, saying, Today, we've covered every single topic of conversation that could end up in a fistfight.

The others nod, proud they haven't resorted to pugilism.

"We touched on some thorny subjects," says the girl.

"Ugh, yeah," says the guy with the curly hair.

We're opposite the Girón building, which is right on the corner of the Malecón and calle E. It is a grimy, elaborate tower block built in the '70s in the socialist realism style, but there's something slightly ostentatious about it that's always caught my attention. As though socialist realism was suddenly trying to be individualistic, to dissociate itself from collectivism. So collectivist, in other words, that it fuses everything to become nothing less than The One, the socialist realist among socialist realists.

Everyone thinks the Girón building is hideous. Built bang in the middle of Vedado, its hideousness is a byword. But it's so truly, truly ugly, and so utterly impractical, that it's unthinkable that neither the architects nor the civil engineers nor the construction workers realized this fact, so much so that I now suspect what we're dealing with is not sheer ugliness, but some curious beauty that we will come to appreciate one day.

The students get to their feet and stretch, walk across the avenue, and disappear into the building. To consider the Girón building as a kind of metaphor would be predictable and pretentious, something I want to avoid at all costs. Before carrying on my way, I notice three police officers standing on the opposite pavement. I look at them for a moment, for a long time, and the officers stand, motionless, so still they're frightening. With nothing to do. Nothing to say. Maybe waiting for a crime that has not yet been committed.

━━

For some reason, from Avenida G all the way to the edge of the José Martí Anti-Imperialist Platform, where it meets Línea, the Malecón is nothing more than a long, dull stretch of wall. No hustle and bustle. No voices. Few people. The authorities, also for some unknown reason, police the traffic of this area.

It's 1:00 a.m., and one woman is saying to another, "No, I've never been to a party. He spent his whole life sitting in front of a chessboard."

Two brothers pass. They seem twitchy, and the elder says to the younger brother, "Are you dumb? Don't you realize I'm responsible for you, and Mom is constantly on my back?"

On a wall there is a photograph from France in May '68 with a slogan that reads, "L'imagination au pouvoir."

A straight couple are falling in love. She's got a silver purse and he's got a huge watch on his left wrist. A gay couple are falling in love. He's wearing a pink T-shirt and he's wearing a beige turtleneck.

A girl on her own is listening to reggaeton, drinking rum, and staring out to sea. The Malecón is a long and lonely highway that leads to a dusty, deserted city. The sheer length of it is beautiful. The beauty is visceral. It stems from its length, its width, its height. Gazing at it and seeing that the wall is never ending, that it stretches far beyond our understanding, is a revelation. Usually, this wouldn't be beautiful, but right now, it is.

━━

A group of good-looking, older black people, two women, one man, sleazy, already drunk. They're beating out a rhythm on the wall with beer cans and singing in a rumba style: "y pienso en ti, mi fórmula de amor. Y pienso en ti, sin ver la solución. ¿Por qué te tengo que olvidar, si yo te amo?"

"¡Agua!" says one woman, red dress, scarf wrapped around her head.

"¡Ahora!" says the other, yellow blouse, black dress, white collar.

They both pick up the tempo. Jiggle their hips. One hand on the wall, the other whirling in the air, ass thrust out for everyone on the avenue.

"Ay," says the one in the red dress, and kicks the beer can.

"La soledad se sienta a mi mesa." The man joins in.

"Let's go get a bottle," says the one in the black dress. "'Cause this ain't gonna work without fuel."

The man has stopped singing but carries on banging the beer can on the wall.

"The Malecón is for partying," says the one in the black dress. "Let's go buy a fuck-off carton of rum."

"We don't have the cash," says the guy.

We're opposite Tángana, the gas station on calle Línea. It's busier around here. People's clothes are different. They wear loud, garish outfits. There are a couple of dumb tourists glancing around like Foghorn Leghorn, as if to say, Okay, so we're here. Now where are all the pretty black girls at?

A mestizo guy in a Day-Glo orange pullover and a Pinar del Río cap is breakdancing, mixing it up with a little guaguancó and joking with everyone. A woman selling popcorn walks by, and he lunges at her. Two police officers walk past and the guy stands behind them, sticks out his tongue, moonwalking like Michael Jackson in "Smooth Criminal." The officers turn around, and the guy whistles innocently and strolls off in the opposite direction. Everyone laughs.

A little farther along, a parked patrol car is surrounded by a lot of officers, twelve of them—too many cops for a callout unless they're tracking a killer. I spot a captain, a hunky lieutenant, and a couple of officers slinking into the background as if they're ashamed to wear the uniform. As though they're shyly trying to convince us that they ended up as police officers by mistake, that life pushed them down this path completely against their will, that they've got no choice. I even see the three stars of a colonel pinned to one guy's shoulder.

They've arrested a couple of young guys. The charge: causing a public nuisance.

"They're nothing but cheap hoods," the lieutenant says, "that's all, a couple of cheap would-be gangstas."

"A couple of dumb fucks," the colonel says, "can't just sit down and enjoy the fresh air."

The lieutenant tells one of the kids to move, but the guy doesn't obey. The lieutenant repeats the order, more forcefully. One of the kid's friends says, "Hey, Piti, c'mon, shift over, dude."

Piti does as his friend says, then launches into his spiel: "You know, the great thing is, it's one fucking day after another. Take me down to Unidad de Zapata y C. Chill, man, I'm chill. I'm an artist, man, nobody around here seems to get that."

"This is fucked up," his friend says. "We'll go on ahead and pick you up from the police station."

"I was just walking along, minding my business. Why do they care how I walk? I can crawl around on all fours if I feel like it."

"Who are you making fun of now?" the second lieutenant says sternly.

"Magician's shoes. Pro."

"Who?" asks the colonel.

"The crooks, man, they come crawling along, begging for cash, and you guys don't do shit. But I have a bit of fun, and just 'cause I've got a record, you bust my balls."

"Shut up, Piti."

"I'm not saying nothing. Let them take me in. Tiger don't care if it earns another stripe. I'm a big guy."

"You're a big guy?' says the lieutenant.

"Me? Five foot six. How many times have you hauled me in? No drama. I'm a professional magician, that's what I am. You can put that on my record."

"If you're a magician," says the lieutenant, "why don't you make those handcuffs disappear?"

━━

A little farther on, two guys with voices like gravel are rapping:

"Esto es problema, problema, problema. / Saca la mano que te quemas. / Que yo me pongo pesao. / Que tú sabes cómo vengo. Guapo y fajao."

"Pero cuál es el foco. / Loco esto es pa ti. / Manos parriba los efó. / Manos parriba los efí."

"Oye que dale, que dale, que dale pal hospital."

In the background, a more placid group is singing "La gloria eres tú." But the rappers are the ones getting all the attention:

"Todo te lo di, todo te lo he dao. / El bonche se calentó./ Manos parriba los efi efó."

"Mi rapeo está potente / dime si no es verdad / le estoy echando plomo al infinito y más allá. / Que tengo yo La Habana súper súper que alterá. / Estate tranquilito que te parto a la mitá. / Pa que escuches mi lírica a la hora que sea, / lo mismo de noche que de madrugá."

"El bonche se calentó. / Completo. Saquen las mochas que después me meto yo."

"Esto es problema llegaron los pesaos. / Esto es problema mañana y pasao. / ¿Por qué? / Porque seguimos guapo y fajao."

"¿Cómo?"

"Guapo y fajao."

"¿Qué dice?"

"Guapo y fajao."

"Repite."

"Guapo y fajao."

——

Malecón at the corner of calle 23: this is where the transvestites hang out. Surreptitious glances, signals, furtive winks. Night condenses to its point of culmination.

In the fountain of the Hotel Nacional there's a trans girl with blue shoes, turquoise blouse, red handbag, tiny white shorts, hair extensions, eyebrows arched so high they look broken. Her friend, who's not as dolled up, is wearing Dupé flip-flops, a mauve blouse, and ribbons in her hair. Both are *mulatas*. The friend is screaming at her. The other girl pretends not to hear as she struts over and back, never losing her disdainful poise.

I look for the masculine traits under the makeup, the handsome, boyish lips beneath the dark-red lipstick. She's not ugly, but she's rough around the edges. The best transvestites, given that to be a transvestite is to camouflage and confuse, are those who succeed in minimizing the more grotesque elements of the male body, trading virility for delicacy, strength for sinuousness.

This kid has promise, but looks less like a woman than a work in progress. Let's say that some of the features are like those of a girl, but others are not quite right. He's got a big ass, the big ass of a slugger.

Some guy walks past and, without stopping, says, "Come on, let's go have some fun."

"What the fuck's wrong with you?" she says.

Her friend, the one who's screaming, comes over and tells him that that she's going to marry this twenty-year-old guy, the cool kid who bought her beer, with his Calvin Klein sweater, his fan, and his leather boots.

In the doorway of the Ministry of Foreign Trade, another long line of transvestites is gossiping. Chiqui, they call one of them, and, from what they're saying Chiqui is in love with a boy with big ears. *Dyke!* they shriek. A blond makes her entrance. The other girls say hi, but don't seem particularly overwhelmed. The blond thinks herself more important than she seems to be. Someone remarks that, a couple of weeks ago, the blond freaked out and ripped her boyfriend's head off. She never does a thing, she's never washed a pair of panties, Chiqui says, referring not to the blond, but to another transvestite.

A chorus chattering about every subject under the sun without ever losing the thread. This corner is their meeting point. This is where they wait until a guy shows up and decides to take one home with him. This is also the setting for some of the typical jokes about the confusion transvestites elicit in horny heterosexuals.

There are no transvestite comedians, or if there are, we're not aware of them. But it would be fair, and even funny, to listen to a transvestite's tale, how she creates the illusion, how she squeezes her cock between her thighs so nothing hangs out, so there is only a glimpse of the delta of Venus that leads to the center of desire, how she walks on eggshells until the guy switches out the light, then undresses, and then shamelessly asks him to take her from behind. And he does. Blinded by a stroke of luck, the guy does it.

There's some hilarious material in it. The successful stratagem, the artifice that succeeded in winning its prize. We like to think that, at the last minute, the guy who has just come up from the provinces notices the deception, but it's more likely that he'll never notice, or if he notices, he'll pretend not to care. He'll enjoy it, then find he wants to be deceived again.

After the first few minutes, the conversation becomes a little tedious. Until Chiqui says her pussy hurts. That pussy is life, it's freedom. But when anyone tries to touch the pussy, they end up touching the dick.

The pussy as paradise lost, as object of desire, a cure for all ills. I would even suggest that a lot of the time when they say pussy, they're referring not to a sexual organ but to an attitude, a presumption, or a struggle. Some are in a struggle with biology, others simply with morality and the law. Transvestites are in a struggle against morality and the law, as are transsexuals, but, first and foremost, the struggle is against biology, against nature, against the motherfucker who saddled them with a body that is their enemy, and here, in the early hours of morning, as I look at their cheap clothes, their desperate desire to appear as they wish to be rather than as they are supposed to be, a thought occurs to me.

Sometimes I've used the phrase "a foreign body" to refer to a splinter of wood, a shard of pencil, a nail. I try to imagine what it would be like if everything about me felt like a foreign body. That *being*, the act of *being*, that part of me that I can touch, can feel to reassure myself that I exist—the chest, the sex, the cheekbones, the feet, an armpit, the smallest pore—are no more than pieces of a body that is not mine, a body I wish I could exorcise, could discard as others might discard a torn dress, a splinter of wood, a shard of pencil, a nail. But I could not discard everything that is inside me, since that would be me discarding my entire self, so I would not be freeing myself from anything. Myself as my own personal jail: it would mean liberating not the prisoner but the prison.

The pussy, in short, as a metaphor for the soul.

Then, at the stroke of 3:00 a.m., I hear the most beautiful words of the night.

"I fuck, I stand, I sit, I spread my legs," says Chiqui.

Someone looking at her, at once mocking and tender, says simply, "I see you as feminine."

OFFSIDE

Madness. Over his sunken eyes, round face, and small mouth are superimposed the enormous eyes, wild face, and restless mouth of physical madness. It's not the madness you see in asylums, which is tranquil and impassive, and can sometimes even be confused with wisdom, with the zen of the desperate—an existential, distant madness.

Boris Santiesteban's madness is a mundane, elegant madness, and perhaps more terrible and definitive. The madness you see in asylums is the final, paralyzing madness, once it has been let loose by the lightness of art or the imminence of death. The madness of Boris Santiesteban is the onset of madness, active and persistent. Events circling around the head like furious spies: the loneliness of the sea, the darkness of the night, the raging swell, the ominous fins of the sharks less than five meters away, the hunger, the thirst, the urine trickling down your throat.

This unruly mask is all he has to show for the period that stretches from the end of 1994, when he first emigrated from Cuba, to now, the beginning of 2013, when he is back there once more. He spends his days on the street, chatting to the other inhabitants of Vedado, playing a round of charades or a bit of football, or taking a brief stroll down Línea or the Malecón.

The night of our meeting Boris is waiting for me, weary and restless. We settled on eight o'clock at the house of a mutual friend who has acted as a point of contact, but Boris gets there at seven thirty. He's come straight from exercise and is sweating, broken by exhaustion. He scans me suspiciously. Then he jokes.

"You're not from security, are you?"

"Do I look like I am?"

"No. I don't know. I don't want anything to happen."

"What could happen to you?"

"Anything. You never know here."

"Rest easy."

"Don't take any photos or use my name."

"Why?"

"I said don't take any photos and don't use my name."

"You got it."

"Or, actually, go on, use it. What difference does it make?"

I say nothing.

"Actually, maybe don't use it. When I read my story I'll know it's mine, whatever name you use. Maybe give me a name similar to mine. Or, no, just put my name."

He keeps on like this, without any letup. Our mutual friend calms him down.

Our mutual friend's grandfather worked as a bodyguard for several of the Revolution's leaders, and photos of Fidel Castro and Che Guevara, hanging from the room's walls, surround Boris and me. Che smoking, Che smiling. Fidel, energetic, giving a speech with his finger raised; Fidel looking roguish in a coat, wearing one of those typically Russian hats that cover your brow and ears. He looks less like a politician and more like Raskolnikov.

Boris rocks rapidly back and forth, drying the sweat from his face with his pullover, which is as wide as a bathrobe, and closes his eyes for a moment to put them in their place. He's done that ever since he began to box, ever since he first received a blow to the face and lost his bearings. He closes his eyes and centers himself. He got into the ring for the first time when he was eight years old. He wasn't wild about it, but it was better than being home with his parents. He preferred gloves, head gear, and an adversary to the commotion, arguments, beatings, and bad tempers he put up with at home.

"Sport was everything to me," he says. "Everything."

Today, he lives with his father. His mother and his two sisters have lived in the United States since 1998.

"Were you good?"

"Yeah, I won medals at youth level."

The mutual friend nods and mentions that Boris has given out a fair number of beatings in the neighborhood.

"That's a lie, I'm a peaceful guy."

"Why did you stop?"

"Because I got KO'd."

"You were KO'd?'" I repeated, shocked that anyone would remember themselves like that, as a loser.

"Took me six months to recover. Right-hand corkscrew. I was sixteen."

After that, he went to university to study physical education, but it was during the Special Period. Students in Havana had their stipends withdrawn, and Boris went hungry often.

"Did they help you at home?"

"Only time they ever did."

Boris talks gracefully, lightheartedly about the knockout and university. But when you mention his family, his face transforms. A look of terror appears. A look of terror that wipes away his normal look, of someone who is mentally unstable. He goes quiet and shrinks into his armchair.

His father is currently sick with pancreatic cancer, and he pisses in corners and defecates on seats. He does everything he can to complicate things for his son.

"Tell me about Sweden, how you ended up there."

He doesn't answer. He asks the mutual friend for a little water.

"You're really not from security?"

I could ask the same of him, but I choose not to upset him.

"No. Of course I'm not."

I start to talk to him about football. I try to make him forget about his parents for the time being.

——

In 1993, the Swedish boxer Lars Myrberg, bronze medalist at the 1988 Summer Olympics in Seoul, gave some lectures in Havana. Boris attended, and they struck up a friendship.

Around that time, his parents got divorced. His father was hitting his mother and both of them were continually shouting either at each other or at Boris, though less than they used to. They didn't even hit him anymore. They couldn't. Boris was twenty-two or twenty-three years old and the physical embodiment of the long-distance boxing style.

Tired of his surroundings, he accepted Myrberg's offer to become a trainer in his private boxing club, and in September 1994 he flew to Sweden.

August had been and gone, and with it the raft exodus, a great spectacle that Boris had watched calmly. The Malecón was like a ferry terminal at the point of collapse, the coast of Havana infested with rafts and homemade vessels used in the enormous, theatrical exodus of thousands of Cubans who were sick of the power cuts, poverty, and hardship that had followed the fall of the Socialist Bloc.

A tumultuous setting. And Boris was making the best of the knockout that had transformed him from an athlete into a trainer.

The beginning of an inverse logic. The logic of physical madness runs contrary to historical logic. Nineteen years later, at a time when Cubans are emigrating with letters of invitation, or at least almost always by more secure routes, when desperate flight seems like an anachronism, Boris will take a raft and launch himself into the sea.

———

Two weeks later, we go back to the house of our mutual friend. Boris seems more stable today. He is a charismatic guy. People in the neighborhood say he was extradited from Sweden because he stole a chocolate bar, but he denies that. First, he says he didn't steal anything, then he admits that he did. Depends on who's asking. Every ten minutes my beard becomes the beard of a government agent, before going back to being the beard of someone who simply doesn't like shaving.

"Myrberg took me to the shops and said I could eat all the chocolate I wanted inside, but that I couldn't take anything with me. So I ate, and when Myrberg turned his back I put some chocolates in my pockets."

"Did the cameras catch you?"

"No, never."

"What about the rumors?"

"Look, I'll tell you the truth. I went to a shop with a Cuban, and this guy took the alarm off a cap and stole it. I did the same, and they got me. Both of us ended up at the police station. But nothing happened to him, because he was white."

"What about you?"

"They kept me in, and Myrberg had to get me out."

"Were there many Cubans in Sweden?"

"Yes, thousands. They used to live in Upplands Väsby, which was like a concentration camp."

"A concentration camp?"

"Yes, a center for refugees, immigrants. They kept them there. It was on the outskirts of Stockholm, and they got paid four hundred krona a month."

Sweden, in need of labor, was taking in an average of 1,500 immigrants each year. Not just Cubans. Also Bulgarians, Africans, Asians, Latinos.

"Were you involved in drugs?"

"No, I wasn't." Unsettled, he decides to confess to some more minor crimes. "I was never involved in drugs. I won't lie and say I never stole wallets, and stuff like that, but not drugs."

He stole out of habit, not because he needed to. He'd visit the immigrant areas to find someone to chat to, pass the time for a while, and then commit the crimes of the displaced. Time will confirm that, wherever he is, Boris will always be precisely this: a displaced person.

To win over Swedish people, he'd offer them some of the chocolates he'd stolen. Using his terrible English, he'd try to strike up conversation on public transportation, mostly with women.

"I had a tough time of it. People don't talk there. Suicide rates are really high, everyone's so withdrawn. The transport is really excellent, though. Sweden was what Fidel wanted for here. Socialism with development, and a place where people would communicate more. Here we communicate a lot, but there's no food."

During the first few months he lived in Myrberg's house. He slept on a sofa bed in the lounge and as soon as Myrberg, his wife, and his daughters went off to work or to school, Boris would turn on the television and drink milk and eat hot dogs or parmesan cheese.

He worked without papers until his boss managed to regularize his position. Soon he was seeing less work. He found Tensta boxing club, third place on the national circuit, and began earning a bit more money. There he made friends and went to live with them.

They were Chukry, a sixteen-year-old Angolan, and Johanet, a seventeen-year-old Ethiopian. From then on, Boris never went to a disco or a skating rink without his two African students. But he did to church every Sunday on his own.

"Are you Catholic?"

"No, but I was homesick. I was twenty-five, and the cold wouldn't leave me in peace."

—

He returned to Havana in September 1995. The situation in Cuba was not improving. There was widespread poverty, cynicism, desolation. His parents wanted him to go back to Sweden. His mother scratched him, insulted him. Then she implored him to think about his decision.

"My folks have no shame, you see." He tenses his face, and his jittery eyes spin in their orbits, like two dice in someone's hand. "I went with my $2,000 to the hotels, mainly Cohíba and the Riviera. I spent everything in three months and then had to go back to the pigsty."

Boris brought hookers home, letting them live in his room. His father reproached him for his addiction to hookers and instability. His mother and his sisters emigrated, and the two of them were left there, alone. Boris worked as a gardener, then he was a caretaker in Miramar, and then he worked as a builder in Cayo Largo del Sur, a small islet where people were beginning to build hotels in an attempt to profit from foreign tourism. He lasted a few months in that position. Boris couldn't accept the fact that the boss was always going off to snack bars and beaches with his sons and his wife while he and the other workers were doing twelve-hour shifts daily, and so he decided to burn his bridges. He grabbed a sports boat and left the site.

"I spent a whole day going around the island, losing myself among the hotels, inviting tourists to ride with me. Then they kicked me out."

Back in Havana, he had to keep looking for work. By that time Gian Luca had been born, his first and only son with Idalmis, a woman from Guantánamo whom Boris had met while pruning trees in Vedado and who everyone, including his father, insisted was a whore. Boris does not deny that he was her pimp, her procurer, but nor does he puff up with macho pride. He just accepts it.

"She left me money because I was the one who looked after the boy. I took him to school, took him everywhere."

His neighbors will confirm that they never left one another's side. They would go out onto the Malecón to play football, but in 2006, Idalmis married an Italian and took the boy away from him. Boris's response to this loss was to shut himself away.

"What happened?"

"Nothing, I just shut myself off. I barricaded the door and stayed inside."

"People say you got food from the schools?"

"Yeah, the dinner ladies in the kitchens of two nearby primary schools would keep a portion for me."

"And your father?"

"Forget about my father. We lived together, but we kept out of each other's way, until now that is, now that he can't even move and I have to make food for him and clean up his shit."

Then he tried to get back on track, but in life, as in boxing, recovery isn't only down to oneself.

"I became a masseur, I did a course, and just when the government was about to send me to Venezuela as a medical collaborator, they canceled my departure because they saw me as a potential emigrant."

"Because of your son?"

"And my mother. But it's the boy I care about."

He speaks of Gian Luca with great pride. He must be around twelve or thirteen now and is the only person Boris shows any love for. It's as if he'd deliberately withdrawn all his love from everyone else and deposited it entirely into this boy, who he says can sing opera and is very intelligent.

"He sends me photos every two or three months. He's so big."

"How long since you last saw him?"

"Three years."

A few months ago, his mother brought the boy to Havana, but they didn't get to meet. Boris was locked up somewhere.

———

Boris was sleeping on the same bed where we are chatting for the last time today when a local friend burst in and said that if he wanted to split, then everything was in place. He confesses to me that he only did it because he'd always wanted to try; it was a kind of adventure and nothing more. But that day at noon he got up and dressed himself with a determination that casts doubt upon these words. Yet somehow you can see that Boris really isn't lying. You only need to look at him to see the coherence, the hidden structure beneath his contradictions. He says his girlfriend at the time, who was from Santiago de Cuba, took care of everything, but that in the end she cleaned him out.

"That shoe cupboard you see there was full. A pair of Nikes, a pair of FILAS, a pair of smokin' hot Pumas, there was everything. She took the clothes too. Eastern Cuban women are the devil, don't ever get involved with one."

The shoe cupboard isn't much of a shoe cupboard. It's the floor of a wardrobe that isn't much of a wardrobe either, more an improvised closet, with no doors, compartments, or drawers. Just a pole joining one side to the other, for hanging clothes on—three shirts, an equal number of shorts, two pairs of trousers—and beneath that a pair of flip-flops, a pair of sandals, his football shoes, and some gar-ish orange-and-green Adidas, which Boris recently bought for forty dollars and which he considers to be exquisite. They're horrible. He doesn't actually say "exquisite." He calls them "killer," which is the way a displaced person describes something beautiful.

"Was this woman on the game?"

"Yeah, she was."

"So, your old man's right."

"My old man's job is to make my life a pain in the butt, no mat-ter what he does."

Boris's room is a makeshift mezzanine, a sort of second floor within the house. There are no photos, but there are two posters: one of Cristiano Ronaldo dummying another player and another one of Barcelona at their finest: Messi, Iniesta, Xavi, Villa, all crouching; thick-maned Puyol, defiant Alves, sly Piqué.

There's an unmade bed, old bits of junk, and a bleak sense of gloom that is brought on by the gray walls and a stuck-on yellow spotlight. The floor is made of cardboard and hasn't been cleaned for some time. There's also a television showing a Premier League match between Aston Villa and Manchester City.

Boris left home one afternoon when his father was out. He's out today too. It's clear to me that his father's presence terrifies him. The slightest noise and he stops in fright, inches open the door—as if he were hiding, or trying to stay out of sight—and looks down to see if he's come in. Then he turns back in relief and starts up the conver-sation again, wherever he sees fit.

He stayed in Hotel Santiago Habana, in the Colón municipal-ity, for ten days, waiting for the contacts who were meant to get him out. There he met seven of the people who would accompany him over the five-night sea crossing. His friend from the neighborhood introduced him to the middleman: a tall, strong black man called Amaury.

The plan was to depart by raft from somewhere on the north coast, between the boroughs of Martí and Cárdenas, and several miles later, nine to be precise, a boat run by Amaury's relatives would collect them and take them to Miami. Except for Boris, no one would pay for the journey. His presence among them was justified by the $5,000 his uncle would pay as soon as they reached the United States.

He bought three packets of biscuits, two tins of condensed milk, a few bottles of water, and left with the others for Martí. From eleven at night until three in the morning, on an embankment, they built the raft from a wooden crate measuring fifty by eighteen paces, using Styrofoam, tires, tarpaulin, screws, and two sets of oars.

"I already knew it was going to be a shitshow, but still I went along to see what happened."

"And why did you know?"

"Because we spent five days in thick mangrove, five days walking, carrying that raft, and we couldn't find a route out to sea."

The only thing they found was two people. One of them was Roberto Lauzurique, a fugitive from Agüica, the high-security prison. He was on the obese side, was passing himself off as a political prisoner, refused to row at high sea because of a so-called paralysis, and once he was in the detention center in Nassau he enlisted twenty or so other Cubans to lodge a human rights case so the United States would give them political asylum. But of those involved, only Lauzurique and three others would be accepted.

"A scammer. He never fooled me. He pretended to faint and we believed him, until one of the girls on board, a nurse, injected him without any medicine and he pretended to get better."

In any case, the group accepted the two new members, and it wouldn't be accurate to say that Lauzurique did nothing, because it was Lauzurique who caught seven snappers and seven sea snails, which no one apart from Boris would eat raw.

"The sea snail has a very strong taste," he says.

A few days later, because of the sea snail, Boris had to jump into the water to defecate, in the middle of their crossing to nowhere. It was early morning, he recalls, pitch black, and he felt like he was somewhere other than where he was—it wasn't that piercing void, like one thousand knives at once; it was nothing like the way anyone imagined the sea, and certainly not like a bathroom.

"And you weren't afraid of a shark or something?"

"No. My belly really hurt and I couldn't think about anything else."

All the same, the sea snail proved to have had a purpose. Many, many hours later, when the rescue helicopter collected them dozens of miles northeast of Havana, Boris was the only one who'd retained a certain amount of physical and mental strength, and who had suffered no hallucinations, fits, or delirium.

Yes, his skin was peeling off him, his hands were bleeding, his fingers were stiff, his eyes bone dry and rock hard; his mouth was rough, his throat was burned from the urine (the water ran out in two days, and Boris prayed to God that "my piss would taste good" and calm his furious, raging thirst), but he was conscious. The raft was adrift, but Boris was still tethered to his own body.

———

"I knew there was no way I'd let go. I always believed."

"Always?"

"Yes. I wasn't going to die there. Who would ever think that?"

"Even when you realized that the boat wasn't going to come and collect you."

"Even then."

"Even when the boats sailed past you without stopping."

"Even then."

"Even when—what was the name of the guy with the gun?"

"Yurién."

"Even when Yurién pointed a gun at Lauzurique because he wouldn't row?"

"Yes, always. I've told you, I always believed."

I think he is telling the truth. He relates the story without any sense of drama. He doesn't exaggerate. On the contrary, he plays it down. He says it was nothing, and indeed there are no visible traces of any trauma, other than the irreversible trauma of his personality. How could someone perpetually traumatized be traumatized any further? Except, as we know, with his parents, and in one very specific detail.

Boris didn't collapse during the days spent on the coast, when he had to sleep covered in sand, or put some kind of covering, anything, between his skin and the midges.

He didn't collapse on Piní Piní beach—the place they eventually set sail from—among all those sinister objects scattered across the sand. Footballs, shoes, dolls' heads, and water bottles that once had owners. People who, God knows how long back, had waited days and nights for a sign that it was time to launch themselves into the water and cross over. Or fail to.

He didn't collapse while rowing either. His hands were red raw and twisted, as if they were being put through a mill. But this torture gradually lost its effect and after that Boris took to it like a natural.

He definitely wasn't going to get upset because of a puncture. He'd put a patch on, get some air in, and stop it with a bolt and washer. Simple.

What terrified Boris Santiesteban, the thing that made him howl with panic, was the sharks.

"One came out of nowhere. I saw it come right up to us, a purple fin, and it started circling us and I hit it with the oars, but it wouldn't go away. It just kept swimming around us, spiraling, then it came back and I hit it again. I thought it was going to jump. The rule was, if someone got bitten, we'd leave them and keep going."

"Leave them and keep going?"

"Yep. There's nothing we could have done."

"And did the shark jump?"

"No, obviously it didn't jump. It tried to take a few bites. It was daytime and we could see well. Then it left and another one came along."

"Another one or the same one?"

"Well, maybe it was the same one, but basically it was two. It makes sense. If you see the same shark ten different times, then you haven't seen one shark but ten."

Everything to do with death requires a calculation, a fresh perspective.

Then they lost interest in everything.

Then all the drifting travelers began to laugh.

Then one of the nurses had sex with one of the guys.

Then they collapsed with exhaustion.

Then a coast guard plane spotted them, near a stone islet—an islet with a lighthouse—and informed Nassau.

From Nassau came the helicopter and from the helicopter came two professional divers who taught him how to breathe: hold his nose and open his mouth so that the water brought up by the propellers didn't suffocate him. The divers took him by the neck and asked him not to offer any resistance. Only then, out of harm's way, did Boris allow himself to hallucinate.

At that exact moment, while his rescuer placed an arm around him and moved him off, he felt as if the thing squeezing his throat was a shark's neck, and that a mauve-finned shark was dragging him along and taking him away.

━━

When he woke up, he knew there was no way he was in Miami. He was surrounded by a great number of black men. They asked them some questions, him and all the others, then they nursed them back to health and took them to the detention center.

"How many days was it since you'd left home?"

"Like, twenty."

"How long were you locked up?"

"Seven months, but I was the first to get out."

The Carmichael Road Detention Center is a warehouse containing immigrants from every country. There were Cubans, Dominicans, and lots of Haitians, along with Americans who were there because of drugs, and Canadians and Europeans. The ones from First World countries got out quickly, no matter what their crimes.

The bulk of the people in that shelter surrounded by walls and fences, designed for thirty bunks or sixty people, were Cubans who'd gotten lost at sea; Dominicans and Haitians undertaking journeys that were too long and who had tripped up along the way; and just as many Haitians that Bahamian companies had illegally hired to do manual labor—they were very cheap—and then denounced to the authorities when the work in question was nearly done.

Nassau was purgatory for those who wanted to get to the paradise of the United States and, for one reason or another, couldn't.

"There was water but you couldn't drink it. There were doctors but they almost never came. Food was scarce. People were sick with AIDS, tuberculosis. The Haitians brought many illnesses with them. Everyone mistreated the Haitians, but I liked them. They were handsome, they weren't cowards, they were good guys. Some of the Haitians had relatives in the Bahamas, and when they brought them food they'd share it with us, but the ungrateful Cubans would steal from them."

"You didn't steal there?"

"No, yeah, not there."

Boris shows me a mark, a faint brown ring on his right forearm, and another on one of his buttocks.

"These spots came from a blood infection. I used to eat with the Haitians, who have lots of antibodies and can resist anything, but it got the better of me."

By February Boris had hardly any relationship whatsoever with the Cubans from his raft. He organized his departure for Havana with the ambassador, and Lauzurique and the others began to accuse him of being an informant.

"If I had been an informant I wouldn't have lasted seven months there. Me not wanting to continue to the United States was another thing. I just didn't feel like it."

"They wouldn't have beaten you either."

"Of course they wouldn't have."

"But now you do want to go."

"I still don't know. I'm thinking about it."

One afternoon, one of the guards stopped him from taking a tray and sent him to the back of the line, but Boris wouldn't comply. They took him out to the walkway that ran around the outside of the warehouse and pulverized him with batons and gun butts. They didn't hit his face or his extremities because they'd already done that to a Haitian two days earlier, and the human rights commission that had visited the place had started proceedings against them for rape and abuse.

While the rest of the group claimed to be political refugees, Boris got the ambassador's number from one of these legal advisers.

"How did the cell phones get in?"

"The guards would sell them, then seize them, and then sell them again. But I met a Cuban who'd kept his, never had it confiscated."

Boris was also in communication with his mother and his uncle. He tried to communicate with his son but couldn't. The weather, the anxiety, and hunger weighed heavy on him, but he didn't do any drugs (the guards sold marijuana at twenty dollars a pound). He didn't even start masturbating in the small hours again. Once or twice a month the guards circulated pornographic films.

"They did it to weaken us," he says.

Then he clarifies: "But I took refuge in the Lord and stopped jerking off, because when I did I'd be completely shattered and spend three whole days in bed."

He began to go on runs on the path that ran around the outside of the warehouse until he was noticed.

"They knew it. I was going to go out through the bathroom window."

He explains his plan, seemingly born out of desperation. It wasn't even a plan, nothing that could actually have been carried out. Jump two walls and two enormous fences, which were impossible to jump over, then run.

At night he'd pray and watch over his belongings. During the day, he'd lie in bed and think about his son. He managed to keep away from the prison gangs while maintaining an aura of respect around himself. The ambassador had told him she was confident she'd be able to get him out of Nassau without delay. His mother sent his passport and his ID card number, and his uncle paid for his flight back to Havana.

———

When Boris came back, the first of the group to do so, he was kept in quarantine, submitted to a series of interrogations, and then set free.

Over the past few months he's done nothing except play football and prowl the outskirts of Meliá Cohíba looking for tourists or hookers. He hesitates when asked practical questions. He doesn't know whether to continue with the complaints procedure his mother suggested would get him out of the country, or to stay in Havana for the long haul, without his son. Boris doesn't have many good memories of his mother. He doesn't have many good memories of being lonely either, but on balance he prefers it.

Today, before his father gets home, he tells me he'd prefer to wrap things up for the time being. The City versus Villa match is almost over. Mario Balotelli is found offside and his goal is disallowed.

"The barefaced nerve," he says. "If it had been Messi or Ronaldo, they'd have allowed it."

"It was offside," I say.

"It wasn't. They just said it was offside because he's black."

Boris gets annoyed and with a jerk of his hand he pulls out the cable and the TV goes blank. Then he looks at me.

"Of course it wasn't offside," he states defiantly. And his eyes, frantic, captive, dart around like two wild birds in an unlit cage.

THE ROAD TO THE NORTH

On this side of the world, November is the cruelest month. And it breeds lilacs out of the dead land, mixing memory and desire.

===

In a cheap restaurant called La Casa Vieja—No. 11, Primera del Poniente, between Avenida Segunda and 4a Avenida Norte—they sell *quesadillas, carne deshebrada,* and *tacos al pastor,* as well as "Cuban food," unspecified. Whatever it is, it is the perfect bait. Low-budget gastronomy for immigrants who have burned their boats and come here panting. At four o'clock in the afternoon, Ricardo Carmona orders *sopa de res,* half of which he will leave behind because it is too spicy, and Ibelys Rivero orders white rice, vegetables, and fried pork.

It is Saturday, November 21, 2015, and the town of Tapachula, in the far south of Mexico, is a gray petal. It has been raining with soporific municipal calm. The quiet of internal courtyards contrasts with the raucous clamor of the narrow alleyways so intimate that everything said there seems to be addressed to everyone. Set next to the Pacific, the town has readapted itself for the new wave of immigrants.

Someday—as was always the way—there will be quesadillas, carne deshebrada, tacos al pastor, but there will be no Cuban food.

═══

Ravenously hungry, surrounded by bundles, they are swigging Corona beer. The owner offers Ibelys a double-filter menthol cigarette and Carmona takes her hand. They are both from Havana. They have been together less than a week.

She is twenty-two, curly hair, glasses perched on her head, with a cheeky little beauty spot on her snub nose, a piercing at the corner of her lips, striped blouse, denim jeans, and a wild expression, as though, from time to time, some untamed shadow flitted across her face. She smokes gravely. She's heavy set. She's pretty.

He is thirty-seven, tall and streamlined, a proud neck strung with yellow Santería beads, a baleful skull, an Orula cap, a convex cornucopia that spills over ears studded with many diamonds. He is a babalawo: a Yoruba priest, a visionary. His native tongue is Cuban slang. There is intelligence in the incipient green of his eyes, and a tattered nobility. The gauntness of a man who has spent a month and a half crossing seven Central American borders is evident in the bones visible through the holes in his sweater and in his face. Three-day stubble, his features droop, as though they are about to fall off. Consumptive and coarse, he looks like a tourist poster for Cuba if it had been painted by Fidelio Ponce.

Where she breaks, or resists, he tenses. She is a club; he is a bent bow. She is white; he is black. She has not yet reached the pinnacle of her strength. He is already on his way out. He is more compliant; she, more impulsive. If they need to fight, they fight. Both of them. They have glorious plans.

═══

In a different time, people left by sea. Sometimes they arrived, sometimes they did not. A law—wet foot/dry foot, it was called, and there are still some months to go before Barack Obama ends the policy—confers legal status on Cuban immigrants who reach the United States by whatever means. No other country has this privilege.

The ninety miles across the Straits of Florida are only ninety miles, but they are also a black hole that swallowed many. Of the eleven thousand Cubans who entered the United States in 2005, seven thousand did so via the Mexican border. Since then, it has become the principal route for illegal immigrants.

In November 2015, Tapachula was home to ten thousand Cubans—more than the number in all of Mexico in 2005. Crisis numbers. At the Estación Migratoria Siglo XXI, the government issues migrants with a safe-conduct valid for twenty days, and they set off north, through Nuevo Laredo, to Matamoros or some other border town, to eventually be welcomed by America.

━━

August 20, Carmona leaves Havana for Peru and from there travels to Quito. His Santería consultations do not fare well. His Ifá board, his black stone statue of Eleguá, his powders and his spells lie abandoned in a corner. Godchildren in Cali suggest that he pass through Colombia, but he is stopped at the border and returned to Quito.

Carmona is bemused. He has lived in Spain, in Venezuela, and each time he settles down, the economic crisis and the shortage of clients has forced him to close his business and pack his bags. He considers going back to his own country, but when it comes to crises, his country is beyond the pale. He revises his itinerary and realizes that he has been able to reinvent himself each time it has proved necessary, but now, stranded in Ecuador, he has no idea what his immediate future holds. In his mental map, the United States does not appear as a destination.

"For years, my sister has been suggesting that I come," he says, "but I never wanted to go there. I had a thousand other opportunities."

A timely proposition forces him to reconsider, however. Two Cuban friends in Quito—Jaime Morel Valladares, thirty-six, and José Carlos Cabrera, forty-two—are up to their necks in the drug trade, and Jaime's mother, who lives in Madrid, is prepared to finance the illegal northward journey that thousands of Cubans make from Ecuador, but only if Carmona accompanies Jaime. He will also have to protect him as best he can. Nothing can happen to Jaime unless it first happens to him. Carmona accepts. The mother is a spiritualist. Relieved, she tells Carmona that he is going to meet a tall white woman, and that this white woman will save him. Carmona, picturing a gringa with a wallet stuffed with Visa and Mastercards, breathes a sigh of relief. José Carlos—Carlitos—brings them together.

On October 12, they head for Tulcán, an Andean city on the Colombian border. A coyote charges them between $100 and $120 each. Then, the Colombian police demand their cut, another $100 for the three of them. They reach Ipiales. Jaime's mother sends more money. Before continuing their journey along the Pacific coast, they agree to stop off in Cali so that Carmona can visit his godchildren. It is three o'clock in the afternoon, and while waiting for the bus that will leave at 8:00 p.m., they decided to have a little fun.

"We chatted to people," Carmona says. "Guys from Havana who are working as mechanics. And Jaime manages to find drugs where there are none. I use a little myself, but I know a lot more about drugs than he does."

"What did you take?"

"Crack. Skunk. Pink cocaine. Base, which is like a yellowish cocaine extract that fries your neurons."

In one go, they blow $300.

Every time this happens—and it will happen more than once— they will have to improvise, to get by on their own. With this first crisis, their roles become defined.

Jaime is the charismatic one, noisy and in-your-face. Carlitos, they say, is like Genaro, the character in the Dominican comedy *Sanky Panky*. Hyperactive, a little obsessive, disruptive, the kind of guy who sees ghosts everywhere, imagines elaborate conspiracies, is constantly convinced he's in danger, sees potential murderers every- where, all of which is nothing more than a wild imagination en- hanced by drugs. Carmona is the even-tempered general, the cool analyst who watches everything from his corner, and, while Jamie is off womanizing and Carlitos is entertaining, falls back on his sor- cerer's aloofness.

On their way to Cali, the bus is stopped at a road block. The bus drives off, leaving them standing in the middle of the road, each car- rying his own rucksack, waiting to be carted off by an immigration truck. Another bus is stopped at the road block, and, while the of- ficers are distracted, they run off into the hills. They keep running, not knowing for how long or in which direction, and wind up in Buga, a small town in the Cauca Valley whose principal attraction is a basilica visited by pilgrims from around the world.

They wander the streets for a while before stumbling on a gang of young punks. According to Carmona, the clothes worn by Cubans make them easily identifiable in Colombia. The thugs demand money. They try to explain themselves.

"We're crooks, too, and they can tell from the way we talk that we're like them."

From this point, whenever they find themselves in a discus- sion with local thugs, they lose their individual identities and be- come simply "Cuba." This is what the local *malandros*—small-time crooks—say, "Cuba, you wanna make money, you best join up with us." They join up and go for a spin on motorbikes with pistols tucked into their waistbands. They like this idea, they can hardly claim they were forced into it. The criminals have marked targets, houses they've spent days watching. This time, they attack some rich guy, but the Cubans just watch, they don't commit any actual crime. They find themselves with walk-on parts in the continent's action movie.

From there, they go up into the hills. Take drugs, drink booze, party into the early hours. The local thugs introduce them to some Colombian girls and, a day and a half later, give them the details of the bus and say goodbye with a round of man hugs. The three are in a hurry. They're eager to get to Medellín to pick up money that Jamie's mother has wired via Western Union, so, ignoring the advice of Carmona's godsons, they don't take the bus, they hire a taxi. A fuck-up, Carmona says, a total fuckup.

The trip should cost about $100. The taxi driver asks for $300. They decide to pay up, on condition that if they're caught, he has to give them back their money. And, of course, they're caught. They demand that the driver give back the money and the driver refuses. They drag him out of the car, work him over, rob him, bribe the immigration officers, who do nothing to intervene, and the same officers drive them to Medellín in a flatbed truck.

Carmona feels the wind whipping at him, feels his hackles rise. He clings to his Yoruba artifacts. He knows things are going to get ugly, but, he thinks, it's all for one and one for all. They dub themselves the musketeers. They are the wild bunch, the clever bastards, the valiant. There's no one more cunning or cutthroat than they are. Molded in the bustling cauldron of Central Havana, Carmona reads the sky. The gods seem to smile on the tragicomic adventure that is to come. On the brink of a journey that other Cubans undertake only warily, with their hearts in their mouths, the three musketeers cannot wait to reach Medellín so they can party all night and get off their faces.

If Jamie's mother thought they'd left their drug-taking days behind in Quito, someone should have told her that drugs are like Cardinal Richelieu: no matter where her son and his friends go, the shadow of temptation will be waiting.

=====

One night in 2012, Ibelys and her brother go down to see some friends on the Malecón. She is spotted by an Italian guy who talks to her and asks how much she charges. Ibelys stops him dead: all the money he has is not enough to buy her. The Italian has mistaken her for a kind of woman she is not, and he apologizes.

So begins a series of events that the Malecón has witnessed many times. The Italian asks for her number. She asks why, and the Italian says because he would like to ask her out. She, apparently, decides to give it to him out of politeness. She is not particularly interested and quickly forgets about him. Some days later, the Italian calls her. They meet. The Italian is an older man. Ibelys does not know precisely how old, but over fifty. He is gentle with her; he teaches her things.

"If he hadn't been nice to me, nothing would have happened," she says. "But the truth is, because of him, I became interested in new things."

Ibelys, who, until them, helped out her mother and her grandmother selling clothes and doing odd jobs from their house in Regla, on the outskirts of Havana, now starts to take language lessons. She passes her driving test, and, after a while, she travels to Italy at his expense.

Once there, the relationship runs into difficulties, and Ibelys travels to Spain illegally. A girlfriend takes her in for a while, and, when she gets fed up, throws her out onto the street. Idelys travels around from Alicante to Valencia, Cádiz to Seville. She sleeps in bus stations, numbed by the cold. Something inside her breaks, something that will never be fixed. Spain was hell, she says bitterly, things happened there that she will never talk about to anyone.

Eventually, in the small Andalusian town of Bormujos she finds a room, sharing a place with a Cuban girl and two girls from Honduras. At the Catholic charity, Caritás, they give her a mattress and find a builder to fix up the room. She tells him she can't afford to pay for the repairs, and the builder tells her not to worry, that he has a daughter her age, and he knows what it's like to be on your own. She cries in his lap. They get married. The builder is not as old as the Italian, but he is older, in his forties.

Two years pass. Ibelys acquires Spanish residency, which, she says, is the thing she's fought hardest to get in her life, and in April 2015 she goes back to Cuba, but quickly realizes the need to leave again.

"It's the only way I can help my family. I see an ornament and I think about my grandmother. I see a dress and I think about my niece. I bought the cushions in the house. And thanks to me there's a shower in the bathroom that lights up with flashing colors when you turn the water on."

In October, she goes back to Spain and tells the builder about her plans. He approves. She looks down at the tattoo on her left side—a defiant line, mantra-like—kisses her Santería beads, and fondly says goodbye.

━━

Between 2006 and 2008, almost 40,000 Cubans entered the United States, 25,000 via the Mexican border. Cuba and Mexico urgently signed an immigration treaty, Article 11 of which states that the Cuban government agrees to the return of any of its citizens who have directly and illegally entered Mexico, or those who immigrated to Central America and are now in Mexico illegally.

Between 2009 and 2012, a little more than 30,000 Cubans en-

tered the United States, and once again 25,000 did so via Mexico.
The flow toward America fell sharply, but the number going through
Mexico did not change, meaning that the percentage increased. What
they signed made no difference. The governments decided to ignore
this issue since, compared to the serious problems of migration in the
region, it was becoming increasingly trivial.

—

After two days in Medellín, the musketeers took a bus to Turbo,
where there are boats that, for $500, take Cubans to La Miel in
Panama. Like Tapachula, all such places have created an infrastructure to accommodate these new arrivals: guides, messengers, apartments, hostels, brothels.

A malandro puts them up in a hostel, personally goes to pick up
the deposit sent by Jaime's mother, and organizes the boat.

"We showed up off our heads on drugs and burned through two-
thirds of the money for the fares," Carmona says. "When they came
to collect us, we had to be up-front with them. Colombians are good
people and we were honest with them, but business is business, and
they can get nasty if you try to fuck them over. I learned a lot about
the underworld. You've got to stand up to them, because if you try to
hide, they'll just kill you a lot faster."

The malandro threatens them but gives them a couple of hours
to come up with the rest of the money. Carlitos is starting to hallucinate, Jaime is getting a little scared, and Carmona suffers his first
disappointment. They argue, they shout. "You guys don't want to
party?" says Jaime. "Let's get blitzed, because we're going to die."
Carmona points out that they are only there to follow him. In the
end, he says, Jaime gets his wish because it was his mother who sent
the money. But what's clear is that they all partied anyway. Now, terrified, all they can do is blame each other.

With the money that's left, Jaime suggests he can save himself. "If you walk out," Carmona says, "I'll kill you before they have time to kill me." They have been friends since childhood, but they are walking the razor's edge. Carlitos has no one he can turn to for help. Addiction has cut him off from everyone. Carmona calls his sister in Atlanta. She is at work and can't get away. He tells her to send something now or not bother sending anything at all, to send what she can, but ideally more than $100. The sister sends him $150.

"Were you very scared?"

"Very. But you can still prepare for the worst. When you think you're about to be killed, there's nothing else to do. That's just how it is: when it comes to money, Moscow doesn't believe in tears."

That afternoon, the malandro shows up accompanied by a fat hitman and the boat owner, Joaco, who is little more than a kid.

"And there we were," Carmona says and suddenly, without warning, he bursts into tears. "Six guys in this tiny little room. Three armed with guns and knives. We give them the money. Jaime takes off his Orient watch and hands it over. I give them a couple of pairs of Nikes. They can see we're not trying to rip them off, but they're still tight-lipped. They don't say a single word, can you imagine? They listen and then they make a call, they can't make the decision. I tell them that's all we've got, so whatever the fuck is going down, let them do it now and get it over with."

The owner, the hitman, and the malandro scoop everything up and leave. The musketeers stand there in stunned silence, still thinking they are going to be killed. It is four hours before night falls and a minibus drives them to the coast. In total, they have paid $800 among the three of them.

"But all I remember now is that, when things got tough, Jaime was only out for himself."

At the coast, the boats don't come in until dawn. There are various sizes of boats, taking ten, sixteen, twenty, or twenty-four passengers. A number of other Cubans are waiting. There is something suspect about the boat that arrives. There are too many passengers.

"It was at this this point that I realized that, though they'd saved our lives, we no longer really figured in their plans."

Though Carmona is a risk-taker, he is terrified of the sea. When he was twelve, his uncles took to the Straits of Florida on a raft with him on board, and one of them drowned during a storm.

"I start to get a really bad feeling. I can't take it, so I say I'm not going. I get out of the boat, Carlitos comes with me. We tell Jaime to go on ahead, to prepare the groundwork and we'll meet him there."

At dawn, an old man picks them up and takes them to Necoclí, a little farther north. He hides them in his little shack, in a village controlled by the paramilitaries. During the day, Carmona sacrifices a couple of chickens and performs a cleansing ritual. The locals ask who he is. "I'm a shaman," he says. And he explains that *babalawo* comes from *baba*, "father," and *lawo*, "secrets." Therefore he is the father of secrets.

Orula is the *orisha* of destiny and of the human form. Orula can also prevent premature death. Not simply physical death, but the death of love or of dreams. The locals and their leaders listen, spellbound. The tablet of Ifá can be used to interpret everything that happens in the world, and 256 *odu*, or signs of the oracle coincide—this is a lie—with the number of bones in the human body.

"You have to throw in a few lies to scare people. That it can cure AIDS, cancer, you name it."

Carmona came to Santería after spending eight years in prison for pimping, and since then, he has assiduously studied the principles of Santería so that the orishas will forgive him his sins.

That night, after performing a spiritual cleansing for the people of Necoclí, and having traveled more than a thousand kilometers, he takes a boat and crosses the Gulf of Urabá.

"Not long after we set out, a thunderstorm broke, the sea was rough, the skies opened, children started screaming. It was like the devil himself was there. Those were the scariest three hours of my life, I was convinced I was going to drown. The boats were tossed around like toys."

Carmona's phobia together with the extreme weather conditions was bad enough, but there was another factor, the most harrowing story of Cubans traveling through Central America. A story like a hammer blow, like a myth, that haunts the mind of every migrant. The story of the couple whose child was swept away while they were at sea, and who hanged themselves from a barbed wire fence the moment they set foot on dry land.

From La Miel, the three take another boat to Puerto Obaldía, a tiny little village with barely five hundred residents. They spend a week throwing parties, selling drugs, practicing witchcraft. They earn twenty dollars working as watchmen on the docks, and they pimp out Cuban women who have ended up penniless, mostly to soldiers and malandros.

"We helped a lot of women. This way, they were able to pay for a light aircraft to take them to Panama City."

"How much did you charge?"

"Depends. Fifty, sixty, eighty for some of them, and obviously we took our commission. The private flights cost two sixty-five. We stirred up a lot of trouble."

The local hostels cost five bucks a night, but to save money the musketeers stay in an abandoned shack. Most of the Cuban migrants they meet during this period follow them around. They call them "the shamans." Wherever they go, they are greeted like artists. Everyone wants to travel with them on buses and in trucks. They are a guarantee of entertainment, and besides, they right wrongs. But later, these people will go their own way. They cannot handle the pace.

On the way to Costa Rica, for example, they stop off in a remote town called David for the night. They go into a store and buy clothes and perfume—"we dolled ourselves up," Carmona says, "smart shirts, blazers"—and go looking for a whorehouse.

In La Esmeralda, the town's only den of iniquity, they take a ringside table near the strippers, as though they were mobsters accompanied by their gangs.

"As soon as we showed up, we saw the place was buzzing, the trucks in the parking lot, the drug dealers, the coke everywhere. Whatever we did, we always ended up coming face-to-face with the devil. We could have decided to stay outside, be sensible, but no. We like the spotlight."

Their grandiose entrance attracts attention, and a little while later, after a lot of cocaine, a *gatillero*, a hit man, comes over to their table and asks who they are.

"What the fuck d'you mean, who are we?" Jaime says. "Who the fuck are you? We're tough guys. I've got a bullet wound in my hand." He flashes a scar on his left finger. "I'm a buddy of Fidel Castro, and I've killed people. That's who I am."

The spotlight is on them. The gatillero lets them talk, Carlitos stares him down, Carmona shakes his hand. Jaime keeps running his mouth. He has "a gift for heating things up within seconds."

"So, you're tough guys?" the gatillero says, coolly lifting his sweater. There are two pistols in his belt. Five bullet hole scars in his belly. "Don't play the tough guys."

Instantly, like a sketch from the finest comedy show, the musketeers start arguing among themselves. About who is to blame for the situation, about whether or not they should leave. Jaime resolves the dilemma. He runs out in a blind panic, hails a taxi, and calls his partners in crime. In a high-speed chase, they escape La Esmeralda, but later, back at the hotel, they decide to go out looking for another strip club, get a little more "fucked-up," which is their slang for "blitzed." They have no limits.

As time goes on, the atmosphere sours. They fight over money, over bad decisions, over old favors, over women. Carmona manages to use his magical chicanery to sleep with two prostitutes for free, while Jaime is forced to pay, and this little joke festers into resentment. At times, they feel like killing each other. But the point is that, whatever happens between them, the shamans will always claim they were a brotherhood, and that this brotherhood inspired a fondness they could never feel for any other companion at any other moment, however pleasant or comforting such companions or such moments might be. At least, that's how Carmona tells it, with absolute conviction, assuming the right to speak for all of them.

In Costa Rica, the problems with drugs and malandros continue. In Nicaragua, they are arrested and held for two hours. When they reach Honduras, their nerves are shattered and their spirits broken. The constant fear, this spinning out of control, has taken its toll on their free and easy manner. The blowouts and the binges, however relentless, are merely a cover for a beautiful and demanding friendship that, despite their best efforts, will sadly founder on the rocks of these events.

===

There are three main reasons for the exponential increase in the exodus over the past two years, peaking at some fifty thousand emigrants in the months before this piece was written: the 2013 Cuban government reforms to immigration policy that eliminated most of the unpopular restrictions on travel, including the need for an arbitrary "special permit"; the reestablishment of diplomatic relations between Cuba and the United States in December 2014, signaling that the wet foot/dry foot policy would probably be repealed; and Raúl Castro's visit to Mexico in November 2015, which led to changes to the 2008 Migration Treaty.

Since 2013, some twenty thousand Cubans have traveled to Ecuador, the only country on the continent that does not require them to have a visa. Once there, the majority put up the average $4,000 for the onward journey and became musketeers after a fashion.

Since Costa Rica imposed a block on migrants on November 12, 2015, the result of intense political pressure following the dismantling of a trafficking network of Cuban migrants by local police, the number of people passing through Tapachula has dwindled. On the other hand, by the end of the same month, at least three thousand more Cubans were granted their eagerly awaited safe conduct documents.

——

From Spain to Amsterdam, from Amsterdam to Panama, and from Panama to Nicaragua. She overcame numerous obstacles by sheer force of character, but when she reached the Honduran border on November 13 or 14, immigration officers refused to grant her entry as a Cuban citizen. She began her travels as a resident of Spain and cannot change her status when it suits her.

Ibelys sobs and almost passes out. She hands over all her savings, except a symbolic five-dollar bill she has managed to hide in her shoe. She crosses the border on a *bicitaxi* rickshaw. The driver insists on being paid.

"I got him to believe that my cheap bracelet was gold, that I couldn't possibly give it to him," she says. "And he fell for it."

Now in Honduras, she asks a taxi driver for help. She needs a telephone to call her family. A hotel manager comes over and offers her a room. She is not sure whether to accept. She knows such offers are never really free. In the distance, someone calls to her.

"¿Qué pasa, la mía? ¿Cubana? Come with me, I'll save you."

Ibelys introduces herself and recounts the broad strokes of her story. As he listens to her, the man is thinking that her account of the incident at the Nicaraguan border is probably just a smoke-screen. Ibelys asks his name. Jaime Morel Valladares, says the man. At this point, Ibelys becomes D'Artagnan. She alone can keep up with the three musketeers.

Together, they go to a hotel in Choluteca. The hotel manager also takes a shine to Ibelys, and she makes the most of this, flirting with him in order to get free rounds of beer. A couple of nights pass between blowouts and hangovers. In the corners of every room, they light the ever-present candles to their patron saints. Jaime is convinced that agents from the Cuban intelligence services have infiltrated the migration route, but no one takes him very seriously.

Ibelys goes to expensive stores with Carlitos; they take selfies in luxury cars and post them on Facebook. Carlitos dresses up and dances so that Ibelys can video him on her cell phone. They create a real-time travel documentary that disguises the abject horror of the journey. To judge from their online profiles, the trek was relaxed and fun, a backpackers' holiday. In actual fact, it was anything but. The tragedy became too personal, too harrowing to post online in every little detail.

"The shamans rescued me," Ibelys says. "In my life, my real fear is uncertainty, not knowing where to go, what's going to happen. I'm not afraid of being hassled by cops. I can deal with that, but I'm terrified of uncertainty. I let my instincts guide me, and I'm almost always right."

She's convinced that her best decision was to follow the musketeers, despite the ructions her presence created between them. Jaime, who starts out flattering and consoling her, goes ballistic when she doesn't seem to reciprocate and ends up insulting and humiliating her in front of everyone. But Ibelys is reluctant to remember moments like this. In her memories, Jaime is sweet and affectionate, hilariously crazy. He is now aggressive and overbearing by nature, but under the influence of drugs.

"He was the guy who gave joy to troubled souls along the way," she says.

But as she and Carmona grew closer, the atmosphere became even more tense.

"If you've got chemistry, nothing can get in the way," says Carmona. "You could bump into . . . what's the name of the actor who was in *Troy*?"

"Brad Pitt?" Ibelys suggests.

"Brad Pitt. You could bump into Brad Pitt and you might go off with him because he's loaded, because he's got serious *moolah*, but if I'm the one, you'll always end up coming back to me."

It is on a patio in Tegucigalpa, lounging next to each other in hammocks on those lost afternoons, that Ibelys and Carmona get to talking and are stunned, they say, to discover that they have so many things in common.

"What things?"

"The stuff we've gone through, not just here but in Spain, in Havana. The way we deal with life," Carmona says. "When I look at her, I know she's mine. Because that whole shoot-out didn't affect me. I know why I'm going to the United States, but I've never had an American dream. I've sorted myself out. Religion taught me what I was worth. When I was a crook, people loved me, but they love me more now. So we're going to Atlanta together, my sister is expecting us. Miami is full of Cubans. If I go there, I'll only lose my way again. When you make a journey like this, it's to radically change your life. If I go there, it's to get a sense of what America is, not get bogged down in the sleaze and corruption of Miami. There comes a point when you've got to leave your past behind."

By the time they reach Guatemala, the musketeers are barely functional. Carlitos keeps to the sidelines, but the romantic complications among the other three exacerbate the situation. Carlitos and Jaime go one way, Carmona and Ibelys another.

"He's not the Jaime I knew anymore," Carmona says. "He's a buddy and I love him a lot, I really love him. And when I'm hard on him, he cries. But he's not like that anymore. The drugs have changed him."

The events of the last night are particularly sad. A coyote double-crosses them and they find themselves in total darkness, stranded in the middle of a road blocked by two felled trees. Sixty Cubans and their fears of dying crowded onto a little bus.

The children are sobbing and an old woman is howling. The driver says to Carmona that if there's a sound he should run for the hills and at this, for the last time, Carmona feels a wave of terror. If we don't give them what they want, the driver explains, they're going to kill us. Carmona says to Ibelys that it's every man for himself now, and Ibelys thinks it's time for them to go their separate ways. Carmona gets upset. He is not leaving her, the two of them are leaving the others; they are one.

"He said, just give me the green light, because right now, no one knows what to do. But then he said . . . what was it you said to me?"

"If I walk, follow. If I stop, push me. If I turn back, kill me."

"And I was strong," says Ibelys.

"Yeah, my woman here was tough," Carmona says, "and it's when you're in danger that you get a true sense of a person."

Eventually, the police saved the caravan from the would-be robbers, and after skirting a sheer, almost vertical cliff during which Ibelys got her foot caught in a barbed-wire fence and was only freed by Carmona with a brutal wrench that left her bleeding, they reached the border, crossed the Suichate River on inflated inner tubes, and reached Tapachula, exhausted but triumphant, on the morning of November 20.

They turn themselves in to the authorities, and while they are waiting to be issued safe-conduct passes, they are separated. Ibelys gives Carmona her most precious possessions: a few family clothes. He asks her to look after his Ifá tablet, even though women are not supposed to touch it.

During the bureaucratic procedures, Ibelys loses her wallet and her money. Carmona borrows five dollars to be able to buy some bread. They meet up again that night, and without a centavo to their name, they have to hand over their safe-conduct documents as a guarantee in order to get a room at the Hotel Palafox.

"We're warriors," Carmona says. "If we have to sleep in the streets, we'll do it. But it didn't come to that."

Familiar to Cubans because of its shabby pink facade and its dismal, narrow lobby, the Hotel Palafox, at the top of 8va Avenida Norte, looks like a rathole.

━━

Curiously, what Ibelys finds most attractive about Carmona is his mild manner, his reluctance to make a fuss. What attracts Carmona to Ibelys is her temperament, a courage and determination that he finds surprising in a woman. They seem less in love with one another than with what they have managed to achieve together. Together, they have reached their pinnacle; it is a relationship forged in the fire, and the few romantic sunsets, of their flight.

"What I'm facing will be tough," Carmona says. "Because my woman here has a ferocious amount of energy for her age. Me, I found Honduras pretty relaxing."

"You need to relax," Ibelys says, "because I'm wild and restless and I've got a bunch of indecent proposals in mind."

"That's what I'm saying. Why does it have to come to that? A trial of strength. There's not need for it. Everything's chill as it is."

"I'm just warning you."

"It's just looking for trouble. I'm not into trouble anymore. I give you advice so you'll learn. What has she experienced that I haven't? I've known all kinds of women—ugly, pretty, black, white, Indians."

"Yeah, but I stole the show," says Ibelys. "Men love me and women resent me."

Carmona looks at her, his eyes limpid, gives her a flirtatious smile, and says, "To tell you the truth, she's not all bad." At the Mexican border they encountered a five-year-old girl and, although Ibelys was starving, she shared her candy with the girl and gave her some clothes. In return, the little girl gave her a bag of oranges.

Ibelys confirms this story with surprising shyness. Carmona says something about the words of Orula, that the sacred books can never touch the floor. Ibelys says she would have liked to write, but she has taken a different path and now she wants to be a therapist. They miss their friends, making a peremptory inventory of their practical and spiritual amulets, remembering those far away who have supported them.

Right now, on the afternoon of Saturday, November 21, they are waiting for some of these people to send money so that they can continue their journey. But if that does not happen, they will find a way to sort things out. Ibelys proudly shows off the tattoo on her right side: a mantra that both of them embrace, a maxim that glimmers in the stormy November skies. If God be for me, who can be against me?

ENGINEERS AND TRAFFICKERS

Mauro Godínez's name isn't really Mauro Godínez, but there are two reasons why you can't know his real name. First, Mauro asked me. Second, Mauro is a personal friend and I don't want him to come to any harm. He also asked that I not portray myself as some kind of hero and steal all his glory and I said, No way, how could I: a boor and a coward?

Both of us were twenty-two, both of us were studying at university, but there were subtle differences between us. I was still getting money sent by my mother, while Mauro was already supporting his whole family. I didn't sell anything, not even my lunch, while Mauro was a notorious trafficker as well as an engineering student, and he was effortlessly successful at both.

He was not what you might call a diligent student, but he was clever enough. In a college that set rigorous standards, he had never flunked a test. He never fell behind on coursework. Meanwhile he ran—more than ran, he guided—a minor mafia, a shady group in whom he had instilled his highly personal and democratic laws.

He was no older than the others, but they trusted him: he was one of those kids who, at fifteen, seemed like he was thirty, and at thirty, looked as though he had seen it all. Pragmatic, a little gruff, and inscrutable. And to his close friends, a gentle tower of strength.

He didn't like—still doesn't like—to stand out, to be the center of attention. His face is not that of an old man, but nor does he look naive. When he decides something, that's what happens. Back then, he often said things that went against logic, but luck favored him and he never lost the status or the prestige he enjoyed with his roommates.

At the Technological University of Havana José Antonio Echeverría—the CUJAE, the most important technological university in the country—most of the students in apartments 28 and 42 of Building 34 were from the province of Matanzas, and thanks to a profitable trafficking business, all those from Matanzas, without exception, were earning twenty and thirty times the average monthly wage of a Cuban state worker.

In a couple of years, they would be qualified engineers and traffickers. A sure-fire combination. And one that could exist only in this country.

═══

It was a Saturday in May 2012 and it had rained. When it rains, the city of Cárdenas—10 kilometers from Varadero, 70 from Matanzas, and 300 from Havana—becomes unbearable. There are places where rain cleanses, and places where it muddies. The red earth had been churned up, and the facades of the buildings further reinforced the curious state of mind conjured by provincial colors.

Mauro, running from a police patrol, knocked on my door. He sat down, wiped away sweat, took a drink of water, explained the situation, and twenty minutes later we headed out, each carrying a rucksack. Less than 200 meters away, there was a taxi rank and from there Mauro headed southeast to the little town of Colón. As always, just before he reached Colón, his friend Fidel was waiting with a motorcycle, to avoid the town center: prying eyes, plainclothes police officers.

Fidel and Mauro had the luxury of forging a friendship not only through their studies but also in the shady world of business, despite knowing that business can mean the end of a friendship and that it's better to come up with the money yourself and do business with people you don't know, people with whom you don't have a friendly relationship. But Fidel and Mauro seemed to be intelligent enough to keep things in order.

That day, in Cárdenas, Mauro had picked up the merchandise from the house of his friend Lázaro, another student at CUJAE. It was a routine trip that happened every weekend. Havana to Cárdenas, Cárdenas to Colón, and from Colón back to Havana. Mauro put his faith entirely in the work. He didn't trust chance. Or luck. Or other people. Only his own cunning and the experience he had gained. But sometimes certain incidents sowed seeds of resentment in him, and at such times he'd laugh it off, or pretend to laugh, to shrug it off.

We sat on a roadside planter, a huge concrete block containing a few spindly, withered butterfly palms. We hid our rucksacks among the palms, walked a little farther on so that they couldn't be connected to us, then waited for a taxi. The patrol car had driven past less than half an hour ago and might reappear at any moment.

The history of Cuba over the past century is a lurid oil on canvas that has been endlessly repainted. My generation—assuming there is something that can be called a generation—has its own particular affectation, an interesting ambiguity.

First came the '60s, the years of social justice. Then the '70s and egalitarianism. In the '80s, the recognition that some things weren't quite as neat and tidy as people had assumed. Then, in the '90s, the breakdown of reality and the realization that not only were things not neat and tidy, but they could and would be much tougher than anyone expected. In the 2000s, the desperate attempt to achieve communism. And now, in the second decade of the twenty-first century, another attempt to start over.

How do you retouch the oil painting? With Mauro Godínez, of course.

=====

As soon as they enrolled at CUJAE in September 2008, Mauro and Fidel knew they would have to find some way to earn a living and so, in an amateurish way, they started buying cookies and spaghetti in Havana for fifteen pesos to resell in Colón for twenty-five (everything is scarcer in the interior of the country). But this didn't last long.

Then they got in touch with farmers who supplied mozzarella in Colón and, having visited dozens of pizzerias in Havana, they came up with three restaurants they could supply. They bought the cheese for ten pesos a pound and sold it on for seventeen. In those early years, a number of factors made things difficult: the informal attitude of buyers, the risks they had to run to traffic goods without government authorization, not to mention the pressure of their university studies.

They even considered giving up, but then, one afternoon, in a store in Miramar, Fidel bought a couple of tires for his father's motorbike for ten CUC,* and was offered more than double the price by a number of interested parties back in Colón. Fidel mentioned this to Mauro, who asked his girlfriend to lend him enough money to buy seven tires.

He used the profits to invest in the rum business, via a family friend who worked at Industrias Arechabala (a distillery in Cárdenas through which rum was smuggled in bulk). He sold the bottles he bought to a student from Pinar del Río who lived in a dorm and he, in turn, sold them at parties held in the university.

---

* Cuban Convertible Peso, officially equivalent to one dollar; exchanged at a rate of 1 CUC to 25 Cuban pesos.

In Colón, both Mauro and Fidel managed to find suppliers for tomato puree, which they sold to the private cafeterias around the university. Needless to say, this required a serious public relations exercise. In his first year, Mauro managed to get three *extraordinarios*— penalties for his coursework—but he managed to survive.

═══

Mauro is a characteristic product of my generation. Someone proactive, someone who knows exactly what to do before things turn even more babyshit-brown than they usually are in Cuba. My father, for example, would never have considered doing what Mauro was doing. And, in fact, never did.

My father was born into a very poor family, went to university without having to pay a centavo, graduated in 1986, and always believed that he could live like a white-collar worker. But he lived like a laborer and earned a laborer's salary. Even so, his profound gratitude, his faith, and the moral and personal debt he had incurred made it impossible for him to be disloyal.

Let's go back in time: the '60s was the decade of the new man. The '70s, the so-called apogee of the so-called new man. The '80s saw the first dents in the shiny exterior of the new man. The '90s, the sudden, seismic collapse of the new man. The 2000s witnessed the dancing corpse of the new man. And now, in the second decade of the twenty-first century, comes the man who doesn't care whether he is new or old, only that he is.

═══

The first and second lessons proved crucial. Mauro learned them one sweltering hot night. He had a spaghetti delivery in his rucksack and was casually walking by the road. He was wearing a T-shirt, shorts, and flip-flops. Seeing an approaching light, and assuming it was a taxi rather than a police car, he first gave a wave, then made a dismissive gesture. The driver did a swift U-turn. The officers asked him for identification and told him to open his rucksack. Mauro invented a story, but the officers did not believe him; they took him to the station where he was fined sixty pesos.

Lesson one: no earrings, no sideburns, no long hair, no flashy clothes. Traffickers all looked alike. They all had tattoos or piercing or their behavior gave them away.

Lesson two: delivery bags had to be anonymous so that, if found, they couldn't be traced back to an owner. No personal items in the bag containing the merchandise: no clothes, no papers, no letters. Nothing that could be used as evidence. Merchandise: packed in a brand-new rucksack. Personal items: in a battered old bag.

It was Fidel who taught him the third lesson. He had taken a state taxi and came within a whisker of being caught, but the police officer stopped before checking the trunk of the car. From Colón to Havana, via Ocho Vías, the route was clear, but from Cárdenas to Havana via Vía Blanca, you could be stopped at any checkpoint.

A state taxi could take a maximum of five or six people, but there was always the risk of being stopped and checked. This was less likely with a bus, and never happened with Transtur buses, since there might be tourists, and the police were not likely to hassle people when there were tourists present for fear of bad press. Even better, if you took a bus you could stuff the rucksack under someone else's seat. Ideally a couple or two women or an old man. If someone got off the bus and a black guy took their seat, you would need to move the rucksack. Because the police—this may sound like a bad joke, but it's not—never left black guys unharmed.

Every week, Mauro was clearing about 1,000 pesos from the rum, without counting the tomato puree. Now, in his second year at university, and the third in his career, he decided to join forces with Lázaro, and they started buying bottles of whiskey in Cárdenas (filched from hotels in Varadero). He gained in comfort, because each bottle earned him five CUC and he could transport four or five bottles without raising suspicion.

The traffic in rum and tomato puree continued. To this he added canned tuna—buying for four CUC and selling for six cans that sold for twelve CUC in a store. He also made contact with a fellow student who lived in Vedado. Mauro had tried to sell the tuna in various quarters, he even had a little speech—CUJAE student, reputable supplier, and so on—but couldn't find any takers until a fellow student—no one really knows why—decided to take the stock and try to sell it in his neighborhood. He sold out within two days.

In Vedado—an area of noble families and discriminating palates—people only buy expensive, hermetically sealed products. And some outlets will only buy in specific quantities. Either you can supply the full order, or no deal. Once he managed to find his way inside, Vedado proved to be a coming of age for Mauro. He was taking risks—he might invest $150 in stock in Cárdenas and make only $35 or $40 in Havana—but there was no way out. Eventually, he found himself selling ham, chorizo, prawns, salmon, and lobster to customers who started out just buying whiskey.

By this stage, there were six or seven other students in the same dorms who were moving stock. Together, they made a small business venture, so a few basic rules seemed appropriate. Mauro gathered all the partners together and they came to an agreement on several points:

1. No two points could ever connect. If Mauro had a client who wanted prawns and Partner B had one who could supply them,

he could not supply it directly. He had to go through Mauro, and Mauro would authorize it.

2. If a partner discovered a supposedly new contact, it had to be submitted to the group, since another partner might already be working with them.

3. A weekly meeting was scheduled to discuss what was happening and share advice: any new incidents, any setbacks, any conditions, any complaints.

4. It was unanimously decided to prohibit three things: trafficking in drugs, tobacco, or beef.

Lastly, they divided up the territories where goods were distributed. In Cárdenas, Lázaro handled foodstuffs; Mauro and Fidel handled drinks.

There was less making it up as you go along. In addition, circumstances seemed to favor them. The government declared—admitted—that it didn't have the resources to run a wholesale network supplying basic commodities to private businesses—at least in 2011–12—thereby tacitly acknowledging that these new businesses would survive using the black market, a strategy they used to try to divert money circulating illegally into established channels.

Mauro and his partners enjoyed almost total freedom. Only a formal denunciation or a serious mistake on their part could topple the empire they had built.

═══

Once, after losing his job, my father seriously considered becoming self-employed. But he never did. He kept waiting for some state job to open up for him. Sometimes, he'd go to the bus stop and the bus wouldn't come for him. He'd wait for three hours and then come home. He'd sit on the sofa, rocking constantly, and didn't speak to anyone.

He had been dispatched to fight in the Angolan civil war in 1985. He was an honest guy. He shouldered the blessing and the burden of an integrity that those of my generation would never know. Mauro would have been incapable of waiting for a bus for three hours (although the bus is real, we could treat it as a symbol)—he wouldn't have waited for twenty minutes. If he lost his job as an engineer, he would have walked away, period. Besides, strictly speaking, Mauro's work as an engineer was never going to make him a living.

The early 1960s were marked by the program of nationalization and agrarian reform. The '70s, by the Ten Million Ton Harvest. The '80s, by the Mariel boatlift. The '90s, by the collapse of the USSR. The early 2000s, by the "Battle of Ideas." And the second decade of the twenty-first century, by the gradual state decentralization.

═══

Many of the staff working in the Varadero hotels were from Cárdenas. How merchandise was shipped to Cárdenas and later trafficked was not particularly complicated. Trafficking even enjoyed a degree of legitimacy. The hotels had vast displays of wines and whiskeys, allowing tourists to choose their drink of choice.

Cooks and busboys took products and resold them privately. The Varadero hotels operated an "All Inclusive" policy so that, on paper, a figure was calculated of the food consumed by tourists. The figure was invariably exaggerated. Any surplus was distributed among the hotel staff, surreptitiously stolen from the hotel after negotiations with the security staff, who were duly bribed, although, it is worth saying that, at the time, none of these acts were considered illegal.

Only maintenance staff were allowed to move between the various areas of the hotel, so it was they who smuggled out the cheese, the ham, the bottles of rums in bags and toolboxes. When, from time to time, a staff shuttlebus was stopped on Varadero bridge it was because someone had blown the whistle.

Sometimes, the head of security would send out the eleventh-hour codeword "zero" or "ring," signaling that nothing could be taken out of the hotel because of a pending inspection. Usually, the accounts had already been settled, so any food and drink that had been signed off had to disappear. At such points, workers and kitchen staff would cut up the ham or cheese and hide it under their clothes, taping it to their stomachs, their backs, even their legs and their feet.

═══

My generation has grown up on the bones of my parents' generation.

Even before he enrolled, Mauro knew that, when he graduated, a professional salary would not be enough for him, that it would be worse than useless. Nonetheless, he decided to go to university.

This is perhaps the one great success of the past fifty years: that someone is prepared to gamble on going to university even when it is obvious—even to those who look the other way—that university educations and utopias can paralyze you and put you in a position of risk.

It is also, perhaps, the one great failure: anyone who is prepared to gamble on a university education has to identify all possible emergency exits beforehand and accept this as something routine.

The routine may not be an indication of optimism but of apathy. Here, every decade begins with a historic jolt. And ends with another.

═══

It was late that Saturday and we were still sitting, chatting. Mauro was showing me his accounts, which were written such that no one could understand them. Numbers, initials, abbreviations. Who owed him money, how much they owed, what they had paid. He had a monthly income of 8,000–9,000 pesos.

Meanwhile, the two officers had parked their patrol car and were now sitting on the huge concrete planter with its withered palm trees. The situation was beginning to feel absurd, though the outcome did not depend on any of the actors involved. The officers were sitting with two rucksacks filled with tuna, cheese, and salmon right under their noses, but they were staring at God knows what. Meanwhile, twenty meters away, the two young men who were up to their necks in this deal seemed to be chatting about nothing in particular. No one would have been able to connect these two scenes, but there were no other clues to connect.

Five minutes later a truck carrying steel and sand drove past and the officers got in their car and gave chase. We raced back to the planter. Some guy had found the rucksacks and was trying to steal them. Mauro told him it would be in his best interests to put them down. The man did not even look at us, but meekly put them back. He was weird: awkward and disfigured. He stuttered something and went on his way. Then a taxi showed up heading for Máximo Gómez—a little town between Cárdenas and Colón—and Mauro climbed in. This all happened in the time it takes to relate it.

That day, Mauro ended up with five extraordinarios. His university career was in danger, but he would have to carry on. He had no choice. It is an old law of business. Never retreat. Never fall short. There are no second chances. This is how rigorous some clandestine schools are.

THURSDAYS WITH RAY

He is the Toulouse-Lautrec of the itinerant Cuban musicians we call *trovadores*—minstrels or troubadors. The Buster Keaton of intellectual songwriters. A subversive jester in the guild of illustrious poets. When you hear him perform live, you feel like devouring the whole world.

It was not always this way. It might never have happened at all. But since it did, for the past seven years, there has been nothing better in Havana. Every Thursday afternoon, Ray Fernández—shantytown showman, rabble-rousing singer-songwriter—performs at the Diablo Tun Tun Piano bar, part of the amazing Miramar Casa de la Música, for four in-your-face hours. A riot of smoke, booze, and blatant promiscuity. It is not a populist event. It is not an elitist event. A bacchanal attracts the righteous and the just.

━━

In Cuba, people often hear Ray Fernández without knowing who he is. It is a sign for posterity: if an artist's work becomes known before he does, and spreads far and wide without his help, it likely will carry on doing so long after he's gone.

The 2000s were withering on the vine. There were unending

shortages and ideological outbursts, and people were starting to sing "La yuca."

With its roots in indigenous Taíno culture, Fernández's song "La yuca" was—is—an allegory of the economic, political, and social situation faced by Cubans.

It goes: "The whole country's getting squeezed now / folks in straw huts hear the sound / there's a shortage now on loincloths, not much *yuca* to go around / now magic's more expensive than medications on the high street / so the local Taína women are turning tricks to make ends meet."

Also: "And they join the big parade to the toot of the flute-oh / that *el cacique* holds the power / and he holds it *absoluto*."

In the long years since the Revolution, a number of songs—from sophisticated allegories to seemingly inoffensive pop tunes—have challenged the prevailing social order. Carlos Varela, Tanya, Pedro Luis Ferrer, and even Silvio Rodríguez once, according to malicious gossips. But nothing as caustic and as hilarious as Ray's first big hit.

===

He's a musician, and he could have been a lot of things, which hardly matters, because even if he'd been something, anything else, he'd have been fundamentally the same. Ray Fernández is the sort of guy who, however things turned out, would have found himself in the opposite lane running traffic lights.

"He spent months threatening to do it," says his wife, Lenia. "The idea was going round and round in his head, and I just stood in front of the door and told him I wasn't going to let him out."

That day, however, after one of his usual blowouts, he didn't get home until six in the morning, and Lenia wavered.

"I figured that given the time of the morning, and given he was shattered, he wouldn't be up to anything."

But he was. He stripped naked, wrapped himself in a blue sheet emblazoned with the letters MINSAP (Ministry of Public Health), took down a Bible, and, as dawn was breaking, went out and started preaching like a madman through the clamorous streets of Alamar, his neighborhood. "Repent!" he howled. He walked for miles along the Monumental, one of the major roads into Havana, railing about the Day of Judgment, reading biblical verses, and spouting gibberish.

"The people in the street recognized him. They all thought he'd lost his mind," says Lenia.

Then Ray wrote a song about it, including a ten-line stanza dedicated to him by a close friend.

"He's a preacher in *son*, rock, and rap / but no one throws open their door / to the man who is spreading the word / in a sheet that's marked MINSAP. / If they want him to shut his trap / this prophet in skivvies and socks / they'll have to reopen the UMAP / and lock him away in a box / this moralistic morning star / the strange apostle of Alamar."

———

"It's a performance," he says, "a shtick, that's all. I get these ideas into my head and I like to act them out. It's like shaking yourself up, challenging yourself. You've got to summon up a lot of courage for this kind of performance. I love the feeling. It's seriously fucking stimulating, like the stuff you read in novels, but real. But you have to be totally committed."

These days, Ray is no longer some nobody. He hosted a television program about trovadores, he's sung a duet with the legendary Omara Portuondo, and recorded an album for EGREM—the national record label of Cuba.

"I'm a citizen of the world and an anarchist. I'm a jester, I'm a cynic, I'm a prankster. I don't have a fixed ideology. I think it's good to joke. I'm a little altruistic."

"Do you think there are any sacred cows you shouldn't slaughter?"

"No way, *broder*. Not a single one."

"Do you think anything is sacred?"

"Life, maybe."

═══

He was born in Báez, a godforsaken hole in the middle of the country, on June 28, 1971. When he was three years old, his family moved to Havana, And in Alamar, his name was duly urbanized and Raimundo became Ray.

He spent his holidays down in the country, and he remembers the black guitar on the wall of his maternal grandparents' house on which local farmers—*guajiros*—played folk songs at parties and on which, in the silent after-parties in the countryside, he learned to play his first chords.

"I was only six years old. I was abusing the guitar strings that, in time, would offer me a way out of here."

As a boy, he spent a lot of time listening to the traditional ten-line form known as the *décima* or the *espinela*, a form that would later make him famous. His grandfather suffered a head injury and spent a whole year reciting décimas. Ray committed the basic form to memory: one four-line stanza, two three-line stanzas with the bridge between lines five and six.

These days, his songs and improvisations are strongly marked by the décima, alternating between pastoral themes and the changeability of seaside cities like Havana.

═══

At the age of fourteen, he started training to be a chef in a school at the Hotel Sevilla.

At fifteen, maybe sixteen, he had his first passionate relationship, which produced the inevitable: the early poems, the inexpressible impulse, the ravening inner mouth we did not know was there until it begins to bite.

At seventeen, someone taught Ray four basic guitar chords, enough of an arsenal for him to head off with his friends to La Playita de los Rusos, a busy Alamar beach teeming with girls where other aspiring Don Juans strolled around with their guitars or the obligatory Selena or Russian VEF transistor radios.

His repertoire was limited to songs by Los Fórmula V and Los Mustang, the legendary minor bands of the '80s—what in Cuba was called the "Prodigious Decade." Just enough to fight his corner. Meanwhile, at home, he finally started to read, books like Patrick Suskind's *Perfume*. All these worlds, the seemingly trivial, the apparently highbrow, would end up fusing into an idiosyncratic style that, like all idiosyncrasies, initially feels unsettling.

There are artists who are so desperate to mold themselves as artists from an early stage that they embark on a rigorous course of training and become militant aesthetes. And then there are those who take life as it comes and wring its neck, use whatever skills they've acquired to become artists.

Ray is the archetypal autodidact. He has the half-spontaneous, half-subconscious style of those who do what they do because they do it. There is nothing he hates more than theorizing.

—

He has read, and set to music, works by legendary Cuban poets Lezama Lima (son), Gastón Baquero (blues), Eugenio Florit (elegy), and Miguel Hernández (bolero), a man who is almost a god to him, which is understandable since Ray and the goliath from Orihuela share the visceral roar of wild beasts.

——

"I'm conflicted. My songs stem from the everyday. They work better that way. It does my head in when I'm writing a song. I get deeply involved in the psychology of my characters, but I try to capture them in the simplest way possible. I don't like pretentiousness. But then I wanted to do something deeper, because all the other trovadores around were big on culture and they criticized me, they said my songs were facile. I don't believe that. I spill my guts onto the page. The problem is poetry. Poetry is also about synthesis, and I favor plain, ordinary language, my language. Sometimes, when you're talking to certain people, you have to use a certain kind of language, but I'm based in Alamar and that's where I write my songs. You can read and understand Lezama's poetry, but that doesn't mean you have to talk like Lezama. I was pretty prolific. I wrote some good things, some bad things, but nothing terribly intellectual, and then it occurred to me to borrow from Gastón Baquero, find the magic in his words, and maybe steal something from him, so I took a fragment from "Palabras escritas en la arena" (Words written in sand) . . . the verse that runs "I am not dreaming life, it is life that is dreaming me." It sounded resonant, so I took it and I decontextualized it. I'm not particularly keen on the trend for importing American styles, but what emerged was a blues song and when I showed it to some trovadore friends, they said, 'You see, that's how it should be done.'"

Thankfully, Ray didn't pay his friends much heed, because the thing, *his* thing, has more thing to it than all of them, and it didn't have to be done that way. Songs like "El gerente," "Matarife," "El obrero," "El hambre," or even "La yuca" made him the most fascinating social chronicler of the last, say, fifteen years in Cuba. His songs provide the most compelling testimony. In full flow, the power of his delivery is more rapper than trovadore.

His songs offer portraits of the social-climbing manager, the corrupt state, the everyday poverty and misery covered up by ideological propaganda, or the well-intentioned parole officer who tells the ex-con why he can't eat beef and the ex-con who gives the parole officer a reality check.

"What distinguishes Ray as a musician is his ability to improvise," says renowned musicologist Joaquín Borges Triana. "He's not a virtuoso guitarist, or a great singer. Far from it! But he doesn't need to be either to do what he does well. When you go to one of his concerts, you expect what you might from a great jazz musician, a familiar repertoire that is different every time, because it's all about the improvisations and the variations."

Love and Revolution. Hippie ideals. People whistle, they pump their fists in approval as Ray sings what almost no one else does.

—

"'La yuca' was the first song that really worked on the Alamar circuit, where they'd already had enough of my maudlin ballads. It was something I wrote in ten minutes. I'd been upset by an incident at Hotel Habana Libre. The doorman wouldn't let me in and I started screaming. This was back in the '90s, when Cubans weren't allowed into hotels. After that, I wrote 'Mr. Policeman,' about police brutality. I felt a real need to criticize, and I love to ridicule things. My love songs flopped, but I was good at satire."

"As an artist, do you feel a sense of social commitment?"

"I'm just having fun, broder. I don't think I have a sense of social commitment; I don't think I can change things. I need to express myself and I'm lucky to be able to play at the Tun Tun every

Thursday. It is like an ecumenical church where we all go to exorcise our demons, but with no pretension that we're going to change people's minds or instill some kind of doctrine. I go and I present my thesis and I'll take any criticism going. Sometimes, I've even apologized for upsetting people. Once a Basque guy got upset because I said 'Long live the king!' Political dissidents like Yoani Sánchez have come to my show and dared me to throw them out. Please, I don't have to throw anyone out. People have ideological differences and I believe friendship can handle that."

"At the Tun Tun you have a freedom that's pretty rare."

"I run the risk of making a fool of myself, of hurting someone, or tearing strips off someone, but people can get up close and personal, broder. It's not like I've got a dressing room or bodyguards."

—

Since starting his Thursday shows on November 27, 2008, Ray has played riffs by Led Zeppelin and Deep Purple. He lampoons politicians, the founding fathers of communism, and himself. He improvises décimas using daringly audacious forced rhymes. He sings songs by El Puma, Roberto Carlos, Rudy La Scala, Enmanuel, Cheo Feliciano, and Silvio Rodríguez. Rescues classics by Matamoros, hymns to literacy. He can shift between rock, son, and tango. He quotes Benito Juárez, speaks Basque, imitates Cantonese, wears mariachi sombreros, pirate hats, elegant all-white suits, or dresses as a junkie or a sheikh, sports a bushy beard or shaves it all off. He sometimes takes off his shirt and plays drums on his belly. Some people assume he goes on stage stoned.

"I don't have the creativity to produce something new every Thursday. That takes work, but when it comes to performing, I repeat myself. For example, this year I've written five songs and, to me, that's a success. Two songs a year and I'm pretty happy. That's why I

don't just sing my own songs, I'll sing anyone's songs, do my inter-
pretations, go from the sublime to the ridiculous."

"And you don't just sing, you act."

"Yeah, it's a performance, a show. I use costumes, get people involved. I unburden myself, I do my own thing. The audiences are
great. Sometimes I'll show up exhausted, with no energy, but I summon the energy. And I have to do it every week, because this is my
livelihood."

"Which of your Tun Tun shows is the most memorable?"

"One day I showed up drunk, completely plastered. I hadn't
slept, I was a complete mess. The audience looked after me. A friend
took off his clothes and lent them to me. I felt welcome."

═══

"Who were your influences? Silvio Rodríguez, Pablo Milanés?"

"I came to them pretty late. My early influence came from what
my parents listened to, the music from the Prodigious Decade.
Music most people hate, although some travadores have started ex-
ploring it again now. They're good songs, they don't have any pre-
tensions, they don't have some objective the way Nueva Trova did.
Of course, I was blown away by Silvio and Pablo, but I never wanted
to emulate them. My songs are very personal. They're stories I can
feel, things that happened to me or to people close to me. I was influenced by the poetic power of Silvio and Pablo, but that's dangerous.
They set the bar so high. You have to listen to them constantly, and
you have to be careful. Their songs stay with you, you can't shake
them off. I never really caught the bug, I managed to keep my distance. I wasn't mesmerized by them. And they're very different from
each other. Silvio could never have written "Yolanda," for example."

═══

The big difference between Ray Fernández and almost every other trovadore of his generation is precisely that. Ray is completely true to himself; he's not just another second-rate follower infected by the Silvio Rodríguez virus, who ended up jumbling everything together, desperate to suffer or to contemplate more than necessary, overloading metaphors or believing that being poetic is boring.

"He represents a breath of fresh air in the trovadore tradition in this country," says Borges Triana. "What some people still call 'Nueva Trova,' and what I prefer to call Contemporary Cuban Music, there is still a grave seriousness, both in songwriting and in performance. Ray is completely different. His focus is on music and performance as play in the true manner of *Homo ludens*. Performance is as important, if not more important, to Ray than writing and performing his own work."

A few autobiographical lines by Ray, from *Romance del guitarrero*, might be seen as a statement of principles: "In the dark days of Chaonda, / of breakdance, of disco, / anything you couldn't bop to / was considered tacky or cheesy. / Then Pablo, Noel, and Silvio / the Cuban Nuevo Trova / stepped into the spotlight / with their lyrics and their rhythms, / and anyone with no guitar / was a pig by any other name. / Performers, trovadores / with a fresh new kind of lyricism / came bursting onto the scene / riving an age-old profession. / True, there were some brilliant tunes, / and melodies—it's fair to say— / that were almost more than songs. / They were pure algorithms, / antiquated equations, / tawdry, tacky meta-sounds, / for meta-intellectuals / creating meta-*tranca*. / And they all sang the same way, / a gravel growl in chorus, / I had no choice but to do my bit / my bid for fatal fame. / Then suddenly it came to me, / a fundamental question: / Who exactly was I writing for, / why would they be interested? / If there's nothing new under the sun, / what the fuck was there to sing about? / So, like the little cockroach / that stumbled on a penny, / I racked my puny mortal brains / until I couldn't see straight. / Whose style should I copy? / Should I wear a three-piece suit? / Or a mackintosh, a bowler hat? / Or a poncho and a long turtleneck? / with cocaleca sandals? / I could go with two-tone shoes, / with long, disheveled hair. / Maybe bald and beardy / best becomes a trovadore? / It was all far too much effort."

—

In addition to tunes filled with caustic humor or biting satire, Ray has also penned extraordinary songs, such as "Tenerte un año," which he wrote for Lenia in the early days of their relationship.

"But he's dedicated lots more to me," she says with concealed pride.

They live in a richly decorated apartment on the fourth floor of a corner block in Alamar's Zone 11. Lenia is a neonatologist, and for the past fourteen years, she has been Ray's emotional guide. She constantly interrupts him, corrects his dates, finishes his anecdotes with that exquisite refinement of female memory, and never for a moment allows Ray to doubt himself. She knows her husband is a warrior, an utterly original character, and she hates the fact that Ray cloaks his talent in reams of modesty.

Their living room has a baroque elegance. Ray's guitar sits in one corner; a tallboy filled with handcrafted vases and bowls, in terra-cotta and other mediums; a coatrack with red and black bowler hats, straw boaters, and tricorns; a wooden table set against the wall; and, to one side, a striking painting, a little anemic in tone, but brought to life by the interplay of swirling colors, as though a feverish palette had been overturned.

Here and there are still lifes; a bushy fern in Lorca green hangs from the ceiling; small lamps; fans; charcoal sketches; cast-iron keys; wicker baskets; bottles caked in wax; more paintings; portraits; furniture; magazine racks; a typewriter; a Cuban flag; coasters; candles and other objects that are impossible to identify.

This is his living room. And his living room resembles him. An accumulation of eclectic pieces that somehow fit together. A room that, despite the description, is small and very cozy, and seems unwilling to part with any of the objects that make it up.

There is also a map, framed in glass, next to which Ray has just been photographed. On this sultry night in the summer of 2015, Ray has already done his show and has allowed himself to be photographed wearing one of the beautiful Russian hats that conjure velvety words like *isba* or *steppe* or *samovar*, while pretending to leaf through a copy of *Soviet Woman*. He's had his portrait taken next to an image of José Martí, in a crate of Presidential rum, and wearing his iconic sweater that is a profession of faith: *I'm a Marxist*, reads the slogan under an image of Karl, Groucho, Chico, and Harpo Marx.

But the photo of Ray next to the map, wearing a black hat emblazoned with a white skull and crossbones, is probably the most expressive, since one of his best-loved songs, "Bucanero," marks him out as a master of allegory. Through the story of a sinking ship, and the paralyzed crew who fail to react to the disaster, his fans see a dazzling sketch of contemporary Cuba.

"When the Government Reform Guidelines* were published, some woman said the Water Provisioning Policy had sprung a leak," says Lenia, "and within five minutes, Ray had written "Bucanero": 'The ship is taking on water, / the hull is peppered with holes / and the mainmast is broken.'"

When you look closely, Ray actually resembles an archetypal pirate. Short, a little plump, but stocky. The pockmarked face, the weathered skin, the wild gestures, the voice like·a rattlesnake, the receding hair, the roving attitude, and a temperament, according to Lenia, that is generous but with flashes of fury.

---

* Basically a public consultation exercise conducted in 2009 by the Communist Party in order to carry out structural reforms in Cuba.

On the living room bookcase, which would be a shelf of harquebuses, a copy of José Lezama Lima's novel *Paradiso* stands out, but since he started working at the Tun Tun, Ray has had no time to read.

===

"I used to read a lot, anything I could get my hands on."

At twenty-three, he was imprisoned while doing military service and his then wife brought him a copy of Lizardi's *The Mangy Parrot: The Life and Times of Periquillo Sarniento*. From there he moved on to Mann, Dostoevsky, Orwell, and some of the major Hispanic poets. Ray firmly believes that he owes everything that he is in equal parts to reading and his tenacious determination to survive.

Later, encouraged by a few close friends, he wrote his first songs. Having studied haute cuisine, he worked as a chef at the DiploJoya in Miramar, at the 1830 restaurant in Vedado, and at El Patio, in Havana old town. In his spare time, he'd go to the Casa de la Cultura in Alamar to play his songs, to read or listen to poetry, and to practice guitar. While working at El Patio, Ray got into the habit of periodically disappearing from the kitchen to join the traditional musicians entertaining diners with sones and boleros, until one night, while he was entertaining, he cremated about thirty chickens and was, as he puts it, dishonorably discharged from the culinary ranks.

He worked as a hotel doorman, as a cook in a teacher training college, and as a busker on the Malecón, a period branded on his memory with white-hot steel, and the subject of one of his songs, in which he says that he has no fear of life for as long as the Malecón has its nights and he has the balls to *fight for his yuca*—a Cuban saying that means "to do whatever it takes to earn a crust."

"I only really enjoyed it at the start, or when people applauded my songs. Having to sing 'Lágrimas negras' to get people to toss ten or twenty pesos into the guitar case is fucking depressing. I'd go down to the Malecón wearing a costume or a mask. I was going to earn my beans and have a bit of a laugh too. I never imagined it was something I could do professionally."

"Never?"

"Absolutely not. People liked my voice, they liked my cover versions of songs by Los Fórmula or Los Pasteles Verdes—I can be a good mimic—but they didn't like my songs."

Every night, Ray would head down to the Malecón at nine o'clock and come home at four or five in the morning.

"He'd work for the State one day on, one day off," says Lenia. "And when he was on shift, he'd head straight from the Malecón to the kitchen where he worked. A lot of times, I'd cook for him so he didn't get fired, or I'd pick the beans and wash them."

Sometime around 2002, Ray took part in the Romerías de Mayo in Holguín where he met a number of the new breed of trovadores, and they introduced him to the editors of *El Caimán Barbudo*, the venerable cultural review, who organized trova gigs at the time.

"It was Bladimir Zamora (a music critic) who discovered him," says Rafael Grillo, the magazine's editor in chief, "and for a long time, until the Tun Tun opened up, Ray was a regular at the magazine events. He even traveled in the provinces with us."

His ascent was instantaneous: concerts, events, auditions in order to gain professional status and get the legal support that, in time, would make it possible to sign contracts and devote himself to music completely.

"I started practicing the guitar for a couple of hours every day, and I got better. Before that, I would hear a song and later, I'd try to play it from memory. It was pretty basic: C, D, E. But there are passing chords, trills, and fingerpicked grace notes that enhance the melody. You learn to think like a musician."

"And this is something you can learn from scratch?"

"Sure. I think you have to have talent. I've got music deep inside me."

"Have you ever written a difficult melody, one you couldn't completely work out and eventually gave up on?"

"I have a lot of fragments, instrumental pieces. They started out as exercises that I played, and they were beautiful. There are maybe seven or eight that I practice every day because they help with my fingering."

At the same time as he started playing at the Tun Tun, Ray recorded his first album, *Entre la piedra y el sueño*, thanks to the support of the Centro Pablo de la Torriente Brau, and began presenting *Entre manos*, a TV program about trova on Canal Habana. But he and the cameras never really got along.

"I found myself having to deal with censorship, not only of my own songs but of the musicians I invited onto the show. Anyway, I don't like television. I think it's tacky, especially Cuban TV. And I hate the fact that nothing is broadcast live, the fear and the paranoia involved. Later I appeared on programs as a guest, but I felt bad doing it. I know promotion is important. But the success of the Tun Tun has all been down to word of mouth. My stuff does get played on the radio, including songs that have been banned from television. Besides, not being on television creates a kind of mysterious aura around you. I'm comfortable now, and I feel no urge to go out, because if I get invited onto a TV show, I tend to cause trouble and to sing things you're not supposed to sing. It's a combative thing. So, I never go. Besides, I should probably add that I'm pretty lazy, broder. These TV shows are recorded at 10:00 a.m., when I'm usually still asleep. My biorhythms are strictly nocturnal. If you want to interview me at ten or eleven at night, fine, but not at ten in the morning. Also, it takes up a lot of time, and I don't want to spend time promoting myself. I know it has to be done, but I'm doing okay as I am.

I want to keep on recording, that's important, so things can stay as they are. That's how I approach it."

═══

The album *Entre la piedra y el sueño* was followed by the *Conciertosky* DVD and the *Paciencia* album for EGREM. In 2015, EGREM signed a contract with Sony Music to distribute its music. And when it did, Ray snuck in.

Ray is well known at EGREM. After he recorded *Paciencia* for them in 2010, they ended up owing him 20,000 pesos. He spent months hassling the company for payment and eventually, frustrated by their lack of a response, Ray walked into the snack bar of the Hotel Inglaterra with a couple of friends, where they drank and ate their fill—"sandwiches, olives, capers, Serrano ham, beer"—and told them to send the bill to EGREM, since he hadn't got a centavo and the record company owed him a fortune.

Hours later, Lenia had to step in and pay the bill, while Ray was placidly digesting his feast in a holding cell at Dragones y Zulueta police station, in Havana old town.

═══

The Tun Tun, late on Thursday nights, is a countercultural space that has only once closed early—on March 24, 2016. The Rolling Stones were arriving in Havana and the Instituto de Música had invited a number of artists—including Ray—to participate in an exchange with the granddaddies of rock.

In subsequent statements to *El País*, Ray, who is like no one else on earth, made his mark. "There they were, the crème de la crème of Cuban music . . . On their best behavior, waiting patiently. But the moment Mick Jagger appeared, they were overcome with joy. They were all throwing themselves at him, pleading for autographs, they looked like they wanted to eat him up. They were like Beatles fans, the girls who used to shriek and pull their hair out," he said.

According to a journalist who was present, Ray was only joking. But anyone who knows him knows that he probably wasn't. This is the thing about the buccaneering pirates of the music world. If they get bored, they pass up meeting Mick Jagger or whoever it happens to be. They destroy the vast armadas of celebrities. They loot and they pillage. They may be jokers, but they're deadly serious.

BROKEN DOLL

Her heart isn't yet hanging by a thread.

But it soon will be. It's the night of May 10, 2015, and in her house in Regla, on the outskirts of Havana, Cándida López receives a call from her daughter, Mayara Alvite, in Quito, wishing her a happy Mother's Day. Cándida recalls a bright, loving conversation, dampened only by the anguish of physical distance. Her daughter seems sparkier and more upbeat than she has been recently.

The fact that her daughter seems more like herself again is reason enough for Cándida to recover a bit of the calm she's barely felt at all since October 2014, when Mayara sold her dead father's house in San Miguel del Padrón and decided to emigrate to Ecuador to try her luck with her girlfriend, Waday, a forty-year-old, half-Chinese woman Cándida has always detested because she is very controlling toward her daughter, who is only twenty-three.

From the night of the phone call on, Mayara, despondent and in an unfamiliar place, becomes progressively glummer until, on the morning of May 12, Cándida receives another phone call from her daughter's number. It is a dam through which the events come bursting.

"When I woke up that day I hadn't felt like having breakfast," she says. "I didn't even want to get out of bed. I had a tight feeling in my chest. I didn't know what was happening to me."

Cándida, petrified, deep in the tunnel where they tell her over and over again that, yesterday night, from a beam in a closet, with a luggage strap,

    your
        daughter,
            Mayara,
                h
                a
                n
                g
                e
                d
                herself.

====

Her blood pressure goes through the roof. Everything Cándida does from now on—her relentless crusade for the return of her daughter's body, the brief moments in which she tries to think about anything else—she will do with her nerves pulverized, sunk deep into a cancerous struggle that will manifest in different ways, with one horrific constant: the feeling of having nothing to lean on, nothing to look forward to.

Forty-five minutes after the conversation with Cándida, Waday—whom everyone calls La China—calls again and talks to Cándida's sister-in-law. She needs $5,000, she says disdainfully, and power of attorney authorizing her to deal with the process of getting the body repatriated.

On her way back from the polyclinic, still unsettled and clinging to the ever fainter possibility that this is some cruel trick, Cándida decides she's not going to send any money to La China, first, because she doesn't have any, and second, because under no circumstances will she give one penny, and far less power of attorney, to that harpy.

And then Cándida gets another idea.

"La China murdered my daughter," she says. "My daughter was full of life. A mother can't be wrong. More than anything, my daughter loved and respected life."

And a while later: "If they bring her, I'm going to dress her up real nice. If they don't let me dress her, I'll kiss her, I'll touch her. I want to do it all."

And so, during that first week, caught between blind rage and unlimited affection, Cándida visits different organizations in search of help. She goes to the Calzada and K. funeral home. She goes to the office for public assistance at the Ministry of Foreign Affairs (MINREX). She goes to the Council of State. She goes to the Ecuadorian embassy. She goes to the National Center for Sexual Education (CENESEX), where her daughter was an activist. She goes to the studios of Kcho, an artist with some influence in political circles. She goes to the cathedral to speak to Cardinal Jaime Ortega. She goes to see the city's historian, Eusebio Leal. She writes letters to President Rafael Correa and—why not?—the Telesur journalist Walter Martínez.

She is accompanied in this process by Mayara's ex-partner Iris Jiménez, who, when she found out about the suicide, could think of no other way to ease her mind than by putting herself at Cándida's disposal. In the end, the information Cándida gathers basically validates La China's demands.

"For the transfer of the body, the family needs to contact someone in the country, a friend or relative, and send them the money, in this case around $6,000. You arrange that through the consulate, and when the flight arrives here they notify us, pay 200 pesos at the airport, and then we make the transfer to the place of burial," says Emir Díaz, from the office for international coordination at Calzada and K.

But $6,000—for the airfare, legal documents, preparation of the body—sounds like compounded punishment. All the money Cándida has earned in her life wouldn't come close to covering that figure.

At this very moment there are two other families who have dead children in Ecuador. A sixteen-year-old girl who was raped and murdered, and a boy who went to receive a prize and was involved in an accident.

You never believe something like that might happen to you, not even in your worst nightmares. That your child might commit suicide . . . That your child might commit suicide abroad . . . That you might have to pay for your child's body to be repatriated, and not only that, but that you might have to pay a fortune. None of it bears thinking about.

"There was one case," Díaz says, "in which a family sent the money, but it got lost, and they decided to cremate instead. It worked out cheaper and easier."

But Cándida won't hear of cremation. She reacts as if someone were brandishing a burning stick. There has to be another option, she thinks.

No one offers her any help, and though she does get advice from MINREX, it is given, she claims, through gritted teeth. After the first couple of days, La China, too, disengages herself from the matter, partly because of Cándida's hostility.

On June 10, an email from the Cuban embassy in Quito reaches MINREX, written in the name of the consul in charge of consular affairs:

> I've been trying to locate Waday for days to ask her why she hasn't cooperated further on the procedure required for the remains to be repatriated. She had begun the process of arranging transportation, but the body is still being held by the coroner and until we give permission, they won't release it.

If the deceased's [*sic*] mother has any information regarding Waday's whereabouts we would be grateful for it, as the information we have is insufficient. In addition, the mother has to give Waday authorization to begin the process of repatriation. . . .

I don't have the results from the investigations since it would seem, according to forensic medicine, that the verdict of suicide is undisputed.

July goes by. August goes by. Entrenched in her battle, Cándida has no resources to move forward. No money. No allies. Neither the charity of an NGO nor the support of a state. She loses her link with the staff at MINREX. Friends from the United States tell her what they've managed to find out: that Mayara has been moved to a funeral home called El Diazepán. Cándida tries to get in touch with magazines or television programs in Miami, like the tabloid show *Al Rojo Vivo*, to bring attention to her situation, hoping someone might come to her aid.

This pileup of impossibilities creates an agonizing sense of confusion in Cándida, and black ribbons of impotence rise up from her insides.

"I'm an honest person, and I'll say what needs to be said: if I have to shout that the president's a homosexual in order for Human Rights to bring me Mayara's body I'll do it. I'm not afraid. They can't get me to kill someone, to carry a bomb, commit an atrocity, none of that. But shouting? I'll shout anything they like, because I want my daughter's body back. Because if you're my government, you're my state, and I come to you, my representative, as the only thing I have, and you won't help me out, so what can a mother do, tell me? Whatever it takes. If I could swim there, I would."

This furious rage is preferable to quiet. In real calm, when she manages to forget about the bureaucratic entanglements, the legal procedures, the institutions' lack of interest, and the impenetrable wall of those thousands of dollars, there gleams an idea far more damaging, one that leaps to her face like acid.

"I can't give in. My daughter, wherever she is, can't find out I've given in, because I'm not the kind of woman who gives in, especially not for her."

That's the idea that comes: her daughter is lost in a dark and distant kingdom, and she needs someone to rescue her.

═══

You'd think that, next to a daughter who has killed herself, next to the concrete fact that she'll never come back, the suffering of not having her body would be nothing. But in reality, it's everything. You'd think that, after the cliff fall of surviving your own daughter, vulgar obstacles would be nothing to you. But in reality, they're everything.

Death can become even more excruciating than the plain fact of death. Death is not just death; there are things that make it better or worse. What Cándida is asking for—without knowing whom to ask—is both nothing and everything.

She just needs one moment. To say goodbye. To look at Mayara. To look at her. And that's it. But until this tiny thing happens she's not going to give in. And then yes, then death. That stubbornness, that brute pigheadedness, that animal obstinacy—perhaps that's what makes us humans.

═══

To commit suicide is to untie yourself. To look at the tree of existence and say: no more. Some, like Mayara, gently undo the knot and skip off. Others—hard, dry, weathered—persist. Like Cándida.

A few months after she was born, her mother abandoned her on a stairwell, where some neighbors found and rescued her. Then at seven her mother took her back, basically turning her into her servant. Her stepfather raped her at eleven, and nine months later she had a son who, she says, she never saw as a son.

"I was a girl and thought of him as being more like my brother, something like that, and not like my son—I had no idea what it meant to have a son. The truth is, I couldn't love him. I looked at him with disgust, because he reminded me of the rape. That man was my mom's husband, not mine. He shouldn't have done that to me."

With a special work license, she began cleaning floors to support herself. At fifteen she met Ricardo Alvite. She was hitching a ride with a friend, and Alvite, who ran a clandestine fleet of cars, invited them to a party. They would remain lovers for years.

Alvite had six other lovers and a rock-solid marriage. The strange thing is, the women all knew about each other. Cándida and his wife even began a friendship.

"He gave me everything," Cándida says. "He got me out of the pigsty I was living in."

Cándida had Mayara in February 1992, when she was twenty-eight. She and Alvite separated when Mayara turned one, but Alvite continued to be a devoted father. He bought Cándida a little wooden house in Regla and did it up little by little. He also took care of Cándida's son until the boy, who showed the same rage toward her that she did toward him, ran off on his own.

In 1996, Hurricane Lili destroyed Cándida's house. She received a government grant for reconstruction materials, but they never showed up. She stayed in the house, which was almost a complete ruin, until someone in the neighborhood emigrated to the United States. Before the government could confiscate their property, Cándida made it her own.

"I'm a force to be reckoned with. I take life on and I'm not afraid, that's how God intends it. I went up onto the roof, got into the little patio, broke the seal and snuck into the apartment where I live today."

When the Housing Department tried to get her out, the neighbors protested. Cándida deserved a decent home. She didn't know whether or not she deserved it, but what she did know, as she stood there, machete in hand, was that nobody was going to kick her out. She denounced the police, went to the Party and the government, insulted any and every official they put before her, and in the end she won the battle.

Mayara was a sickly child. Cándida, who knew what it was like to have no protection, reacted by overprotecting her.

"As a mother I was always on the lookout, ever watchful, and I always used to say to teachers, 'Wherever you go, I'll be watching. Make sure you don't touch her because I'll kill you like a dog.' No, I didn't understand."

Cándida, the attack dog, tirelessly sniffing around.

"My daughter had a diary and I never thought twice about looking through it from time to time."

"I knew she was a homosexual by the time she was four. I saw it in her."

Cándida, the sensitive oracle, predicting, presaging, from day one.

"I went to my mother's house—she raised me—and said to her, 'I have to tell you something. Mayi's going to be a lesbian.' And she said to me, 'Hush, child, the devil will hear you.' I don't know why—she was feminine, she played with her girl cousins. I bought her dresses, dolls."

Claudia Rodríguez, one of Mayara's closest friends, tells me, "We knew each other from the age of eight. We used to play house, and she always wanted to be the daddy."

At one point, among many scattered memories, Cándida mentions one unsettling detail: "Scarves. My daughter loved scarves."

=====

When Mayara began primary school, Cándida started working at the school as a cleaner. She followed her through secondary, and when Mayara started at accountancy school, Cándida would wander around the outside of the building. When, as a teenager, Mayara would go to Park G in Vedado at night to hang out with her friends, Cándida would make surprise appearances.

Her mother's presence was a disagreeable one, embarrassing.

"To be a homosexual is to belong to a very dirty world," Cándida says. "It means fighting against homophobia, but it also means fighting against twisted and shameless homosexuals who do bad things with one another. Am I wrong?"

How much did her mother's obsessive surveillance affect Mayara? Her interference caused problems early on in their relationship.

"She used to say to me, 'Mom, how many times does God forgive people? I forgive you every day. Why are you so pigheaded?'"

Mayara was already coming out to others by the time she turned sixteen.

"She used to confide in me and Dayana, my girlfriend and her best friend," says Claudia. "And at the time Mayara was in love with some little girl from school."

After reading her daughter's diary from cover to cover, Cándida sat her down and begged her to tell her what she'd always known anyway. Mayara told her she didn't feel male, that she was a woman before anything else, but she wanted nothing to do with men, and she was disgusted by the idea of a man touching her.

Cándida went to the kitchen and took a knife to bury it in her own heart, but Mayara, Cándida says, took another knife and told her that if she couldn't share in her happiness, then she didn't want to live either. Cándida asked to be forgiven, said she was stupid, that she loved her, she really loved her. She went out onto the street, rented a lesbian porn film, and sat down to watch it with her daughter. Shock therapy? Solidarity? Cándida battled between excessive love and her concern about what she considered to be a defect.

"She asked me why I was showing her these obscene things, said I didn't respect her. I told her to pay attention, because that's what she was going to be doing from now on."

Mayara offered grudging comfort, telling her that while her father was alive she'd have no relationships in public. Her father was an honorable man, with different principles, from a different era. She was spending a lot of time in her father's house in San Miguel del Padrón, and he was a mentor to her.

But the deferment didn't last long. Ricardo Alvite died within months. And Cándida—of course, it was Cándida, it was always Cándida—found Madelín for her. Her twenty-one-year-old neighbor; her first, fleeting daughter-in-law.

===

There's a rather strange photo of Mayara. She's young, older than four, maybe six or seven. She has light and intentionally scruffy hair, a fringe hanging over her brow. Her lips are like a pink communion pyx, her solemn nose dead center in her symmetrical face. Her mauve blouse hangs off her slight shoulders, and you can make out the faint semicircle of bags, like the inevitable shadow cast by her immense, deep-blue eyes.

We'll never know exactly what, but something—turbulent, unshakable—is gestating in her. At six or seven, she was a girl whom any other boy or girl could have fallen in love with.

"If it weren't incest, I'd have been a lesbian to satisfy her," Cándida says. "To stop others from harming her or from messing with her mind. Or her heart."

═══

The nation's news bulletins announce that Pope Francis will arrive in Cuba on September 20 and give a mass in Havana Cathedral. Cándida comes up with a plan: she will interrupt the mass, tell the pope about her situation, and commend herself body and soul to the most holy. She's heard that the pope is an apostolic leader, renowned for listening and attending to the needy. She looks in her wardrobe and rifles through her clothes to decide what to wear for the occasion. She says she doesn't care if the police arrest her, mistaking her for a political dissident.

But September 20 comes and goes and Cándida doesn't go anywhere, and after speaking to La China again, her mental state flips from religious and devout to violent, demonic.

"I'll rip your heart out and eat it, I don't care," she tells her at the end of one of their last conversations.

She keeps count of the days. Four months since Mayara died. Eleven months since she left Cuba. Seven months since her last birthday. Et cetera. A dead child hits one milestone or another every day. She takes amitriptyline, she's prescribed floral essences. Her breasts are inflamed with psoriasis, her diabetes spikes, sometimes she forgets things, and she's started wetting herself and uses muslin diapers because the disposable ones are too expensive.

"They want to admit me to hospital. I'm not doing well. I've been driven to despair."

A psychologist prescribes Cándida a certain melody that she has to listen to at regular intervals throughout the day to help her relax. Some strangers visit and ask her if her daughter had taken communion, if she was Catholic. Cándida probably suspects they won't help resolve anything, but she chats away regardless. She needs to let it out, let it all out. She knows that God sees suicide as a sin and gives the visitors a detailed lesson on the subject. When a person hangs themselves there's a sudden yank and then they wet themselves and their tongue droops out. But her daughter was sitting down, like she was trying to force herself up with her legs. That's what MINREX told her. Her daughter was a dark-blue color, which means she'd been asphyxiated. Then she asks them, as she's asked so many others, if they know anyone who could go to El Diazepán funeral home and take some photos of Mayara for her. There's an instantly recognizable tattoo on her left hand.

"Don't look at her eyes, they're sure to be different now. A tiny little tattoo, that's how you'll know. A moon with two angels. One sitting on one tip, the other on the other tip. That's how she got it done."

===

By the time Mayara turned twenty, in 2012, she was already living alone in San Miguel del Padrón and had begun to frequent CENESEX, where she became a fierce activist for the rights of the LGBTI community. She attended conferences, went to talks delivered by specialists, and joined circles of exchange where each member had to reveal some of their personal secrets or explain why they were there, what their motivations were, and other empathetic exercises.

She met Iris Jiménez, who was the same age as her, at one of these meetings, and they became romantically involved.

"She was very pretty, with lovely blue eyes. And her personality was magnetic," says Iris. "Extroverted, entirely lacking in reserve or self-pity. You'd talk to her for five minutes and feel as if you'd known her all your life."

Mayara was her first relationship, the one she discovered everything with. Romance, long conversations, a way of being in the world.

"People looked at us like we were weirdos. It made me sad, as I wasn't used to that. She told me not to let myself be intimidated. She told me she cut her hair short and wore shirts simply because she felt like it."

Their relationship lasted barely a month, but it left such an impression on her that three years later, she didn't think twice about contacting Cándida and putting herself at her disposal. Without Iris, Cándida wouldn't have been able to knock on as many doors as she did, though they haven't got her very far.

It hurts Iris, bothers her, that Mayara got together with La China only a few days after they broke up, and she still can't figure out how the hyperactive girl she'd been so close to became the submissive, dull creature who would end up hanging herself with total disregard.

—

They met at a party in Virgen del Camino and started living together straight away. La China had a son whom Mayara doted on, and Cándida initially accepted La China, but turned against her once the abuse started.

"Mayara would get furious whenever I got involved in their relationship. She turned against me, because Waday was everything to her."

It was an unequal relationship from the start.

Claudia says, "La China would tell her to her face that she had no job, that she was a deadbeat. She even told some of us, her friends, that she didn't like Mayara, that Mayara was a whiny brat. But La China kept on going to her house, brought her son over. To be honest I never really understood that relationship."

Cándida did, though, and she summarizes it succinctly: forty years old versus—at the time—twenty-two. Mayara, however, didn't see it as a battle.

"She wouldn't accept any criticism. We all warned her not to get attached," says Claudia. "But there you go: she was in love. She didn't even mind that La China hit her. There were beatings and insults, breakups. There was this wall of shame that, even after she'd started to work—selling clothes and soaps—cornered her, in ways I couldn't imagine. La China always decided to 'give her another chance,' although—everyone thought—all she did was use her."

"They'd fight, but every time my daughter made some money, she went straight back to her," says Cándida.

Then, in the midst of the darkness, like a flame ignited and accelerated by youth, Mayara started thinking about emigrating.

"I remember La China saying that what she needed was to leave and leave for good, that she didn't want anything from Mayara. But in the end, she did want something," says Claudia.

Mayara sold the house in San Miguel del Padrón for $12,000. She went to the cemetery in Colón and, standing over her father's grave, promised him she'd get the property back. She bought her plane ticket and—according to the diary Cándida managed to peek at—a $500 air-conditioning system and a $300 stove for La China.

"I gave you life, I fed you," Cándida told her a few days before she left, "but if I have to kill you, I will, because that bitch is abusing you."

At that moment, Cándida hadn't even suspected that Mayara intended to pay for La China's tickets as well.

"She didn't call me again, and she didn't say goodbye, but I stayed strong. I didn't call her either."

Mayara arrived in Quito in October 2014, on a five-day tourist visa. La China arrived in November. Sometime later, she brought her ex-husband.

That was the final blow for Mayara—illegal, exposed, her money gone. As she wandered alone through harsh, foggy Quito on the night of May 11, the delicate threads that tethered her became unraveled, and in her apartment in the La Floresta neighborhood, on Sevilla N24-606 and Vizcaya, she finally let herself go.

=====

Two days after the suicide, Dayana Stincer—Claudia's ex-partner, Mayara's best friend—calls La China, and the conversation, for some reason, is recorded.

"Tell me it's all a lie," Dayana says.

"Child, how on earth . . . Look, Dayana, how could you think it's a lie, something like this? I mean, wow. How could I call Cándida and say to her, 'Cándida, your daughter's dead'? Of course it's true."

La China tells her they were already separated. "But she couldn't find work, she was depressed, she'd also tried to end her life the month before, she cut her wrists in front of me and I had to tell her all manner of things. Then she calmed down, she was very calm, but I have a job you know, and look, I'll say it again, we were already separated. I'd go over, leave her money for food, rent, for all those things. And also things like helping her with her papers, so she wouldn't be illegal. Every time I went we'd fight, and you know the way me and Mayara used to fight. That Monday I went over, we argued as usual, and then I went out to get her some food because she didn't have any. I get back, put down the things, go into the room, and then I found her, hanging, in the closet. I cut her loose and then I went running to call an ambulance, but by the time the ambulance arrived it was way too late. And I'd taken my time in the shop. I never thought Mayara would go and do that, go figure. The coroner came, the police, and I was caught up in that whole fucking thing until 3:00 a.m., and then in the morning I called Cándida. Now I have to wait for Cándida to send me power of attorney, but that takes time. Then I have to send over Mayara's stuff, her clothes and shoes, her belongings. Cándida wants me to send it and I will. I don't want anything that belonged to Mayara. What for? I have no use for any of it."

"And how are you doing, *mami*?" Dayana asks.

"Well, right now I'm still experiencing the shock of finding her. I'll say it again, I never thought . . . I spoke to her many times, told her that though we weren't together anymore, she had to stay strong, keep going. She wanted to go back to Cuba. I told her that if she wanted to go back I'd pay for her ticket and she could go back, but that's not the point. The point is you have to keep growing in life, face challenges. Mayara was never like that, she wasn't strong. All of you who were close to Mayara knew that she was in love with me, that she wouldn't leave my side. All Mayara thought about was La China and you know it."

Four months later, in October, Dayana had already immigrated to Miami, and having said on Messenger that yes, she would talk, she finally says she won't. She doesn't want to keep remembering.

May she be forgiven, she says. Her friend will understand.

———

Once Mayara was in Ecuador, Cándida says they spoke often, the way you imagine a mother and daughter would speak, but she can't forget that the last time they saw each other they both ended up screaming. And she blames herself.

"I'm going to say the saddest thing now. I didn't deserve my daughter. I was too tough with her. I persecuted her, didn't let her be."

Those cries come back to haunt her today and, right or wrong, Cándida, the fighter, cannot dispel them. The noise of the past is not something that can be silenced.

———

On November 9, after many attempts, La China finally answers her cell phone in Quito. She doesn't seem agitated or apprehensive, she reacts naturally, she says she's ready to talk and asks to be called back later. But no such talk ever takes place. She doesn't pick up again, doesn't answer any messages. Her silence is a stance in itself, and perhaps also an answer.

On November 11, exactly seven months after the suicide, it's confirmed that the El Diazepán funeral home doesn't exist and Mayara has been in the fridges at the Pichincha Department of Forensic Medicine in Quito the whole time.

"There have been several cases, in Ecuador and elsewhere, where a long time passes, the family doesn't send the money, and the corpse ends up in a communal grave," says Emir Díaz, in Havana.

Sergeant Luis Armando Quispe, from Pichincha, explains that the department signs annual agreements with the city's funeral homes and that, once approximately a year has passed, and subject to availability, they do the necessary preparations and the unclaimed victims are buried.

Quispe doesn't allow Mayara's corpse to be viewed; the authorization of a family member is needed for that. But he will share the forensic ruling, the police report—including La China's declaration—and the letter from the Cuban consulate. Time of death: 7:55 p.m. Cause: hanging.

In the photos, Mayara is wearing brown slippers, a blue sweatshirt, and pink trousers. Her lower lip is split and she has bruises on her shoulders and cheeks: the consequences of rigor mortis. There is a broad welt on her neck. The stiffness of death has come to rest on her face. Unless there is some miraculous solution—thousands of dollars found for her repatriation—Mayara will end up in a communal grave, or in some medical school where her organs will be used for clinical studies.

On her left hand, on the canvas of her deathly pale skin, a faint tattoo shows three stars and a waning moon. One angel is sitting on one tip. Another sits on the other tip, breathing.

THE NATIONAL PERFORMANCE

It is December 17, 2014, and Tania Bruguera is in Vatican City, watching and listening, something she does frequently, intently watching and listening to what is being said and what is happening around her. She has a keen and subtle intelligence.

Pope Francis I is giving his weekly public mass, and Tania, who has developed one of the most powerful bodies of work in Ibero-American installation and performance art, is there to offer the Argentinean–Third World pope some ideas for his campaign Dignity Has No Nationality from her latest project, a public policy platform called Immigrant Movement International.

On a train back to Venice, where she's taking part in an International Performance Art Week, Tania learns that, after a year and a half of clandestine negotiations, with Pope Francis acting as one of the principal intermediaries, Cuba and the United States have just reestablished diplomatic relations. And Tania's head is spinning, like everyone else's.

"I felt a lot of anxiety, fear, and hope, all at the same time," she says. "This draws a line between the present and the past. And you ask yourself, 'Now what should I do? What should I do with what I'm feeling?' Because something like this means everyone's role has changed. It's like a reshuffling; old metaphors take on new meanings, everything is recontextualized."

True to her principle of performing at all times, even in bewildered astonishment, on December 19, Tania posts an open letter to Raúl Castro on Facebook. It turns out to be the first action in YTE—*Yo También Exijo* (I, too, demand), a civic platform made up of a group of friends and colleagues, for which Tania will be the main spokesperson.

"I found it suspicious that the government was selling the idea that everyone was happy about the treaty between Cuba and the United States. The government has always considered itself an *owner*, and as the only body that can legitimately speak to the feelings of its citizens. The way I saw it, people weren't happy. What the people felt was shock, and a glimmer of hope, something they hadn't felt in many years, the hope that something might change, but that's not happiness, it's wariness."

"Why did you decide to act?"

"The president of Cuba merely informs us. He dictates new resolutions, and we don't know what pressures or objectives are brought to bear, because in Cuba there is no such thing as governmental transparency. And a president has a duty to steer his people through a political process, which is also an emotional process. To my mind, to say, 'you have to do this' is just as violent as saying, 'you cannot do this,' especially when the very people you are encouraging are those you previously censored, without acknowledging their own role in the process."

Tania immediately announces that she intends to rehearse in a public place, preferably the Plaza de la Revolución, the symbolic heart of government. She previously performed the piece she is rehearsing, *El susurro de Tatlin* (*Tatlin's Whisper*), at the 2009 Havana Biennial. It offers a temporary platform for free speech and consists in giving everyone an open mic for one minute to say whatever they want, on whatever topic, in whatever way they want, except for calls to violence of any kind.

When first performed, *Tatlin's Whisper* caused serious headaches, so the suggestion that it be performed again is not likely to be well received. The machinery of political propaganda grinds into gear, and, over the following days, a number of blogs, magazines, and online press sites controlled by the government attempt to discredit Tania, portraying her as a pawn serving the interests of subversive elements or those in favor of annexation.

Raúl Capote, a former agent with the Seguridad del Estado turned blogger, writes, "These people aren't looking for peace or freedom of expression. They're looking to create conflict, cause confusion and disorder, at a time when fascist right-wing forces in Miami are trembling at the prospect that their hegemony of terror will end, that time is against them, that the great business venture that is the war on Cuba is collapsing." Tania's attempt to create political intervention through art is instantly interpreted as political opposition.

On December 26, Tania returns from Europe and lands at Havana airport, where she is greeted by the political police, who film her from the moment she emerges, and set about tracing and monitoring her every step. The campaign against her gathers momentum.

"In the moment when it's all happening, you don't have time for things like vanity. You're in the moment. I've never been so in the moment. It is a state where you're keenly alert, attempting to work out the semantic consequences of your every action, how it will be interpreted. And trying to stop others from hijacking your narrative."

This is symptomatic of everything that follows. Pablo Helguera, director of Adult and Academic Programs with MoMA in New York, defines it: "It is impossible to think of a relevant artistic action in the second decade of the twenty-first century that hasn't been mediatized—or in which mediatization does not form a part of the work itself. Tania's work is precisely that—a campaign, within which anything that happens or doesn't happen is part of the work. It's hardly surprising that the government fell into it the way you might fall into a black hole."

There are those who point out that the performance has already been hijacked by dissident political groups within the country, activist groups that are quick to show support and solidarity, but whose support and solidarity further strain the atmosphere because of the relentless repression to which they are subjected by armed forces and the ideological tools of power.

Tania says she feels that, at various points, her work has been seized on by various forces with diverse histories that do not include her, who suddenly happen on something they can use to their own ends. But faced with the accusations, she thinks, she has worked with activists and dissidents in Europe and in the United States who have exploited her work, so why not do the same in her own country?

On December 26, she sends a letter to Pope Francis I asking him to speak out on freedom of movement and freedom of expression in Cuba, and in the days that follow, there is a battle between Tania and the Cuban cultural bureaucracy. She visits the Municipal Police, the National Police, meeting with officials to request the permits to perform the work, and none of them has an answer. There is a legal vacuum.

In two separate meetings with Rubén del Valle, the president of the Consejo Nacional de las Artes Plásticas (CNAP), it is suggested that Tania consider alternative spaces to the Plaza de la Revolución. But the Plaza de la Revolución is an integral part of the work, because, at the end of the day, the performance is nothing more or less than the Revolution itself. This is what it is about. Nevertheless, Tania accepts the alternative proposals, such as the Museo Nacional de Bellas Artes.

Just as they are about to reach an agreement, after many hours of discussion, Del Valle tells her that, as an institution, the Museo reserves the right to decide who will be admitted, and who can and cannot participate, a stipulation Tania interprets as the death of the project. She has previously agreed to curtail the public elements of her performances from an indefinite period down to only ninety minutes, but she rejects this stipulation. At this point, Del Valle calls an end to the proceedings.

"He tells me that from here on it's my problem, that he washes his hands of it, that he's got nothing to do with what's going on from a legal standpoint. Later, I realized that he already knew what was going to happen."

In an interview, Del Valle gives his side of the story: "I thought it was crucial . . . to come up with a collective, constructive solution, possible alternatives to her desire to probe and question, but stripped of political manipulation. She wanted to meet and talk to ordinary Cubans, she made much of the stereotypical idea that Cubans are afraid to express themselves. . . . I suggested the possibility of staging the project in factories, universities, at bus stops, at agricultural markets. None of these proposals proved acceptable."

Eventually, Tania—who insists that a number of these alternative spaces had been suggested by the YTE project itself, but that she refused to accept the state's stipulation that the work be postponed for five years and undertaken jointly—decides that the only possible location is the Plaza de la Revolución, because she feels it is important to make a stand that demonstrates the need for a law, to which an addendum banning political hatred will be added, that will give Cubans free access and the right to use their public spaces. At this point, someone suggests that the best way to reappropriate the Plaza de la Revolución would have been to leave it empty, rather than burdening it with another gesture, another scream. But Tania says that, to her, it's become the Plaza de la Censura—the Place of Censorship.

Tania Bruguera is stocky and pale skinned. Her mouth and eyes are small. She rarely breaks into a smile, but when she does, it reveals her youthful face. Most of the time, Tania is cerebral, but not cold, utterly unpretentious, and comfortable with her forty-eight years.

She was raised by her parents in an apartment in the Altamira building in Vedado, and later moved to her current home, on calle Tejadillo in Havana old town, to look after her grandparents. Her father, Miguel Brugueras, was a member of the underground resistance movement against the Batista dictatorship and, after 1959, a valued diplomat who was trusted by the revolutionary high command. Even his family didn't really know what Miguel Brugueras did on his travels around the world, and according to Tania, his father never talked about it. As a young woman, in a kind of parricidal gesture toward Miguel, Tania decided to drop the last letter of her surname and with it any possible physical or symbolic inheritance. It was her first political break.

From 1980 to 1983, she studied at the Escuela Elemental de Artes Plásticas in Havana. Afterward she enrolled in the Escuela de Artes Plásticas de San Alejandro, where she studied until 1987. In 1992, she graduated with a degree in painting from the Instituto Superior de Arte (ISA), also in Havana. It was a time of great upheaval in the Cuban arts movement.

According to the Cuban essayist and intellectual Rafael Rojas, "Between the '80s and '90s, a generation of visual artists reinvigorated cultural life in Cuba. A generation that, while still part of the Soviet Bloc, was aware of the disruptive currents in Western art and tried to assimilate and adapt them to a Cuban context. One of the most representative artists of that transition is Tania Bruguera."

While best known in Cuba as a professor at the Instituto Superior de Arte, where she launched the distinguished Cátedra Arte de Conducta (Behavior Art School) in 2002, over the following two decades Tania built a major international career and earned much-deserved fame as an unsettling artist. She delved deep into issues such as migrants' rights, the use of weapons, drugs in Colombia or border violence in Mexico. She was a professor at the University of Chicago and at the École Nationale Supérieure des Beaux-Arts in Paris. Her awards include the Guggenheim Fellowship and the Prince Claus Award.

However, by Christmas 2014, all of these things seemed a little hazy. And for good reason.

"This was the first time Tania had embarked on a project with a political context specifically related to Cuba," says Clara Astiasarán, an art critic, curator, and member of YTE. "All of her work is political, but this time she was directly challenging the president of Cuba over a foreign policy decision that has been one of the building blocks of the Cuban nation for the past sixty years: the notion of anti-imperialism."

Late at night on December 29, having spent three days in meetings and discussions, and some eight hours in the office of Rubén del Valle, for the first time in her career, Tania feels afraid. She goes for a stroll through Havana, feeling a little bewildered. The performance is scheduled for December 30 at 3:00 p.m., but friends have already warned her that she will not be allowed to attend.

She considers possible ruses: she could sleep at someone else's house, disguise herself as a homeless person, and wander through the city until the appointed hour, then suddenly appear on the Plaza. But why should she behave like a criminal? she thinks, and walks back to her mother's house in Vedado. She starts making calls, issues invitations to artists and friends, tries to get into a routine, as though this were just another exhibition.

Tania believes that things are still being dealt with by the

Ministry of Culture, but by this point, the State Security service is listening in on her every conversation. Héctor Antón, a respected art critic, recalls that "with her fearless defiance of authority, the Cuban artist . . . forced the visual arts authorities to wash their hands of the whole business, leaving responsibility to the state systems of search and seizure." At 5:30 a.m. on December 30, someone knocks at the door, and from her balcony Tania sees a bustle of Political Police officers around the building. Finally realizing what was about to happen, Tania sits down with her mother and her ninety-four-year-old aunt and tells them to stay calm, whatever happens. But it is not until noon that—imagining the possible reactions of those on the Plaza if she does not appear, and fearing that it might trigger a violent incident—Tania decides to take off her earrings, her glasses, her ring, and open the door. She cannot see anyone. She calls out and two officers appear. Tania has already tried to contact her sister in Italy, to ask her to announce that the performance has been suspended, but ETECSA, the state telecommunications company has cut off her landline and her cell phone.

Tania is charged with three offenses, including resisting arrest, a charge that is later dropped since Tania did not resist arrest. They confiscate her Cuban passport, the only one she has, charge her with contempt and inciting public disorder, and usher her into the first of more than thirty interrogations. The Kafkaesque machine roars into life.

═══

At 3:00 p.m., the Plaza de la Revolución is the eye of the hurricane, a place of utter, almost bucolic, calm. Nobody would believe that this—which is nothing—is the center of a raging storm. It is a tragicomic contrast. Accredited members of the foreign press are in attendance, there are cameras on tripods, and the usual imposing symbols: the statue of José Martí, the steel sculpture of Che Guevara on the facade of the Consejo del Estado, and, in the background, one of Camilo Cienfuegos on the facade of the building that houses the Ministry of Information and Communications, the Library, and the National Theater.

There are also dozens of onlookers in small groups, waiting for Tania to arrive, surreptitiously watching every junction, trying to work out by their clothing who is an undercover agent and who is not. Cars and buses continue to move along the Avenida Boyeros as always. An hour later, the onlookers gradually begin to disperse.

The damage, the disaster, is taking place elsewhere. Some days earlier, in the pervasive atmosphere of contempt, the graffiti artist Danilo Maldonado, aka "el Sexto," painted the names Fidel and Raúl on the backs of two pigs and, when he attempted to release them onto the streets, was arrested and imprisoned. The arrest of Tania—who is taken to the police station at Diez de Octubre and Acosta—is just one of a number of arrests of activists and prominent political dissidents, many of whom had no intention of taking part in the work.

As a backdrop, on that same day, the CNAP issues an official statement: "Given current circumstances, it has been deemed unacceptable to proceed with this alleged performance in the symbolic space of the Plaza de la Revolución, especially considering the extensive media coverage and the manipulation of the media to disseminate a counterrevolutionary message."

At the police station, Tania is ordered to change out of her clothes and into a prison uniform and is locked in a cell with a woman who is clearly a government plant, since she bombards Tania with questions about dissidents.

"At that moment I learned that injustice was not merely an abstract concept," says Tania, "that it had a physical manifestation. I refused to eat, not because I was brave, but because I believed what

they were doing to me was unfair and that was the only way I could
communicate it."

She is interrogated by a number of officers, some persuasive, others brutal. She is referred to some kind of psychologist, whose questions seem so inane to Tania that she wonders whether they are
trying to drive her to despair or merely playing for time. What television programs do you watch? That kind of thing.

Back in her cell, determined not to talk, she lies down and tries
to sleep for a while, although she has no idea what time it is since
it is a windowless cell. On December 31, she is released, and, when
she discovers that a number of dissident leaders are still incarcerated,
she goes to the Monument to the Victims of the USS *Maine* on the
Malecón, and heads for the Plaza de la Revolución. Once again, she
is arrested. The international press roundly condemns the violation
of her rights.

"The second time, there was another woman who I assumed had
been planted to keep an eye on me," she says. "I didn't feel like
talking to anyone, and she was quiet and polite. We didn't talk about
anything much. She just asked whether I planned to eat anything
and I said no. She was combing her hair and I ended up braiding it
for her, without saying anything."

Tania is fast getting to know the three State Security officers who
take it in turns to interrogate her. Agent Andrea, Agent Javier, and
Kenia, the investigating magistrate in her case. Andrea is young and
inexperienced. Javier seems a little more experienced; he knows a lot
about Cuban art of the 1980s, seems familiar with Tania's career,
and uses the memory of her father in an attempt to emotionally manipulate her. But it is with Kenia that Tania establishes a more sys-
tematic relationship during the course of these interrogations.

"There was something interesting about Kenia in that she seemed
honest. I don't know whether she was. When you're being interrogated, nothing is what it seems. She was the only one of the agents

who talked about her private life, her family, her mother, her relationships, in between revolutionary tirades and arguments about principles and ethics. This was her technique."

A few hours before the New Year strikes, under intense pressure from the foreign media, the authorities once again release Tania. She welcomes in 2015 with criminal charges, no passport, and a warning not to leave the city. As Pablo Helguera says, "The performance turned out to be not so much what didn't happen at Plaza de la Revolución, but the high-handed, hysterical tantrum thrown by the Cuban government. . . . Cuba is in a constant frenzied attempt to manipulate the message, and anyone—artist or otherwise—who succeeds in tipping the scales will naturally be greeted with fear and outrage."

===

One of the few artists or critics who dared to publicly question Tania's work (others claim they were and are unwilling to play into the hands of the government), Lázaro Saavedra, former winner of the Premio Nacional de Artes Plásticas, penned an article that triggered a heated controversy in which he wrote: "Just as she did with *Tatlin's Whisper* in 2009, Tania will leave Cuba having scored another 'goal' on her artistic curriculum. Armed with thousands of anecdotes, she will be criticized but also celebrated for her audacity and her bravery in artistic circles and on social networks. Certain critics or curators will opportunistically include her in contemporary art publications, exhibitions, etc. Thousands of Cubans will carry on fighting for civil rights in this country, and, as always, hundreds or thousands of people outside Cuba will be cheering them on: but the cheerleaders are not the ones who get beaten."

Also: "If we accept that, on the side of the scales, #YoTambienExijo made a modest contribution to the struggle for civil rights in Cuba, and on the other, a contribution to YTE in itself, it becomes clear that Tania Bruguera's YTE represents a provocation rather than a real advance for civil rights in telling us something we already know, something we have been told over and over: the government doesn't allow 'open mics.' They do not want all voices to be heard."

That is precisely one of the points on which many experts might have touched, had they been able to express themselves in a less drastic framework, without fear of arrest or abuse: the issue of political art that works within society but finds its rewards outside it, curricular empowerment in a project that should be completely detached. Had Tania performed her work in a gallery, they argue, she could have stymied cultural leaders. But outside the context of a gallery, not only did it leave the cultural sphere unscathed but from a political standpoint, the work was inconsequential: it had little public impact.

To return to Saavedra: "The most interesting (and, of course, the most difficult) way for the project to achieve its goals would have been to use art or artivism that creates a genuine, effective way to 'open the microphones' to hear 'all voices.' By this I mean that Tania should have found an intelligent way, sidestepping censorship and the formal structures of social control, of seeking, of creating (after all, she is a creator) a temporary autonomous zone (TAZ) in which it would have been possible to 'open the microphones' to hear 'all voices.' But she failed in her attempt. The voices are still waiting to be heard."

———

On January 2, 2015, after Tania had been arrested for the third time in seventy-two hours, more than two thousand international cultural dignitaries signed a petition demanding the return of Tania's passport. On January 5, in a letter addressed to Fernando Roas, the deputy minister for culture, Tania returned the Orden por la Cultura Nacional that had been awarded to her and canceled her membership in the Unión de Escritores y Artistas de Cuba (UNEAC). Two weeks later, she was informed that her case would be number 25 on the 2015 judicial program.

Throughout January, there are further subpoenas and interrogations. Tania is required to report to the police station at 21 and C, in Vedado, where they put her in a car and drive her around the city to interrogation houses whose addresses she will be unable to identify, with the exception of one specific house in Playa, near the ISA. Some acquaintances question her continued willingness to cooperate in these interrogations.

"For the project to work," Tania says, "I had to comply with the law, because the subject of the project was tolerance, and at this point I needed to show the internal control mechanisms within the system and the legal paradox in which we live in Cuba."

At the end of January, YTE send a letter to Raúl Castro and María Esther Reus González, the minister for justice, demanding that freedom of expression be decriminalized and that all charges against Tania be dropped. In response, Kenia, the investigating magistrate, informs Tania that the public prosecutor has not yet made a decision about her case and she will have to wait another sixty days.

In the months that follow, international solidarity is galvanized. Tania is unable to attend the various biennials around the world that have invited her to participate. Meanwhile, on social networks she is publishing a kind of chronicle about her unprecedented experience. On April 28, 2015, in "Los ojos del poder" (The eyes of power), she writes, "I have spent four months staring into the eyes of power and resisted its gaze, embarking on a journey that gave me access to a different Cuba, a Cuba reserved for those who demand the right to free expression. Today I find myself in a Cuba that cannot be seen by tourists, cannot be accessed by businessmen assessing the risks of investing on the island, cannot be witnessed by artists who come to the Havana Biennial since they will be cocooned in the art world bubble." On May 20, during the Havana Biennial itself, Tania stages a public, continuous reading of Hannah Arendt's *The Origins of Totalitarianism* in her Havana old town home, something that might be dubbed an embryonic Hannah Arendt Institute of Artivism. Which is what it is, although for Tania the *performance* has multiple endings and, in all probability, is not yet over. The final note is yet to be played.

"I felt this particular work was successful because I explored a number of my theories about political art. I had written about these theories, I had talked about them at conferences, I had explored them separately in other works, but here they are all clearly manifested. One of the concepts, for example, is what I call creating work for a specific political moment, that is, when the work is a response, not to the personal, intimate desire of the artist, but to the political conditions in which it will be developed. That was very apparent. Another thing that was integral to this work is the research that I have been doing for more than twenty years about the limits between art and life, the creation of moments in which those limits lead the viewer to the fertile question of whether what they are being exposed to is art or not."

On June 29, 2015, after arduous and protracted bureaucratic confrontations in which Tania demands a permanent solution, the public prosecutor informs her that her case will be dismissed. In July, her passport is returned and on August 21, after joining in several protests led by Las Damas de Blanco (The ladies in white), one of the major dissident groups in Cuba, during which she was physically attacked by the forces of law and order, Tania finally leaves Cuba.

"The project was a success at the time for two reasons," explains Clara Astiasarán. "It forged a bridge between the creative world and the political sphere, and demonstrated a way for differ-

ent agendas to become sovereign as well as politically and ideologi-
cally independent."

On April 8, 2016, after months of painstaking organization abroad
through the YTE team, INSTAR is officially born, funded by a
Kickstarter campaign that raised more than $100,000 from some
nine hundred donors. Tania declares, "The principal goal of the
Hannah Arendt Institute of Artivism (INSTAR) is that the future of
Cuba lies in the hands of Cubans. We cannot simply wait for things
to be decided by politicians, we do not want to wait for the situation to be irreversible before we go out and demand our rights. Now
is the time for us to intervene as stakeholders in the future of Cuba
through art and activism."

A month later, Tania flies back to Cuba, and is stopped and interrogated at the airport. Her house in Havana old town at Tejadillo
No. 214 bajo is now the headquarters of INSTAR—a more powerful
and pluralistic extension of what Tania's own work has always proposed: civic education for Cuban civilian society, to be carried out
within the public sphere.

"This time of polarized feelings, when citizens lack the means
to change the course of events, makes it necessary to reclaim public space as a civic space rather than a space for propaganda charac-
terized by institutional tolerance and a lack of transparency; while
the state stubbornly insists on defining things in simplistic terms as
'good' or 'evil,' I prefer to create and share complex concepts and
emotions with others, concepts such as forgiveness."

Six months later, in October, INSTAR launches its first two concrete actions. Via video, Tania asks that "we make the most of the
2018 elections to change the climate of fear, the culture of double

standards," and ends, with an audacious challenge, by announcing that she will be a candidate for the presidency. A few days later, INSTAR donates $10,000 from its funds to aid the victims of Hurricane Matthew, a Category 4 hurricane that has devastated the province of Guantánamo, probably the most impoverished in Cuba.

At certain junctures, the Cuban government has tolerated art that is critical of power, but with little social resonance. It has allowed art to bear witness, to flirt with the evidence, but not to be transformative. Was Tania constrained within these narrow margins, or has she managed to break free of them?

In all of this, there is something nebulous, like the smile of the Cheshire cat.

PANAMA SELFIES

At 9:00 a.m. on her last Saturday in Panama, in the doorway of the crowded shelter she has spent the past couple of months sharing with hundreds of other Cubans, Árelys Trujillo shaves her forty-five-year-old legs with reckless swipes that move from ankle to knee, from midthigh to the crease of her buttocks. She rinses the blade in a blue bucket full of soapy water, while nearby several of her friends are handwashing panties and T-shirts in similar buckets. Arelys flashes a contagious thousand-watt smile that, as recently as three days ago, she wouldn't have been able to muster, despite the fact that in every situation she is positive and cheerful.

"I'm finally leaving," she says. "Really happy. Uh, yeah, really happy."

Having been deported once, and undertaken two arduous journeys through Central America, Arelys is on the brink of making it to the United States. Earlier that week, Thursday, May 5, 2016, the president of Panama, Juan Carlos Varela, gave a press conference announcing that his government would launch a new humanitarian operation to gradually move the 3,500 Cubans who have been trapped on the Costa Rican border since last December—in Paso Canoas, Chiriquí, or Los Planes de Gualaca—to northern Mexico. It is an ultimatum, intended to put an end to the catastrophic crisis in the region that began in November 2015, when Nicaragua closed its borders to Cuban migrants, and Varela also makes it clear that this would be the last explicit offer of help from his government since Panama, like Nicaragua and Costa Rica, has already begun to close its border with Colombia. The last Cubans trickling into Puerto Obaldía from Ecuador have been greeted with clubs and tear gas.

Nonetheless, whether President Varela likes it or not, the crisis of the undocumented migrants will carry on for some time. Not all of them can afford the trip out: it costs $835 to get a bus to Panama City followed by a flight to Ciudad Juárez, in the Mexican state of Chihuahua.

"We expected tickets to cost $500, maybe $600, but not $800," says Lorenzo, a melancholy forty-year-old man from Cienfuegos who speaks ambivalently on behalf of himself and his two friends on this dazzlingly bright morning.

Unlike Arelys, who has just shaved, Lorenzo's face is darkened by an unkempt beard that gives him a somber, sickly air.

═══

Arelys Trujillo: forty-five years old, Quemado de Güines, Villa Clara

On July 26, 2012, while the Revolution was celebrating the anniversary of the assault on the Moncada Barracks, Arelys left Cuba for the first time, heading to Quito, Ecuador, on a T-3 visa. Some months later, she started her journey north, only to be stopped by Mexican authorities in Hidalgo in August 2013. Arelys had been uncomfortable but safe traveling in a truck transporting fruit, until the driver panicked as he came to a checkpoint and forced her to get out and take a passenger bus. After twenty-eight days in prison, she was deported to Cuba. She landed at the Rancho Boyeros

Airport wearing cheap flip-flops, took a taxi to the home of relatives in Marianao, and then traveled on to Quemado de Güines, from where, a year later, she set off again, following the same plan, but this time via Guyana. From Guyana she crossed over to Boa Vista, in Brazil, where she stayed until she could apply for residency. Then, on October 26, 2015, with the migrant crisis blazing in Costa Rica, she threw herself back into the ring. She bribed a stranger to take her to the Venezuelan border, hid out for several days in Turbo, Colombia, with no food, no washing facilities, and little drinking water. It took her two days to cross the Darién Gap, where she encountered African migrants and climbed a hill called Loma del Cielo—the Hill of Heaven—which nearly cost her her life. "I could tell you how dangerous it is, but you still wouldn't really understand," she says. In Puerto Obaldía, Panama, she slept in tents, survived by eating "a lot of bread," and on the morning of March 11, 2016, she eventually reached Paso Canoas on the northern border of the country. Tomorrow afternoon, Sunday, May 8, she will fly to Ciudad Juárez, where, since she has previously been deported from Mexico, she will be detained for a few hours. She will pay the penalty and on the afternoon of May 9, after a grueling four-year struggle, Arelys will set foot on US soil for the first time. True to her nature, she will not make a big deal or overdramatize. Just her usual smile and her thick mane of curly hair.

Leydiana Rivera: forty-three years old, Guanabacoa

She never really considered immigrating to the United States. She lived comfortably in Quito with her son and her husband for two years. She has a degree in management and economics, and worked as an administrator at companies like Sony, until one of the partners prohibited employing Cubans. The growing xenophobia toward

Cubans in Ecuador meant that Leydiana ended up working as a receptionist while her son worked as a security guard nineteen hours a day for almost a month. In the end, neither of them was paid a cent. They considered filing a complaint with the Labor Committee, but the bureaucratic process would have been more expensive than any compensation they might get. By now desperate and barely able to pay rent, they sold their $3,000 car for $1,000, all of their furniture and household appliances at really low prices, and headed north. Along the way, they encountered neighbors with whom they shared the hardships of the journey.

Juan Carlos de la Torre: thirty-four years old, Camagüey

Computer engineer. He claims that back in Cuba he was a political dissident. He claims he daubed dissident slogans in public places and expressed himself too freely on more than one occasion. In Ecuador he hawked cheap jewelry at traffic lights or washed dishes. He hit the migration route with less than $1,000 in savings. Now, in Paso Canoas, he is penniless. He has no friends. He has no relatives in the United States and, except for his mother, no one back in Cuba. His face is a mask of sorrow, the intense sadness that initially inspires rejection, because it seems fake, but which, after a few minutes, saddens those around him and awakens genuine compassion. He says he set out in search of freedom and that there is no way he will go back to Cuba. Anything but. He even uses a phrase that has long since fallen out of favor among Cuban migrants: "I won't go back until the Castros are dead." When asked whether he would go back to see his mother, de la Torre doesn't answer, and his eyes well up with shame and confusion. Looking at him, anyone would assume de la Torre has many more things to say, truly important things about life in general, but he cannot find a way to get the words out. He wears his cap turned backward and has a bedraggled ponytail.

Two moles on his face. He looks much older than his years. But he is a man who carries the weight of his experience.

———

Right now, the heat is oppressive, almost granular. It scratches at the skin the way a piece of grit can scratch your eyes. The Hotel Millennium in Paso Canoas, a hundred yards from the Costa Rican border, is a concrete fish tank three-stories high glazed with shit-brown glass and, from what people say, terrible facilities, as though the Millennium were a journey that the architects, engineers, and construction workers abandoned midway through. The first floor boasts air-conditioning, water, adequate lighting, and the basic partitions you might expect in any decent room. The second and third floors, on the other hand, consist of vast, soulless cubicles—with no water, sweltering heat, and absolutely no privacy—where migrants group together according to affinities, the provinces they hail from, or the order in which they arrived, until they form travel-weary groups of twenty or thirty. They sleep on mattresses on the floor, next to their belongings.

"No, no one steals anything. Why would they steal? There's no need," says Mirka Oviedo. "Clothes are cheap here, everything is cheap here. It's not Cuba."

Despite the conditions, there seems to be a genuine feeling of fraternity among the migrants, fueled by the knowledge that no one can improve their precarious situation without making things more precarious for someone else whose circumstances are just as fucked as theirs. It's well known that few things unite people as much as extreme situations. And the Hotel Millennium is just that.

Currently it houses about five hundred Cubans, a figure that will fall steeply as the first groups leave over the next three days. Even so, some remember a time before the Panamanian government established migrant camps, when the Millennium housed more than a thousand lost souls, so five hundred does not seem particularly alarming.

"I had to sleep in the doorway and there were people who spent weeks living outside," says Arelys.

The constant transit, which has been going on for five months, has turned the Millennium into a typical Cuban building, instantly recognizable by an islander aesthetic, filled with folk trappings. Which simply confirms that the definitive Cuban aesthetic, when not dictated by improvisation, is dictated by necessity, or both. The brown-glazed windows are hung with laundry that was hand-washed minutes earlier by disheveled women who wait in line for the only running water available outside the hotel. Sometimes, a dark-haired woman from Bayamo leans out the window, waving a clothes hanger rather than a flag. Dark hair piled into a supercilious bun, mixed-race features. All that is missing is a hibiscus blossom tucked behind her ear.

The only communal space is the hotel lobby. On a green card, taped to a window by the entrance, is a list of instructions that Cubans must comply with on pain of a $250 fine or one day in prison for every dollar unpaid. The phrasing of some of the instructions sounds as though it has been comically copied from some provincial police station: wandering around after curfew, breaching the peace, failing to comply with police regulations, affronting public decency and good manners. In the Hotel Millennium, which is a veritable hive, Cubans are prohibited from tasting [sic] alcohol on the public thoroughfare. Doors are locked at 9:00 p.m.

"We don't pay them any heed," says William Carralero, a man from Las Tunas with a face spattered with freckles. "We stay out until ten or eleven, talking, killing time."

"And they don't penalize you?"

"How would they do that?"

He's right. A sanction would entail withdrawing some form of comfort. What comforts does a stranded migrant have? Some of the other rules sound like they were copied from a nursery school: no throwing stones on the roof. On the lobby wall there are posters—pitched somewhere between educational and precautionary—offering advice on dealing with the A/H1N1 virus and the flu pandemic more generally.

There is also a sweet, naive, absurd mural of the kind you might find in an elementary school. A yellow background, framed in purple, with words scrawled in freehand that read:

I

HAVE O

H   P

E

Stuck here and there are little paper hearts—white, red, orange, pink, and green—the repositorites of personal, private wishes that, once read, turn out to be the same.

"I want to go to America to help my family."

"I want to go to America so I'll have enough food."

"I want to go to America to study and help my family."

"To be happy."

——

Leonel Sánchez: fifty years old, Santiago de Cuba

He claims he's been in Panama for four years. He says he has a daughter back in Santiago de Cuba and a grandson he has never met. He has committed one of the worst sins a migrant can commit. He has allowed his passport to fall apart to such an extent that it is nothing more than a mass of ink and paper on which it is almost impossible to identify a name or face. If you look at it closely, though, the passport is a perfect metaphor for Sánchez's life. In the doorway of the Millennium, he waits for who knows what. In the afternoon, he looks after the hotel barber's equipment if, for some reason, the hotel barber is not around. He chain-smokes, and behind the pall of cigarette smoke lurks the face of a child. Or a villain.

Toochi: eight months old

She is not and will never be Cuban, and yet Cuba has defined her. She has never had a home beyond the vortex of a space-time tunnel that is difficult to define. She looks like José Martí's *Black Doll*, though it is probable that, when she grows up, whether in America or elsewhere, José Martí will be only a vague reference, if she has heard of him at all. Everyone says she has behaved like a perfect angel.

Beads of sweat trickled over her forehead while her mother was crossing the Darién Gap, but she never whined. Hers is one of the most striking faces of this crisis, but she does not understand what is happening, nor will she remember it. Asleep, her chubby little body seems invincible.

Danilo Garma: twenty-eight years old, Havana

In January 2016, Danilo and his girlfriend boarded a boat in Turbo so they could cross the Gulf of Urabá. Two days earlier, in a skirmish between paramilitaries and coyotes for control of the area, a boatman was murdered, and halfway across, for reasons relating to the murder, the boatmen ferrying Garma and his girlfriend decided to hide. They spent several days aboard the boat, moored in the tangle of a mangrove swamp, shitting and washing where they sat, sharing meager rations of food with other Cubans and with African migrants from Congo, Senegal, and Mali who had crossed the Atlantic in order to make this same journey. Then the coyotes separated the Africans, and Garma crossed the Darién Gap on his own. Once in Paso Canoas, he managed to find work as a freelance civil engineer for a group of Arabs who control the real estate business along the border between Costa Rica and Panama. They paid him about $100 a week. With what he saves, Garma will be able to pay passage to Juárez for himself and his girlfriend. Once in El Paso, in the United States, he will catch a Greyhound bus and spend $220 traveling across the gringo south—Louisiana, Mississippi, Alabama, Georgia—as far as Miami. The architecture, the buildings, and the streets that Garma will see flash past the window of the bus as he eats peanut butter and raspberry jelly sandwiches will make a deep impression on him. He will decide to set up a business and, in the medium term, to create a real estate company he can use to invest in Cuba.

Mirka Oviedo: forty years old, San Leopoldo, Centro Habana

She lived in a small room on calle Escobar, with her mother and her two children. In order to get out of Cuba, which had always been her plan, she sold a plot of land she had inherited for $3,000. She had previously made two illegal attempts to leave Cuba by sea, first in 1994 and again in 2006. On both occasions, the boat was seized. On her shoulder, she has a tattoo—since forever—asking her mother's forgiveness if she has ever failed her. Her sister, who is already in the United States, refuses to send money so that Mirka can continue her journey. Meanwhile, since her children do not know what is happening, Mirka does not phone Cuba so as not to worry them. Lunch at the Millennium—white rice and spicy fish—has aggravated an old ulcer.

——

Between ten and eleven in the morning, the atmosphere at the hotel becomes more restless. A supply truck from the Catholic charity Caritas delivers food parcels and a short, sullen lady feigns interest as she jots down a list of the names of migrants who don't have enough money to make the journey. Everyone adds their name to the list— after all, it can't do any harm.

"It's very informal," says Juan Carlos de la Torre. "They don't take your passport number, your room number, or anything." Like many others who have no savings and no possibility of having money sent to them, de la Torre is pinning his hopes on people with dubious intentions or, at the very least, a crude and vulgar manner: Miami TV stars dressed like messiahs visit the migrant camps and, brashly, self-importantly, promise to pay for the journeys of those in dire straits.

In the Hotel Millennium, those preparing to leave and those who will have to stay are easily distinguished by their manner, their gestures, and a number of trivial details—how they walk, how they dress, how often they go in and out of the hotel, how often they speak without being asked a question.

When asked who he works for, the cameraman filming the food delivery says he is from a Panamanian TV channel, although it's obvious he works for Caritas. The Catholic Church has the crassness and bad taste common to all charities: it records all the good deeds it does.

=====

María Caridad Rodríguez: forty-two years old, Camagüey

She worked as a teaching assistant at the Joaquín de Agüero Special School in Jimaguayú, before immigrating to Ecuador in mid-2014 with her husband, Evans González, a butcher. In Quito, she cleaned houses and looked after children while her husband worked as a carpenter or in fast-food joints. For a whole year, Evans spent every moment of his spare time studying Google Maps, and this, together with a compass, allowed him to cross the Darién Gap with María without the help of coyotes. Given everything he now knew about Central America, Evans could have gone wherever he wanted. They both believe, to an inordinate extent, in God. María's profile page on Facebook features a quasi-mystical image of her and Evans in the middle of the jungle, staring into the heavens, apparently heedless, smiling or ecstatic, convinced that the Almighty will guide them. But, with or without the help of the Almighty, neither Evans nor María is the kind of person to sit idly by, and they have earned a certain fame among migrants making the journey because in Puerto Obaldía, having borrowed a pot and a grater from some local residents, they started making and selling croquettes, *frituras de harina*, and *coquitos*. In Paso Canoas, María set up a little stall, four crates, a tablecloth and a couple of salvaged chairs. She bought a stove, glasses, and crockery, and opened a little café where, for the past few months, she has been serving *criolla* food to the delight not only of Cuban migrants but also local Panamanians. María usually charges her friends and family less.

William Carralero: forty-four years old, Las Tunas

A native of Puerto Padre, a seaside town, Carralero spent his time spearfishing for sharks and hawksbill turtles to sell on the black market. He used his savings to go to Ecuador, where he worked as an accountant for an events agency. In Turbo, he paid $240 to join eighty other passengers aboard a boat with a maximum capacity of thirty on the very day that paramilitaries murdered the boatman. Injured, Carralero spent four days hiding in the mangrove swamps and another four days in the jungle. In Paso Canoas he has been working in construction. He has a wife and two children back in Cuba. He has no plans to send for them. "You have to take life day by day," he says.

Deny Jesús Tartabull: thirty years old, Jesús María, Havana old town

Her name is Kinella, the flower of Catalea. She has placed a new name over her own; in a sense, it is something she has been doing her whole life: placing one thing over another until she finally becomes herself, the person she truly is and always should have been, not the person she was by mistake. She wears a scarf over her hair, two gold hoops in each ear, a hand of Orula. Just above her shaved eyebrows are tattooed eyebrows, elegant and well defined. Beneath the smooth chest, depilated to remove the loathsome traces of masculinity, are two round, evenly proportioned breasts, which cost her $600 at the Hospital Miguel Enríquez. She and a number of her friends visited a doctor who did breast implants until he was arrested and now no trans women in Havana can have the operation. "The dream of femininity makes you desperate," she says. In her last six years in Cuba, Kinella was an activist with CENESEX (the National Center for Sex Education), and they are the only good memories she has of her country.

As a child, Kinella dressed up in wigs, brassieres, and panties. As a teenager, she studied food preparation, although she calls it culinary art. Kinella mostly hung out at gay venues: the gas station at 23 and Malecón, La Rampa, the Parque del Quijote at 23 and J, Vedado. But this did not stop her being harassed.

"It's like you've always got a spotlight trained on you. I wouldn't have dared to get on a bus, it would be like a clown getting on."

"Do you get used to the way people look at you?"

"You get used to it, but you're always an outsider, always looking at people askance."

"Did they call you names?"

"Pájaro, huevú, Shemale, the Ball-Less Wonder. Even the local chief of police used to get in on the act. There's no life for me in Cuba. I left because of police harassment, not for any other reason."

Kinella was abused in her own home, in front of her family, only to be later arrested on a trumped-up charge of aggravated robbery.

Neither in Ecuador, where she mopped hospitals floors and later sold fruit juice and pastries, nor in the other countries she has visited on her journey, has Kinella experienced anything remotely comparable to the discrimination—tacit or explicit—that she suffered in Cuba. In Central America, she says, no one ever looked at her as a freak. She crossed the Darién Gap with a trans friend and a number of migrants from Nepal, but she didn't spot "any tigers or savage beasts. A couple of cheeky monkeys, that was all we saw." In Puerto Obaldía, a smart-ass police officer tried to send her to the men's toilet.

"I told him I was a woman, that I identified as a woman, but he didn't understand so all he could do was try to make me feel uncomfortable."

Since then, authorities have shown her solidarity.

In Turbo, in Colombia, Kinella contracted a bacterial infection from the water in a river where she washed and drank. For a while, she suffered an anal discharge of reddish pus but is much better now that she has been treated with metronidazole. Now she is hoping that some of her old friends will send her the money to get to Miami so that, God willing, she can register in a new country as a woman.

——

Around noon, the weather suddenly and unexpectedly changes. Rain is threatening. The sky closes over like a grim vault. From the Hotel Millennium, the view is particularly bleak. A highway of constantly rumbling buses and trucks with, beyond, a dreary wasteland that seems to lead nowhere, and the increasing commercial activity around the rural border posts. It is the perfect setting for the mindless evenings typical of Cuban life to unfold in all their glory. For a long time, people in Cuba have had nothing to do and no way to entertain themselves, and so they meekly sit or stand on balconies and street corners and allow the passing time of the barrio to gnaw away at them.

A motley group gathers in the doorway of the Hotel Millennium, engaged in no particular activity. Some sit, others stand, leaning against the wall, their arms folded; others wander in circles. What are they waiting for? Sometimes they will make fun of a passerby, smoke a cigarette, make a comment about someone who is not there, lie on pieces of cardboard and chew their nails, or scroll through their Facebook timeline without seeming to read any of the posts. The profound absurdity of people gathering together in order to do nothing has always seemed to mask some important, mysterious reason that is impenetrable to those on the outside.

Meanwhile, there are those who do things, lots of things. Arelys spends two dollars to take a van down to the National Immigration Office at the Chiriquí Mall in David. For an hour she's subjected to the most excruciating music ever composed. A sound like dripping fat, a sonic screwdriver that turns music inside out. Insipid reggaeton, bachata interspersed with ad break commercials that the van drivers play at full volume.

The palpable torpor of the Chiriquí Mall is much like that of the Hotel Millennium, and in that sense, is the epitome of the national character, the indolence best described in the works of José Lezama Lima. That almost perpetual inactivity that erupts in chaos, a blare of conga, that spontaneous uproar of which we're so proud.

In the mall, migrants are lying between the tables, sitting on window ledges, buying food, shouting and screaming, disrupting the peace and calm, desecrating this small temple to consumerism. They bring to the mall—shopping malls always so sterile—a rare sense of possibility. On one of the windows of the Immigration Office is a printed list of the names of the lucky ones scheduled to travel to the United States on Sunday, Monday, and Tuesday. Two hundred and thirty-eight between Sunday and Monday, and a hundred and fifty-four on Tuesday. There are also two long lines of people who have been waiting since Friday afternoon. The first line is the migrants waiting for a three-day visa to be able to travel to Panama City (Arelys, Garma, María); the second is people hoping to buy tickets to travel on Wednesday or Thursday.

Though everyone is exhausted, no one seems particularly discouraged. This is the final hurdle, the most exquisitely pleasurable anticipation: better than pensioners waiting for a handout of free bread, better than retailers waiting outside a wholesaler to buy cheap products—many, indeed most, of which are scarce in Cuba—which they can sell off at a premium.

"As soon as I get to Miami, I've got a job lined up that pays twenty dollars an hour," says Yandriel Siberio, a computer scientist. "And once I've got my work permit, I won't take less than forty. The problem is that I have to pass a test. I'm not particularly good at maths. I took mathematical analysis at university because I had no choice. But if it's algorithms, or working in some computer language, I'll ace it."

In addition to all known species of migrant, Cuba has a particular endemic species: academic migrants.

It's clear that a migrant has not truly left his country until he finally arrives at the place he wants to be. The migrant's journey is a curious form of purgatory, no matter how far he travels or how terrible the journey, and for as long as he is traveling, the migrant is still in limbo. Caught between convulsion, illusions, and hope, however much they may have adapted, these migrants are still living in Cuba.

But when they reach Miami, where the majority will soon end up, the languid tempo of life that they have been used to will be dramatically different. In the hectic atmosphere of Miami, the slow metabolism instilled in them by a society that asks little of the individual—where it is possible for people to coast, to go with the flow—will not survive twenty-four hours. People who have never learned to ride a bicycle will have to buy a car and learn to drive within the week, to negotiate the broad expressways that zigzag through the city, to negotiate with dealers, to work ten hours or more a day, pay rent and taxes they barely understand, adjust to the grueling habit of punctuality, of obeying superiors, of applying for debit and credit cards, and other things about which they know nothing.

And they will thrive, because they carry within them a memory of the place they came from, a country that sadly had little to offer them, but it won't be a piece of cake. There are almost no documented cases of Cubans who legally traveled to Miami later deciding that they made the wrong decision. Fewer still for these people, who have burned their bridges.

At 4:00 p.m., in the midst of the unending bustle, Chiriquí Mall holds a canine fashion show. Dressed in style, dogs of every breed stroll down a catwalk while a Major Lazer tune booms from the speakers.

At the bus stop, an archetypal Cuban twentysomething—baggy harem pants, loose-fitting red T-shirt, New Balance sneakers, also red—waves his passport and, skipping over all the necessary periods of residency, yells to another: ."This ain't worth shit no more, broder. I'm already an American. It says it right here. A-m-e-r-i-c-a-n."

Outside it has started raining furiously. It is Saturday, May 7, 2016. In the stark gray of the Panamanian sky, a crack has opened up, like a stretch mark on skin.

ALCIDES, THE UNPUBLISHED

He looks like a god, but he is a heretic. He looks as though he is carved from stone, but he is a live wire. He looks like the first man, but he is the ultimate survivor.

Writing about Rilke, the great Russian poet Marina Tsvetaeva said: "Rilke is neither a command to our time nor a display of it—he is its counterweight. Wars, slaughters, churned-up flesh of dissension—and Rilke. Because of Rilke the earth will be absolved of our time."

At the age of eighty-two, Rafael Alcides is Cuba's counterweight. Political lackeys, a population consumed with cynicism and coward-ice, wasted, fruitless lives heading nowhere, shot through with bitterness or fear—and then Alcides. Thanks to Alcides, our country will be forgiven.

At the age of eighty-two, in sacred communion with the world, reconciled in equal measure to defeat and to light, Alcides is both all that he appears to be and all that he is: a poet. Someone who once wrote, "When a funeral cortege with only two cars / passes and no one turns to look, I tremble, I shudder, / I quiver; I feel afraid to be a man."

He lives in a garage he has turned into an apartment—almost a
cave—on the corner of a quiet street in Nuevo Vedado in Havana.
This is not the shambolic home of a tormented genius. This is not
the ostentatious home of a famous writer. This not the suffocating
home of a bureaucrat. This is not the empty home of a suicide. It is
the quintessence of "seasoned homes, / where action does not allow
itself to be usurped by word."

The force of will that is Rafael Alcides is contained within an
ideogram. The narrow sofa, almost at floor level; the cushions decorated with small tremulous flowers; the still lifes in ceramic vases;
the chairs of polished wood; the rattan furniture; the wax candles;
the austere paintings of the everyday and the funereal; the fading
light; the tentative cold of Havana winters; the plasticity of evening;
the vague murmur of seemingly uninhabited places; and the incon-
stant barks of a raw-boned dog with mismatched eyes and droop-
ing ears.

Regina Coyula—his wife, twenty-three years his junior—is
brewing coffee in the kitchen, when, through this aroma of domes-
ticity, Alcides emerges from the depths of the apartment. A man
who can only be described by an interjection that these days, from
anyone but him, would sound ridiculous: Oh!

He is wearing heavy gray trousers, a Prussian-blue sweater, black
socks, and slippers. His full white beard, his elegant bald pate, his
weathered copper skin, his wrinkled brow, and, set deep in his face,
howling, his feverish dark eyes.

He is reciting a poem by Darío.

"Margarita, how beautiful the sea is: / still and blue. / The orange
blossom in the breezes / drifting through."

The deep, booming voice combined with his quick gestures com-
mands a certain fascination.

"The skylark in its glory / has your accent too."

His hands seem to break into a little dance, urged on by dizzying rhythm. The long, gnarled fingers tell the words like beads, as though all his powers of expression are connected, as though nothing in Alcides is discrete. When he speaks, he does so with his whole body.

"Here, Margarita, is a story / made for you."

His ears are filled with water, he cannot hear his own voice, and at a distance of a few meters, can see only shadows. He has spent the past two months in bed, except for the days when he goes to the hospital to be examined by doctors.

This is how he has come to find himself in a city he no longer wanted anything to do with, one he has consciously avoided in its final stages of destruction.

"For more than twenty years, Alcides has lived his life within a radius of a single kilometer," says Regina. "From the apartment to the market, from the apartment to the winery."

Last November, surgeons operated on Alcides for colon cancer only to discover it had metastasized, and fitted him with a colostomy. He still has not decided whether to undergo chemotherapy. Apparently, he would rather live out his last months peacefully, no matter how few, rather than dragging things out between bouts of vomiting and nausea.

But what is surprising about all this is that it has rekindled his ability to celebrate concrete details that others would dismiss as minutiae. It is something that no cancer—not the cancer of power nor the physical cancer he now suffers—can rob him of. Today is January 19, 2016, and Alcides has just read with delight a recent review of his work by a devoted reader.

"I'll make a handsome corpse," he says, "lovingly remembered." But Alcides is not dead yet. He is Cuba's greatest living poet, and probably its most honest, its most unfairly silenced, the one who has paid the highest price for his nobility, the one who has never been swayed by fashionable trends or corrupted by the small change of politics.

His work, published intermittently, has brought rewards that cannot be classified. The fact that, in the 1980s, prison inmates traded packs of cigarettes for copies of his collection *Agradecido como un pero* (Grateful as a dog). The fact that his books—wrapped in nylon to protect them from the sea—were the only thing taken by the migrants who launched themselves on rafts into the Straits of Florida. The fact that, after reading his work in a secondhand bookstore, young people from the province would make a pilgrimage to his home.

He is not a champion of exile. He is not a victim of the *quinquenio gris*—the five gray years of censorship that blighted the 1970s. He is not part of the system. He did not become cynical or bitter or resentful or wary or violent, and he never submitted. For some inexplicable reason, his personal fortunes matter less to him than the death of his country.

══

"If I lose my book, after all the years I've spent writing it, I'm the only one who loses. It is a personal defeat, whereas we are talking about the defeat of a people. And that's something sacred, it's a tragedy. Cuba is a patchwork of capitalism and socialism that is worse than useless. Go try to buy some food. You won't find any. Just look at the prices. Is the blockade to blame? It's fucking ridiculous. It's just not serious. Does our food come from London? Do yams come from Paris? No. Life is constantly in motion and it's like a game of chess. With every move, the board changes. You can't stay still. Things are the way they are because Fidel and Raúl are in a standoff with the United States. And the whole thing is a barefaced lie. Raúl says, 'We can hold out for another fifty years.' Well, yes, obviously, *you* can hold out. But the people can't hold out. I don't feel proud at all.

I feel like the construction worker who's helped build a prison. I'm one of those bricklayers. But if I had to live my life again, in the same circumstances, I'd fight that war all over again, I'd do all the things I did. I'd sign up for this adventure again. We thought we were heading somewhere. But in the end, we got nowhere."

"What about your writing?"

"I'm not talking about my writing. My story is simple. At the end of the day, I've only ever written first drafts. In my filing cabinet there are three or four meters' worth of novels, and that's where they'll stay. More than thirty years ago, when I moved into this house, I burned another couple of meters."

"Doesn't that upset you?"

"There was a time when it upset me, because that was what I lived for, that was what I spent my life doing, but after a while it doesn't bother you so much. Why? Because there have been greater losses. The greatest loss has been the Revolution itself; for people like me, that was the dream. There was an opportunity, we had an opportunity, but that train has gone, we won't see it again."

===

Previously, in an interview with critic and writer Efraín Rodríguez Santana (*Cuba Encuentro*, no. 36, spring 2005), Alcides admitted that he burned his novels to unshackle himself from a future burdened by so many drafts he could never complete. In that sense, you might say the Revolution is the great unfinished, total novel that authors keep trying to write at the wrong time. Politicians are politicians precisely because they cannot comprehend the generosity of true poets.

===

"Cuba needed a revolution. The problem is that the Revolution quickly stopped being a revolution and became something else. Fidel started doing whatever he pleased. He was waging wars around the world, wars in which he didn't fight the way Alexander, Hannibal, or Napoleon did. His children didn't even fight."

"If you had to pinpoint the moment when the Revolution stopped being a revolution . . . ?"

"The moment the body of laws was written. When it was set down that black and white were equal, that everyone had the same rights, that the state controlled the means of production, that's the moment when the Revolution ended. At that point, there is a contract between the individual and the state, the individual and society, the same social contract that has always existed, in which the citizen produces and pays taxes, while the state collects and distributes, builds schools, pays the salaries of civil servants, soldiers, the salaries of Fidel and Raúl. This is the point when the state is responsible for giving you a scholarship if you have the right results, provides free education, which is absolutely crucial, provides hospitals, doctors. The revolution ended in '65 or '66. And then what happens? Fidel is clever, he's intelligent, he's a genius, no doubt about it, but he's malevolent, and he clung to the concept, the abstract notion of the Revolution.

"Why? Because that's the way to keep citizens owing things to the Revolution. But since the Revolution has no face, it's not a person, you have to identify with someone. Your father was a garbage collector, but you ended up becoming a doctor or a lawyer thanks to the Revolution, which is to say thanks to Fidel Castro. You owe everything to Fidel Castro. No! No! Fidel Castro owes everything to you. Everything he is, whatever glory and power he has he owes to the people, to me as a citizen. I pay him a salary to govern, place my trust in him. This whole 'The commander in chief orders . . .' thing is bullshit. No way! Sovereignty is vested in me, not you. You doff your cap to the people, they are the sovereign power, it is they who can grant and they who can take it away. This, obviously, is a state governed by the rule of law. Here you can't take anything from anyone. But he can take things from you. He can take your life."

"Was there ever a time when you admired him?"

"Of course, I followed him, he was the chief."

"Did you love him?"

"Love is a strange word. Love is one thing. Appreciate is another. You can respect someone, admire someone, feel part of something. I felt part of something. Besides, you have to think of yourself as a giant octopus, because you love people for lots of different reasons. You're a leader, you're a commander, you represent an ideal, and lots of your friends are also friends of mine, and they have died; we are all part of an ideal. And when I meet you, we are bound together by the affection of these people who love you, these people you love, or that I assume you love. We are all part of one big family. It's not a question of whether I love you or not. You're a part of me, and because I trust you and we're part of a great venture, every decision is the right one. Besides, Fidel was the man who was making our country's dream a reality. For example, one of the greatest things he did, one of the most beautiful, was the literacy program. And giving land to farmers. Who wouldn't agree with that? Anyway, it was a wonderful time, honestly. Fidel could have been one of the Christ figures in the history of mankind. He was headed that way. People loved him, they gave thanks to Fidel. Fidel, your home is my home. All these things happened, things that could make you weep. Socialism seemed to be the political and cultural fulfillment of man as a species. Opening up the hospitals to everyone. Even though he didn't build the hospitals, they had already been built, and then the doctors emigrated, he hounded them out. All wisdom drained away from the country, leaving it to begin again with people he trained from scratch, people who owed everything to him. But yes, it was a glorious time. And we were making history. You don't take the money, you take the glory. We were rebuilding the world. Ushering in a great era."

━━

The life of Rafael Alcides is a pretext for nostalgia. Going back to Rilke, it seems fitting to say that Alcides embodies the last lines of the Eighth Duino Elegy: "Who then has turned us around like this, that we, whatever we do / appear like someone about to depart?"

The beginning—he was born on June 9, 1933, in a tiny village in eastern Cuba, "a sprawling savannah with only ten or twelve houses"—the middle, and the end of everything is this: "I can never stop being from Barrancas. / From a Barrancas that today exists only in my dreams." So it's understandable that remaining true to his moral convictions has been a relatively easy task for someone who has succeeded in salvaging what is most important: integrity of self.

Alcides is a pillar of memories, and time has finally forgiven him. Regina, his wife, describes him:

> One of the extraordinary things about him is how he looks. When we first got together, my niece, with the artlessness of a ten-year-old, asked whether I was dating the poet Eliseo Diego. Even then, Alcides was prematurely bald and had a white beard. His contemporaries looked like his younger brothers. He played a trick on them: he never got any older, while they gradually lost their loooks, their hair, their physical and mental agility, sailing past him until eventually the roles were reversed. All this despite a series of medical issues, which he hides well.

Alcides grew up in a wooden hut, with a dirt floor and a roof made of guano. His first heroes were the founding fathers of independence: Maceo, Gómez, Calixto García. When they played together, he and his brother Rubén fought over the leading roles, sometimes even coming to blows. Both of them wanted to be Maceo, until eventually Alcides persuaded Rubén he was better suited to Ignacio Agramonte: young and handsome.

"This was our literature as children," he said. "This was our cinema."

He already thought of Cuba as an epic work of fiction, the raw material from which his creativity would flourish.

He attended elementary school in Bayamo, and in 1946, when he graduated from the Escuela Pías de San Rafael y Manrique in Havana, he moved back east, only to come back again. In "Poema de amor por un joven distante" (A poem of love for a distant young man)—dated 1989—Alcides, sounding like a protective father, recounts the typical experience of a callow youth from the provinces arriving in Havana—that first, terrifying, Balzacian confrontation with a city he has heard of so often. In fact, like Whitman, in his affectionate address to a distant young man, Alcides is actually addressing himself, comforting and embracing the youth—"solitary and alone, the loneliest of men"—that he was on that June 22, 1952, which was "longer than a century."

It was in the 1950s that Alcides experienced his baptism of fire in the struggle against the Batista dictatorship, clandestine conspiracies, joining rebel groups, acts of sabotage. There are moments and events that haunt him, youthful rages that he would not endorse today, that he does not even mention. Those were fearful, violent, years, and he was in the prime of life. What could he do but sacrifice himself to the fierce ritual of justice?

"Once, while we were at the university, the police showed up and started shooting. We threw ourselves to the floor, and the following day, when we looked, we saw that the bullet holes were at least a meter above our heads. But we only found out in hindsight. That's exactly what happens in life."

In the early years of the Revolution, Alcides was assistant to the commander of the Rebel Army, Manuel Fajardo Sotomayor. He was involved in the literacy campaign, took political positions with the Organizaciones Revolucionarias Integradas (Integrated Revolutionary Organizations), and wrote two forgettable rites-of-passage poems: "Himnos de montaña" (Mountain hymns) (1961) and *Gitana* (1962). In 1963, in the magazine *Únion*, he published "El caso de la señora" (The case of the lady), a poem that caught the attention of Nicolás Guillén—later a close friend—and made its mark on the buoyant literary scene of the time.

Alcides adopted a conversational style that would come to mark Cuban poetry for decades to come. Though spontaneously adopted by Alcides and other poets of his generation (Pablo Armando Fernández, Manuel Díaz Martínez, Roberto Fernández Retamar, Fayad Jamís, Heberto Padilla, and others), it would later become obligatory as the stylistic manner or appropriate tone with which to praise the feats of socialism.

Meanwhile, for the Instituto Cubano de Radio y Televisión (Institute of Radio and Television), he wrote scripts and presented the radio program *En su lugar la poesía* (In its place poetry), whose guests included many of the most important poets in Latin America. If this were not enough, he had begun work on a number of narrative projects. In 1965, under the name "Brigada 2506," he submitted his novel *Contracastro* for the Casa de las Américas Prize. Mario Vargas Llosa fiercely championed the novel, but the title—which translates as *Against Castro*—created bitter division. It was eventually decided to award no prize for fiction, though Alcides was given an honorable mention.

"It wasn't a counterrevolutionary novel, quite the reverse. The decision was probably made by Haydee Santamaría (then president of Casa de las Américas), a wonderful woman, a great woman, though she considered Fidel beyond reproach, so a title like that would have been like a red rag to a bull in a china shop. I later found out that, during a trip to Vietnam, she asked for a copy and decided that yes, they would publish it."

But they asked that he change the title, and Alcides declined.

"Maybe that's where your disappointment with the Revolution starts."

"No, it wasn't that. It was something very specific. This was back in January '65, a romantic year, when anyone could write about anything."

In 1967, *La pata de palo* (The wooden leg) was published by Letras Cubanas, and his first poem, "El agradecido" (Grateful), is enough:

My whole life has been a disaster
for which I feel no regret.
Deprived of childhood I made myself a man
and survived on love.
Prison, starvation, all these things:
all these things were salutary:
the night-time stabbings
the father I never knew.
And so with what I had
everything I am was born: all too little, I admit,
yet huge, and grateful as a dog.

Since that moment, Alcides has been an exemplum. Delicate, yet profound. Forceful, but evocative. Between them, the forthrightness of his actions and the purity of his poetry end up creating something vast. An epic that he painstakingly ground to dust. He sat at his kitchen table, took *la Patria*, the Motherland, put it in a coffee grinder and started to grind, sometimes with his left hand, sometimes with his right. His colloquial style is ambidextrous. Like a blind, omnipresent god attentive to all things, it demands the right to move mysteriously, arrogate the ability to create, like a skilled potter, an exquisite shard of the everyday.

The collection *La pata de palo* found an immediate echo in some of Guillén's late work, such as *En algún sitio de la primavera* (Someplace in spring), and in Roque Dalton's defining collection of poems *Taberna y otros lugares* (Taberna and other places). The poet and essayist Virgilio Piñera, writing about "Carta hallada en los bolsillos de un monje" (Letter found in the pockets of a monk), said:

> A reader looking to find the "trembling" of Saint John of the Cross, the "imagery" of Góngora, the frisson of Baudelaire, the dazzling flares of Rimbaud, or the "silences" of Mallarmé will make nothing of this "Letter" in which poetry is something other than trembling, imagery, thrills, flashes, and silences. Perhaps there's a measure of such things . . . but couched in very different words to those the aforesaid writers used in their poems.

In the braid of Alcides's existence, in which History with a capital *H* is interwoven with lyrical intent (and cannot be untangled without being destroyed), *La pata de palo* was quickly followed by the Prague Spring of 1968, Soviet tanks rolling into Czechoslovakia, the Cuban government's approval of the Soviet invasion, the brutal dagger of realpolitik that ripped the poet's glorious illusions to shreds.

Next came the literary and artistic purge, censorship codified and enshrined in law, the increasing Stalinization of Cuban society, abusive methods of so-called ideological reeducation, the famous "Padilla affair"—accused of writing "critical and antihistorical" literature, the poet Heberto Padilla was imprisoned on charges of seditious activity and later forced to publicly read aloud a mea culpa straight out of the Moscow show trials—and the resulting wholesale rejection of the Revolution by Western intellectuals.

"You need to understand the enormous cruelty involved, the gaping wound inflicted on Cuban culture. Everything disappeared into a black hole. Someone shifted the points and the train set off on a very different course. We began to replicate the USSR model, utterly betraying the ideals of Martí: a republic of all the people, for the benefit of all people, an economic program based on small and medium-sized landowners. This demonstrated that a fundamentally human program, seemingly led by men, was carried out by people who strived to be seen as gods."

In 1970, Alcides decided to make his disillusionment public, and submitted a notebook titled *La ciudad de los espejos* (City of mirrors) to UNEAC (the National Union of Writers and Artists of Cuba), only for it to be unsurprisingly rejected as being "nihilistic, unfit for the New Man."

Knowing that he, too, would be pushed out, he decided to stand aside. He would have no further contact with UNEAC. Nor would he submit books to publishers. He would not attend exhibitions or cultural events, or go to cinemas, concerts, or public events. So began Alcides's long *inxile*—a word he coined to describe exile in one's own land.

"The only other possibility was to tear down what I had helped build, and that was something I would never do."

In the deliberate and complete solitude of his home, Alcides wrote radio scripts and drafted prophetic verses. He subjected his soul to a disciplined military regimen:

Past and future have already passed.
Everything we had, we lost,
and it was more than anyone could wish.
All that remains is this whisper. This
pile of sorrows scattered by the wind,
timeworn, and timeless.

This whisper
of what it was like
our life before the future came.

It was a time of great fear in Cuba. No one visited anyone. "César López and Pablo Armando saw each other from time to time. Manuel Díaz Martínez worked for a radio station where he wasn't allowed to use his own name; Heberto (Padilla) did translations of Mayakovsky he couldn't put his name to. At the time Virgilio was also doing translations he couldn't put his name to. Everyone was scattered. It was an assault on the very intellectuals who had championed the revolution, who had fought at Playa Girón, slept on the jagged dogtooth rocks along the shoreline. People who cherished the Revolution. These same writers began to have ideas, to embark on literary criticism, and in doing so infuriated those who had climbed on the high horse of Stalinism. That's the story in a nutshell," says Alcides.

Later, many of these banished intellectuals were welcomed back into the fold and gratefully accepted the perks of the State. Alcides never did. He was a very sentimental, perhaps even melodramatic poet, but one who had the courage to write the most passionate confessions, and to walk the tightrope of excess. But also a poet possessed of a dispassionate lucidity. He firmly believed that what the Revolution should expect from true revolutionaries was not faith, but doubt: "A poem can be / a conduit for emotion machine / or a conduit for intelligence / (Emotion is fleeting)."

———

"Poetry gets mixed in with stories, with novels, with everything. Poetry is something that happens in bursts, it's like love. You have to write what you are feeling. This is your only chance; you don't get a second turn at life. That's the secret. It doesn't matter if no one else sees it. A creator risks his death, others risk their lives. Poets who seem transcendent today will be forgotten by tomorrow. It happens to every writer. Poetry is the mystery, the gift that has the words to beguile. But it is not a safe place. Today, people blow you kisses, they embrace you, but tomorrow . . . There is so much poetry out there. That's why you have to take the risk. A poet doesn't write for the present, for me, for you, for anyone. You are writing for your contemporaries, by which I mean for the future. For truth. If it turns out well, so be it. If it doesn't, it doesn't. Never lie. Never ever lie. The hand of the liar withers," says Alcides.

===

It is easy to trace the important moments in Alcides's life, since they all appear, undisguised, in his own work. He married Teresa— "Without loneliness to dupe us, / Teresa and I no longer eat but drink in poetry / like potage and like coffee and so we feed, / and laugh to see, bubbling in a jar / or sizzling in a frying pan with butter / our future Collected Works"—and it was with Teresa that Alcides had Rubén, the most famous of his four children.

When, in the early '90s, Teresa—having been divorced from Alcides for some years—emigrated, taking their son with her, Alcides wrote "Carta a Rubén" (Letter to Rubén), one of the most harrowing elegies about the trauma that afflicts so many Cuban families: "But we, / we the lonely, / the sorrowful, / the homesick, / what new homeland is this? . . . / A homeland far from everything we love? . . . / Where life is ringed by walls and locks / This too is exile."

He wrote poems to the humble flower ("Canta para los dos"), to the tomb of his only general ("At the Graveside of the Common Man"), and even to government ministers, in a poem in which he confesses, "Every time I hear of a friend / who is about to become a minister, / a silent hand erases a passage from my life." A quick glance over the list of cultural commissars or ex post facto sacred cows—who have included many poets from the "generation of the '50s"—it is clear that the unseen hand of power has erased more of Alcides than should be erased of any man.

In 1984—during a period of thaw—*Agradecido como un perro* (Grateful as a dog) was published, creating an explosion that could never be erased. There was a shower of plaudits; stunned, attentive young readers woke up to Alcides. The Revolution gets a mention in the title poem. But the poem does not wither, which so often happens; instead, the Revolution carries on. After so many tone-deaf singers and dishonest public speakers, in the end, the Revolution owed its survival to a dissident.

In the late '80s, believing that idle nonparticipation made no sense, and borne up on what he calls "the deceitful winds of perestroika," Alcides rejoined UNEAC and took part in meetings and conferences.

"My attitude had always been that of a man who didn't want to rail against something he once loved, and still loved, something he would still give his life for, because he still hoped that we could fix it."

Out in the world once more, he met Regina, then working as an official at the Ministry of the Interior. She knew his poems by heart, and Alcides captured her heart with his elegance, his manifest disinterest, with silences interrupted only by the affable voice booming as a radio presenter.

"I first saw him at a funeral vigil and we didn't speak, but I was impressed by his brooding expression, as he sat in his chair in the chapel of Funeraria Calzada y K. Later, at UNEAC, someone introduced us, and there was a fellow feeling, but nothing more. On December 31, 1988, through the connivance of a friend, we met again, and the rest, as they say, is history."

In 1991, following the furor surrounding the "Letter of the Ten"—in which ten intellectuals were expelled from UNEAC and suffered administrative sanctions, false accusations, and a shameful smear campaign for daring to sign the letter which, according to one of the signatories, Manuel Díaz Martínez, was little more than a "list of moderate requests to the government"—Alcides felt convinced that nothing would change, so he once again retreated, preferring solitude to the company of contemporaries he still loved but whose pusillanimous silence in the face of events made them complicit.

At around that time, his forgotten notebook *City of Mirrors* was published by Letras Cubanas under the much more bitter title *Nobody* (*Nadie*), which summed up all of Alcides's frustrations. It was his last book to be published by a state publisher, and Alcides never again appeared in public. At some point, they tried to tempt him, awarding him the National Prize for Literature, but he refused it.

As alternative means of expression gradually became available in Cuba, Alcides shifted from silence to critical participation. He has been open about everything, in interviews, in articles, and at the talks and events to which he has been invited by political dissidents. Over the past twenty-three years, his poetry has only seen the light thanks to the Sevillian publisher Abelardo Linares, who knocked on his door one day and rescued him.

═══

On his eightieth birthday, Regina wrote, "Alcides is no longer able to travel by *guagua*, by *almendrón*, by *panataxi*; he's no longer able to walk two hundred meters even to meet a celebrity. But he is still a wonderful host, so warm and attentive that he instantly makes new acquaintances feel completely at their ease.

"In this age of ideological polarization, he still retains that affection, that intense fondness, whether for a senior government official or for a senior opposition leader in exile. He forgives (but never forgets—he has an excellent memory) arrogant fools, whether fledgling poets or civil servants who, from their lofty new positions, deign to treat him coldly. He still regrets the error of omission of failing to dedicate a poem to Roberto Fernández Retamar in a book recently published in Colombia."

A year later, various online media outlets published a letter, signed by Alcides:

Havana, 30 June 2014
Attn: Miguel Barnet, poet
President of the National Union of Writers and Artists of Cuba

My Friend Miguel,
Given that my books are no longer permitted entry into Cuba either through customs or by mail, which is tantamount to banning me as an author, I hereby resign from UNEAC. Enclosed, you will also find the Commemorative Medal celebrating the fiftieth anniversary of UNEAC, given to me as a founding member. All that remains of that great association of which, in other times, I was a part, are memories, and since these are mine alone, I take them with me. Among those memories are those of the close friends I made at the Union, the treasures of my youth, all that remains of that great failed dream, people I still love though they do not think as I do, and who love me though they dare not visit me. That's all, Miguel. To forestall the possibility that the text of this irrevocable resignation might be expurgated, I have taken the liberty of making it public.

And so it has continued. Since late 2015, a YouTube channel run by the filmmaker Miguel Coyula has published a series of short videos—powerful visual haiku—in which Alcides talks about the lost dream of the Revolution, about the Cuban people, about beauty, Fidel Castro, artists. Meanwhile, the Spanish publisher Verbum has just published a collection of his poetry, which feels definitive, of which Alcides has only one copy.

Still, he is not bitter; still, he fervently believes in God.

——

"Over time, you have gone further than anyone of your generation."

"No. Like everyone else, I have evolved. I'm sure that we all think much the same thing. There are only two dissidents in Cuba: Fidel and Raúl Castro. The rest of us agree that this isn't working. The difference is that some dare to say so and others don't, because some are in the game and others are out. I don't need to travel, so I don't agree to trips, and since I don't need them to move me to a new house, or want them to give me a car, or have a landline, I am in a position to speak out."

"But that in itself is going further."

"No, it is not."

——

Manuel Díaz Martínez has said, "Rafael Alcides still cherishes— they live on in his actions and his writings—the revolutions and the desires that once were the common currency of our now tumble-down generation. So it should come as no surprise, then, that in the cave of Polyphemus, this Ulysses of the Caribbean continues to dream of reaching Ithaca. Across the wide Atlantic I see him, a sailor of steadfast dignity, resisting the songs of the sirens amid a swampy sea of betrayal and surrender."

=====

"Did you ever consider leaving Cuba?"

"No, never. This is where I am from. Truthfully, I wouldn't know how to live anywhere but Cuba. But the problem is to continue the struggle. It doesn't matter whether it's here or there. And I believe that everyone who ever fought for change, whether they are here or elsewhere, has the same right."

"Do you feel lonely sometimes?"

"I don't feel lonely. I have a lot of friends out there. Because the friends I once had no longer exist. They are part of the past. They don't come here."

"Do you still love them?"

"Yes, I love them in the past tense. Not even God can erase what has been, and I respect everything. Now, those friends don't visit me anymore. If by chance we see each other out there, some embrace me, others turn away. I've become invisible."

"How does that make you feel? Sad?"

"Not anymore. I know they can't do anything else. I know they're afraid. I feel a little pity, because I know they haven't stopped loving me. Because I haven't stopped loving them. I love them in the past tense, but I love them. I have great respect for the choices made by others, in every sense, but they have to respect my right to disagree. If a future Cuban government is going to be as intolerant as this one, I'll stick with this one, because at least I've grown used to it."

"You're not particularly convinced by the radical positions of old exiles."

"No, I don't believe in radical positions, radical positions are stupid. We haven't come to terms with it yet, but we've suffered a terrible tragedy. Thirty, perhaps forty thousand people drowned. Today the word *Patria*—homeland—no longer exists. We have drama. And literature, novels, poetry, are fashioned out of drama, out of pain. This will soon be over. The time has come to start telling the tale."

FIDEL, THE BUTCHER

The butcher's name is Fidel, the shop's name, 26 de Julio: a kind of impregnable barracks on the ground floor of a stoic-looking *microbrigada** building. The neighborhood, which adheres closely to the aesthetic precepts of socialist realism, was built in the mideighties, after a cyclone destroyed the houses along the town's coastline and the state decided to compensate those affected by constructing this new community, judiciously sheltered a few kilometers back from the sea.

The buildings surrounding the shop all have five floors, and on their roofs you can see several water tanks, some dilapidated wooden dovecotes, and a bunch of illegal antennas, unashamedly visible to the public, which intercept transmissions from Miami TV stations. Clothes hang from the railed balconies and there are overflowing garbage cans on the pavement.

Cárdenas—two hours' drive east on the highway from Havana—is one of Cuba's biggest municipalities and, since it's less than fifteen kilometers from the tourist hotspot of Varadero, also one of its most

---

* The microbrigadas were an initiative put forward by Fidel Castro in 1970, whereby workers in a particular office or factory were given the opportunity to build their own housing.

prosperous. Direct access to foreign currency and the vast black market created from the theft of hotel supplies has allowed the town to continue to grow into poorly tarmacked areas dotted with luxury stone-built mansions.

There's no sewage system here and on the streets there is a constant flow of buses carrying workers, bicycles, and horse-drawn carts. There's a port, a famous rum distillery, a hotel where the Cuban flag was raised for the first time in the mid-nineteenth century, a train station, and a bus terminal. Food isn't as hard to come by here as it is in the rest of the country, though it is more expensive.

Fidel Albelo is a crucial part of the municipality's food distribution network. Sitting on a parapet behind the granite counter of his establishment at the end of calle Tenería, the doors flung wide open, he is something like the area's sheriff. His relationship with and influence on the lives of the two thousand people and six hundred families under his jurisdiction is far greater and more effective than that of other public servants—shopkeepers, postmen, chemists—and even than that of the nurses and doctors at the medical consultancy. In Cuba, this is success of the highest order.

This is perhaps owing to the fact that the fiftysomething Fidel, bald, with white skin and a six-foot display window, has spent more time in the shop than anywhere else except, since 2004, the town cemetery. The 26 de Julio unit has been his only place of work. He started there in 1987, aged twenty. He knows nothing else, but within these walls he knows everything.

Most of the locals maintain close ties with him, which is strange for such classically antagonistic enemies as a butcher and his customers. They bring him coffee in a flask, tolerate his filthiest jokes, and shout greetings to each other at the top of their voices in the middle of the street, with words of genuine affection disguised as insults, like "faggot" or "prick" or "motherfucker." It's not that they don't know Fidel steals, or that the goods he steals should rightly go to them. It's more that, since they have to steal at their jobs to survive, they know Fidel must also do it in his job. Or maybe it's that Fidel never hesitates to throw an extra, overquota piece of chicken into the package of a hard-up family who really needs it. Or that Fidel's persona—his multifaceted charisma, his brash personality, as contagious as a lethal virus, his strict adherence to the ethical code of the streets, which demands he be a good son, an even better father, and an astute crook at all times—seduces and bewitches them, and they end up loving him. After spending a few hours in his company, this seems to be the most solid hypothesis.

"Each of us has, how to put it, their own professional gift," he says. He pulls up his sweater and strokes his enormous belly. "To find out what it is, you've got to hustle behind a counter and serve two thousand customers. And those two thousand customers are never content. Those two thousand customers are always looking for a fight, because why would anyone in Cuba ever go to the butcher's in a good mood when they know what's going to happen there every time. They're already worked up in advance." His voice is deep, his body at rest. "And they get worse when you serve them. Rightly so. Because it's not just the shit they're due, the tiny chicken, the tiny eggs, the pound of mincemeat. Even though they're only due a paltry amount, you still have to steal their shit. You have to take your share of their ration. When it's right in front of you. And how do you keep two thousand customers content when you're hitting them while they're down? Ah . . . ," he concludes, and leaves the question hanging, without revealing his secret.

As in any state butcher's, here in Cárdenas the main products are subsidized and each customer has the right to a quota of rationed foods via their supplies card. Namely: a pound of chicken every other month and six ounces of chicken to substitute for fish, a few ounces of soya mince or the exuberant sum of five regulated eggs per month.

Nine years ago, the state also liberalized the sale of eggs and withdrew the other rationed five. The government thought there would be enough for everyone. The facts, however, are irrefutable.

A case in point: in March 2015, nineteen workers at the companies for the Collection, Distribution, and Commerce for Havana faced charges of embezzlement, wrongful appropriation, and falsification of bank documents, and possible sentences of between eight and twenty years for the theft of eight million eggs. The vessel of public administration is nothing more than a rusty piece of scrap that has run aground in the swamp of personal survival.

This explains why, on the day the eggs reach their points of sale—small markets, grocery stores, cafés—there are genuine pitched battles between shoppers. Today is one of those days in this Cárdenas neighborhood. There is a horse cab stand just on the corner of Fidel's shop, and half-starved horses are constantly trotting down the road, wearing down the tarmac with their hooves.

Spurred on by necessity, residents from every rung of the ladder hurry out. Word has spread. The neighborhood is a chaotic hive. A long, restless, and disgruntled queue of thirty people gathers halfway down the block from the shopfront. It's early in the morning, and it's always the same clients arguing over the eggs on free sale—generally housewives, punctilious grandmothers, and retired old men.

It's a picturesque local scene, touching somehow. Fidel knows every one of them and they all know Fidel. The line unfurls and at certain points gets tangled up in knots of three or four, or curves and curls around itself, like a boa digesting on the pavement. People's fabric bags are hanging from their forearms, and their disposable bags are scrunched up in their fists or in their back trouser pockets. There are several ladies in the queue, regulars to whom Fidel has given nicknames, and to whom he is now shouting. Mireya is Mireya la Plebeya, the commoner. Victoria is Vito Corleone. Fidel serves them and they trundle off contentedly.

Later there is a short argument about one of the unanswered questions regarding the ancient practice of lining up: whether or not it is acceptable for someone to call another person when they are at the front of the queue so that that person can come along and buy their eggs without having gone to any effort. And whether someone can buy in someone else's name, as one of the ladies is now attempting to do.

"No one buys in anyone else's name in this shop," Fidel bellows. "I say it every month."

The butcher's shop is a refurbished microbrigada apartment. Behind the sticky counter there are two stools and a rusty green fridge whose handles recall the old American Westinghouse fridges, which until very recently were still struggling on in Cuba, a country that out of necessity became a theme park for classic cars and household appliances from the fifties. There are cartons on the floor, thousands of eggs piled up against the wall and, in one corner, a box of soy mince. There is also a neighboring room that should function as a storeroom, but Fidel, who never stores anything, has turned it into a garage.

Tempers flare in the queue. It's shameful, someone says, it's always the same people who get the eggs.

"I can't serve anyone in this chaos. Control yourselves or I'll shut up shop and no one will get any eggs today."

He's not exaggerating. Although the shop does have set opening hours, from eight in the morning until midday and from three in the afternoon until seven at night, Fidel can open and close whenever he feels like it, whenever it's more convenient to be open or closed, rather than when the rules say it is. There appears to be no public establishment as private as his shop in the whole town. That must be one of the reasons why, despite everything, it functions, as far as a butcher's shop that only receives products from time to time, and that never has enough when it does get them, can function.

━━

In 2014, the Provincial Poultry Company in Matanzas, in charge of egg supplies, declared that the scarcity was due to stress in chickens affected by low temperatures, lack of sun, and strong winds. No one here wants to hold anyone else to account because they don't want to be held to account themselves. The big Cuban corruption cases all have something in common: the exact number of losses is never published. It is precisely this informational void, this shamefully absent detail, that reveals the magnitude of the theft.

In mid-2011, Ofelia Liptak, manager of Río Zaza, an important food distribution company, was sentenced to five years' imprisonment along with ten other employees. According to an article published by the *Granma* newspaper, those sentenced "diverted or permitted the diversion of raw materials from their intended destinations, falsified information, adulterated documents, and carried out other fraudulent activities, abusing the responsibilities and the proper contents of the tasks they were charged with carrying out in order to benefit from the lucrative interests of unscrupulous individuals, to the detriment of the interests of the country's people and economy."

That same year, the Provincial Court of Havana handed out a sentence of fifteen years' imprisonment to the food industry minister, Alejandro Roca Iglesias, who was buying juice, milk, and other foodstuffs at an inflated price from a Chilean company owned by Salvador Allende's former chief bodyguard for whom his son was working. Just how many millions of dollars were lost in these scuffles is something *Granma*—one of the most discreet newspapers in the world, which isn't exactly ideal for a newspaper—will carry to the grave.

By contrast, if there's an art at which Cubans excel, it's petty theft. They all know its measurements, its weight, the risks and benefits, because there's barely a soul who hasn't had a go at it at least once. The fine web of constant, small-scale embezzlement and various other immoral acts has become a heroic form of resistance in the face of the state's ineptitude and hypocrisy. That's how people see it anyway. They make furtive purchases of black-market beef from some slaughterhouse worker or a hospital nurse or administrator working at a hospital who has stolen it from the food meant for the patients. A kilogram of powdered milk—which in the shops where foreign currency is accepted, costs almost six dollars, or 150 Cuban pesos, a quarter of the average monthly salary—can be found on the street for three dollars, or 75 pesos.

It stands to reason that a devastated material base is unable to produce white-gloved, scandal-ridden millionaires. Cuba is a country held hostage by a political regime whose plans for economic development seem to be little more than Fidel Castro's latest attempt to overcome our congenital, tropical underdevelopment through whimsical methods as fantastical or overblown as you like, provided they bear no resemblance whatsoever to capitalism.

What we have in Cuba is a sharing of scarcity, an equitable distribution of embezzlement. Unproductive socialism made us top students at school and thieves in the workplace. As recently as July 2017, our greatest criminal masterminds were two employees at a shop in Trinidad, a historic town in the center of the island, who were sentenced to fourteen years in prison for stealing a quantity of cement valued at 4.7 million pesos, some $195,833. Those are our Lilliputian masterstrokes.

Back at the start of the twenty-first century, Fidel Castro declared in one of his speeches that certain regulatory measures being put into action at the time—like getting groups of workers at city gas stations to keep an eye on other groups of workers—would shed light on large-scale fraud, the loss of $100,000 a day, a mountain of minor infractions. And this was before the group of workers meant to be monitoring the others inevitably joined in on the game.

The great political watchword has always been that nobody should get too rich so as not to create an imbalance in the general jackpot of scarcity, thus ensuring the endurance of the status quo. The system realized that it could continue indefinitely as long as it socialized corruption and so, because everyone needs to get by on something, the $100,000 siphoned off each day was divided into one dollar per person, never more. Cubans have managed to survive—especially since the fall of the Soviet Bloc—thanks to the pounds of rice, the slugs of detergent, the defrosted chicken breasts, and the three or four liters of yogurt that, whenever possible, have been diverted from the state's intended destination and ended up instead in their pantries or on kitchen tables.

This is what the Revolution sought to achieve in the long term: a collective of workers striving for the common good.

=====

Each month Fidel has forty-five boxes of regulated eggs assigned and ten for free sale. Each box contains eight cartons and each carton contains thirty eggs. That makes a total of 10,800 regulated eggs and a mere 2,400 free eggs, little more than one egg per local resident. The regulated eggs cost fifteen cents each in the national currency, less than one US cent. Before the state withdrew them, additional eggs cost ninety cents, free sale eggs one peso and ten cents. Eggs resold on the black market fluctuate between two pesos and two fifty.

Like many, Fidel has, up to a point, found mechanisms for alleviating the scarcity and solving, with the least possible emotional damage for his customers, this confusing equation of free eggs and regulated eggs and additional eggs, which no longer exist.

"It's simple: if an egg falls, it breaks. And if there aren't enough of them, then there aren't enough. This whole problem, this whole discussion, exists because we don't have enough."

In theory, the first person to arrive can buy all ten boxes of liberalized eggs, but Fidel has imposed his own regulations. He won't sell more than two cartons to anyone, a smart policy through which he has managed to find the right balance between providing for his customers and personal profit.

"If a confectioner from a particular business comes and asks me for all the eggs, I have to give them to him, but what about what's mine?" he asks as he serves, using his blue pen to draw crosses on supply cards. "Shouldn't I fight for what's mine? No one can tell me anything. If an inspector asks me why, I'll say, How do you expect me to turn away these old dears with no eggs, when they've been waiting there since eight in the morning? Who's going to argue with me?"

Around midday, once the cartons that are to be sold have been sold, and once those that are to be put away have been put away, the excitement dies down and the space in front of the shop empties out. There are whites from broken eggs that have spilled onto the floor. The sun is no longer shining so fiercely. Sitting on a high iron stool, behind the sticky counter, Fidel leaves everything in place and looks out calmly upon the neighborhood.

Sitting alone with him is not to be recommended. Fidel is a three-hundred-pound, six-foot wonder who shrivels up like a raisin when no one else is around. His voice is deep, but not as deep as his silence. He resembles both the good-hearted, effusive small-town butcher and Bill Cutting, the terrible slaughterman from *Gangs of New York* whose spite is crystallized in the form of his glass eye. There's a reason for all this. On the right wall, above the steelyard and the mince box, near a broken television, a small altar, with a crucifix, a bunch of yellow roses, and an enlarged portrait of a ten-year-old boy, is on display.

Fidel goes to the back of the shop, where he has built a garage for his 1990 Volkswagen and his TS-250 motorbike. Resting one hand on the open hood of the car, he frees the fuel pump, which has got blocked, inhales, and breathes out slowly.

＝

Havana's restaurant directory describes La Mina, located on 109 Obispo, on the corner with Oficios, as "a colonial mansion that has recreated an atmosphere as *creole* as traditional Cuban food itself. With a patio notable for the greenness of its vegetation, a fountain, and peacocks on the premises, it has welcoming rooms with stained-glass windows and rustic furniture with stools, marquetry designs, and Cuban saddlery."

Bolstered by these clichéd credentials and located in Havana old town, normally packed to the brim with tourists wearing bright shirts, their cameras hanging around their necks and wearing shorts that show off their pale calves, La Mina holds every qualification it needs to be just what it is: a generous source of dollars.

In the summer of 2004, at a collective birthday party for the restaurant's workers, with beer and music and food and friends of friends, Raúl Suárez, shop assistant, is talking to the chef's daughter and her boyfriend, Adrián, who is twenty-three and lives in the center of Havana. He is listening with great interest to all Raúl has to say. About how they change the prices of the dishes in La Mina to overcharge tourists. About how the staff buy the meat and the drinks at a low price on the black market and resell it in the restaurant, making a decent profit. About how much money he makes there, and how he keeps it in a safe in his brother's house in the provinces.

Raúl and Adrián become close. He's a nice kid and Raúl likes the way he hangs off his every word. Besides, they both breed dogs and bet on underground dogfights. One day, a few months after that birthday celebration, Raúl has to go to Cárdenas, his sister's town, to buy a purebred. His adviser pulls out at the last minute and he gets Adrián to accompany him.

After a two-and-a-half-hour journey, they arrive at his sister's house. Her name is Nancy Suárez; she's thirty-six and divorced. Nancy lives with her mother, sixty, and Ronald, ten, the son she had with Fidel Albelo, who used to be her husband. The family and their guest have lunch and talk. Then Adrián goes out onto the patio and takes in the scene carefully. A while later, the two men say goodbye and leave.

==

At six in the evening, Peyuco arrives with his son. Fidel, covered in grease and encased in a raw petrol smell, interrupts what he's doing and addresses them.

"Well then, Peyuco! Tell me, old friend, what is it?"

Peyuco, a slight, elderly man, needs Fidel to make use of his contacts at the Municipal Commerce Company to get a friendly staff member to sign a false letter claiming that Peyuco's son works there.

"No problem at all, Peyuco, old friend."

Peyuco's son is leaving the country for the second time and he needs proof of a place of work in order to be granted the visa. They did it that way the first time and it worked like a dream.

"Wait for me at my house tomorrow, at seven. When I shut up shop, we'll go see the partner and he'll sign the letter you need."

Peyuco's son is already twenty-two and the boy has a special place in Fidel's heart. He was his son's childhood friend.

Fidel had a son when he was basically still a teenager, another son with Nancy Suárez, his first wife, and he also has an eleven-year-old daughter with his current wife. Today, for no apparent reason, the girl has sent him a souvenir postcard in which she doubtless tells him how much she loves him, and Fidel is very keen to get home so he can sit down and read it while drinking a few measures of whiskey. He lives in an expansive property: a lounge covered in ornaments, a forty-inch plasma TV, three air-conditioned rooms, a tiled bathroom, a kitchen with a fridge and a freezer, and a covered patio with a barbeque oven and an unfriendly-looking dog, maybe a pitbull or a bull terrier.

Since he has been a butcher for thirty years, no one is surprised that Fidel lives a comfortable life, but in reality, he says, most of his money comes from buying and selling cars, motorbikes, and spare parts. Clearly, if everything he owns had come only from his skill at butchery, he wouldn't have lasted so long in the role. But we'll never know how much he earns from one thing, and how much from the other. It's his greatest secret and he wouldn't think of confessing it. He keeps his cover.

He only ever says things like this: "When a truck brings the meat, and you're the one who's going to mince it and distribute it, it's only logical that you keep a piece for yourself. You take what's yours. You follow me? And the state knows that. It knows that I have to make ends meet because they don't pay enough. But that doesn't matter to the state."

"The state lets you run with it."

"Yes. Now, what you can't do is run and jump at the same time. Do you want to see me lose my shit and smash someone's head open?" He gives me a stubborn look. "Let them come here and offer me one hundred pounds of meat."

"Right."

"The state won't allow that. They'll break your legs."

Fidel is referring to the handling, theft, and slaughter of large livestock—specifically cattle—punishable by law since 1979, a crime that can incur up to eight years in prison. It's no coincidence that the joke that it's more expensive to kill a cow than a person is a linchpin of Cuban humor.

When Fidel Castro came to power, Cuba had six million inhabitants and the same number of cattle; in 2019, there are eleven million of us, and official figures state that there are two million fewer cattle than there were sixty years ago. In September 2015, the government pardoned some 3,500 prisoners ahead of Pope Francis's visit, but the

amnesty did not include murderers, rapists, violent pedophiles or—
yes—those found guilty of the illegal theft and slaughter of large livestock. That's how serious it is to steal a Cuban cow.

Butchers' shops, like any other gastronomic places of work, in
commerce or in supplies, are ticking time bombs, but Fidel still has
no administrative sanctions on his file, no proven illegality, and not
a single previous offense.

His most nerve-racking moment, he recalls, took place in 2003.
The chief of the municipal police's Rustling Department (yes, there's
a department just for that) summoned him to his office and interrogated him with a very common technique used by domestic intelligence: appearing to know more than they actually do.

I know what you're up to, he told him. Fidel asked him what exactly he was up to and the official answered that he had information
saying he was selling beef on the black market. Fidel told him he was
wrong. How else was Fidel able to maintain his living standards, the
official asked, with a car, motorbike, and a luxury house? Fidel told
him he was going to speak from the heart. It's true, he had his comforts, and it's true that he did his business and sold his pounds of
meat, or of chicken, or his cartons of eggs when they arrived at the
butcher's shop. That was true, everyone knew it.

Now, he asked him, if you had the things I have, if you lived the
way I do, would you risk it all by accepting rustled meat? No, the
official said. Then why do you think I would do that? Fidel asked.
Resigned, the official agreed, but reminded him that once you are
being watched, escape is impossible. Fidel answered that he who
owes nothing, fears nothing.

A few years later, their roles were reversed. A straight-faced local,
Efraín, proposed that he join the ranks of the Revolution, in State
Security. Fidel had the ideal cover. He was sociable, a businessman,
not completely corrupt, at least on the surface, and people believed in

him. Besides, his shop stood at the mouth of the mighty river of local rumors. In other words, if anything out of the ordinary happened, beyond the usual infidelities, Fidel would be the first to find out.

He spent several days thinking about how to explain his answer.

"It was no, of course, but you can't just say no to these people," he says, summing it up as succinctly as possible. The exchange was a short one.

"I can't serve the government that failed to execute those who killed my son."

—

On November 4, 2004, Adrián and two friends are skirting the northwest coast of the country on the Hershey train, which goes from Havana to nearby Cárdenas. In Santa Cruz del Norte, a medium-sized town, one of the friends has second thoughts and turns back. At midday, Adrián and Alain, just a boy, reach Nancy's house, and tell her that they have come from Oriente and that they don't know how to get back to Havana. Nancy invites them into the room, gives them two omelette sandwiches and some fruit juice, gives each of them sixty pesos, and shows them the way.

She needs to go to the shop, so they leave with her, say goodbye, and then go straight around the block and back to the house. Nancy's mother opens the door to them. They push her around and extort her. They ask her for the code to her son's safe. The old lady doesn't know it. They push her around some more. She screams with fright. They take a butcher's knife from the kitchen that Fidel left there after he split up with Nancy. They stab her and slit her throat. They drag the body and hide it under the bed.

They lie in wait for some five hours. When Nancy comes home from her day, they grab her and hit her on the head. Stunned and probably still not understanding what's happening, she tells them to wait a second because the driver who brought her home is outside and she has to pay him. Adrián goes out onto the street and pays with the twenty pesos Nancy gives him.

Alain is a little on edge now. For a second he seems to have grasped what they've done: who knows what doubts go through a murderer's head when he's on the brink? The ruthless Adrián spurs him on. They keep on pummeling Nancy. She must have felt torn. Tell them the code, it's curtains for you. Don't tell them, get beaten some more. What to do? Tell them. Nancy tells them.

Now they have the money, the wads of dollars Raúl has accumulated from years of ripping off diners at La Mina. The two men stab her repeatedly. Adrián tells Alain to cut her throat. Alain says she's already dead, no need to overdo it. Adrián insists. Alain is scared of him, he knows that Adrián is quite capable of killing him too. Later, at the trials, Adrián will confess it: he was about to kill his friend.

So Alain slits Nancy's throat, and just as they are leaving, young Ronald, arriving home from school, rings the doorbell. The murderers will say he struggled, and that he managed to scratch one of their arms with the blunt knife he used for sharpening pencils. He was only ten, so they didn't cut his throat. That was supposedly the only sign of compassion they showed.

━━

It's midmorning on a Sunday in Cárdenas cemetery. The sun falls on the niches of the columbarium and the old marble memorials, bringing the dead some warmth.

Two minutes: that's the window of time the coroner, after reconstructing the case, said would have saved the boy. If only he'd arrived two minutes later.

"What I think, after thinking about it so much, is that he was born to live the life he lived," Fidel says. He parks his motorbike and removes his helmet. "You have no idea the dark, dark places this head has been."

After his son's death Fidel tried to hang himself in the shop, tied to the freezer with some old ropes. But Ronald appeared to him from somewhere and spoke to him and told him that what he was doing was cowardly. Fidel reconstructs this improbable scene with obvious pain.

"Everything in life has a name. If you like men, you're a faggot. If you like women, you're a lesbian. If your husband dies, you're a widow. If your mother dies, you're an orphan. But if your son dies, what do you call it? There's no word for it, nothing. It has no name."

Fidel considered bringing Ronald's remains back to his house, but since he wasn't allowed to, he goes to the place that houses Ronald's mortal remains. He's constructed a lavish memorial on the cemetery's main alley, probably the most popular pilgrimage site in the town of Cárdenas.

It's a solidly built construction, three meters high and four meters wide, with a small tower above it and a white, solid marble cross. Up on the roof, his son's name in mortar. The gravestone reads:

THIS MEMORIAL WAS BUILT IN MEMORY OF LITTLE RONALD ALBELO SUÁREZ WHO OFFERED UP HIS LIFE IN DEFENSE OF HIS MOTHER AND HIS GRANDMOTHER WHO WERE VICTIMS OF A CRUEL MURDER. IT IS DEDICATED TO HIM BY HIS FATHER WHO LOVES HIM AND WILL NEVER FORGET HIM.

Fidel opens the entrance gates and walks toward little Ronald's ossuary.

"Hey!" he whistles. "Daddy's here! How you doing, son?"

One corner of the ossuary is smeared with Fidel's kisses. The wall is also smeared in the exact place where he rests his head when he sits on the floor.

Adrián and Alain, his son's murderers, were sentenced to life and put in the maximum-security wing of Havana's Combinado del Este. Fidel wanted them dead. At another time, it's very likely they would have been shot. However, the murders took place just a year after Fidel Castro, seeking to make an example following several thefts of boats intended for Florida, had ordered three young people who had hijacked a transport boat with thirty passengers on board, though without causing any physical harm, to be shot after a summary trial that lasted less than forty-eight hours. The international scandal was so big that it made the government rethink. Since then, the ultimate penalty hasn't been applied to any guilty person, though it remains constitutionally possible.

Furious at what he sees as an injustice—shooting those who don't need to be shot and not shooting those who should be shot—Fidel whistles to the dead in the cemetery. He's celebrated Ronald's birthday here, Christmas, Father's Day. He plays music, eats cake, serves soft drinks, and prepares ham paté sandwiches. He's stopped doing this, though, because he knows the cats always end up eating the food.

"I talk to him all the time, I tell him my problems, my business at the shop," he says, sitting on the floor. "He's up to speed with all of it. And he knows he has to look after his mother and his granny, he knows it."

Fidel pauses, runs his hand over his face.

"Look, I'm not crazy. I know he can't hear me. He's in another dimension. But it makes me feel better."

That he's been able to spend thousands of dollars building a memorial for his son that is equal in size to the pain he feels has only been possible because Fidel is both butcher and businessman. Almost any other father would have had to make do with a modest tomb, hidden away in the cemetery's inner streets, with a brief inscription that the wind and the rain would have by now begun to wipe away.

Fidel walks through the cemetery, playing the tour guide. He knows every corner of it, and every bit of business the gravediggers conduct in the shadows. A few years ago, all of the employees, from the humblest to the most important functionaries, were fired from the Communal Services Company for the illegal sale of land and plots in the cemetery. In fact, Fidel's memorial, like many others, is built on the border, a line of lawn that should have remained untouched. But even that has been sold.

"The boy's memorial is sacred. No one can mess with it."

Fidel says this because the town is one of the birthplaces of *abakuá*, the secret *ñáñiga* society that originated in Africa, specifically in southeastern Nigeria and that, at the beginning of the nineteenth century, spread rapidly among the mass of slaves on the western side of Cuba, as well as among the poorer white and mixed-race communities.

The spirits play a major part in the fraternity's religious ceremonies—they provide the framework for the rituals. So much so that today, in an era in which the ethical codes of abakuá seem to have fallen apart ("anyone who works in Varadero and steals from the hotels and can pay four pesos can now become a member of or form a new *plante* [ceremony]," says Fidel, who has belonged to a plante since childhood), the desecration of tombs is the order of the day.

The bones of the dead are valuable and are constantly being sold to the abakuá in the town's cemeteries. Now Fidel is talking to one of the gravediggers, a fiftysomething mixed-race man of medium build, hidden among the niches, who has been working in an open grave for almost an hour.

In a country where no state jobs are worth doing for the salary—between twenty and twenty-five dollars a month on average—but only for the extra slice of the pie they offer, gravediggers openly remove crosses from recent graves and marble angels and Latin inscriptions from the flamboyant and now decaying memorials of the nineteenth-century aristocracy and the republican bourgeoisie. There aren't that many really well-executed designs, so they take it in turns to help themselves.

Four winged angels, which originally guarded the memorial of a famous police chief in the town who was shot up by delinquents in the 1940s, came into Fidel's hands. He sold two to a buyer in Havana for $1,000, and the other two now watch over Ronald's ossuary.

When asked why he didn't commission some sculptor to do the angels, he goes over to a neighboring memorial and points to an angel, cast in an ordinary mold, eroded, lacking the elegant marble veins, its body shrunken and its head way too large. The individual fingers cannot be told apart, far less the cuticles, and the folds of the wings are clumsy, so thick as to be vulgar. "I don't want that for my son," he declares.

——

Petty corruption in Cuba is no longer recognized as such. It has become the primary state of personal relationships, even close ones. It's the unheroic driving force of a cunning society that still wears the makeup of its political dramas and the weight of its recent history but that, for those who live within it, functions in a tribal manner, like a gang of thieves.

Fidel spreads out his rows of eggs; a neighbor asks for help forging an administrative document; the police believe he is stealing in large enough quantities for them to arrest him and then try to recruit him because they know he doesn't steal enough for it to be considered serious; the leitmotif of his son's murder is the theft of money from an uncle who had also stolen part of that money from the state; and in turn, in the cemetery, the bones of the dead are stolen for a secret society's rituals, or some decoration expressing one

family's mourning is unscrewed and removed to express the mourning of another family, or a vault or plot is sold to some desperate bidder; and so on. Because that's how things are—the hordes
of swindlers, the daily plotting for survival—prosaic corruption contains you, and whatever your own drama is, it must be settled in those
lands. The most crushing thing about it is the way it appears to be
inconsequential

Close to midday, Fidel climbs onto his TS-250, says goodbye to
the gravediggers, and crosses the town in twenty minutes, though he
could easily do it in ten if it weren't for all the people who stop him
in the street to say hello. Some of them will visit the shop tomorrow,
perhaps to buy eggs, do a deal on some car parts, or ask some favor
Fidel will find it hard to refuse.

He arrives home, parks the motorbike, leaves the helmet on some
furniture in the living room, and heads straight for the kitchen. He
takes a piece of potato omelette from the fridge and chews it with
gusto. He's a three-hundred-pound wonder who looks upon things
like a ferocious buddha.

A TRAPPED (AND MULTIPLE) TIGER

At two-thirty in the afternoon, several minutes late, the plane touches down on the asphalt runway outside Terminal 3 at José Marti International Airport. It is December 5, 2016. After nine days of intense national mourning, and a cross-country tour of the island, today is the first day of eternity for the ashes of Fidel Castro, which have just been interred in a large boulder that, it is said, was brought from the Sierra Maestra to the cemetery of Santa Ifigenia in Santiago de Cuba.

From the window of the plane, I gaze at the perimeter fence that encircles a lush green patch of land, preventing this swirling riot of color from encroaching on the airport. Fidel Castro was the marabou that spread its implacable wings like a plague over a historic time in Cuba. I have not yet stepped off the plane and already my mind is whirling with thoughts of him. I want to see how long it will take, on this first day after, before someone mentions his name.

Last night, in his farewell speech, a visibly exhausted and grieving Raúl Castro announced his brother's last wishes: Fidel wanted no monuments or statues to him, no buildings or public institutions to bear his name. We should be grateful to Fidel Castro, who knows exactly the kind of people he leaves behind, for sparing us one last patriotic-revolutionary offensive in the form of an

onslaught of new facilities that would further fuel the symbolic greatness of *el líder*.

The propaganda machines are already applauding his decision,
and the gist of their message, recognizing their own absurdity, is,
"Fidel Castro is a genius, he knew that we're so fanatical we'd have
spent the next decade praising him until we were blue in the face,
and he's freed us from this folly." If the country hadn't been brain-
washed with ideological propaganda, Fidel wouldn't have needed to
warn us. The idea wouldn't have occurred to anyone, and there would
have been no need to waste time on something as disastrous and
sterile—yet sadly unsurprising—as the cult of personality.

Fidel was the shield of his people and later his people served as
his shield. He bit into the heart of the country the way someone
might bite into a fruit; he sucked out the flesh and has left us with
nothing but the stone. Coverage of his death confirms him as a tow-
ering figure—the determined chin, the unbowed body, the stern
gaze—looming over the rubble that is our theater of war.

═══

The immigration officer checks my passport. In the past year, I have
racked up a dizzying number of stamps. In a few months, I've visited about six countries, something that, for a Cuban, is unusual to
say the least. "Do you live in Cuba?" the blond woman asks, half-
suspicious, half-impressed. I nod. A current Cuban passport, in
constant use, leads anyone who inspects it to speculate and wonder, "Who is this guy, what is he up to, why is he traveling all the
time?" Or, "He must be pretty famous if he travels so much."

In this country, "airport" has metonymically become a zone of
conflict and hostility. There is a notion of success that is powerfully
linked with foreign countries. To Cubans, the idea of leaving Cuba,
escaping Cuba, breathing the air somewhere other than Cuba is, in
and of itself, a higher stage of evolution. People from the Cuban di-

aspora, who once lived here and know how outsiders are regarded, are particularly presumptuous and rude. Cubans landing on the island can swagger past the immigration and customs officials with embarrassing arrogance and the immigration and customs officials, in turn, treat them with calculated hostility, when they are not officially confiscating some household appliance or stealing a suitcase full of clothes.

In Cuba, an airport—which should be the place where a country should begin to be reconciled to itself—continues to be the most vicious of wrestling rings.

=

The news of the death took me by surprise while I was in Miami. My best friends and my father all live around Coral Gables, Kendall, or down by Miami Beach, and I like to visit them regularly. I considered going down to 8th Street or to the Café Versailles, the historic centers of Cuban exiles in the city, to watch the outpourings of joy that have been going on, uninterrupted, for days and nights since the early hours of November 26. But in the end, I stayed home and watched it on TV. Apparently, they owe not just the tragedies of exile but also its joys to Fidel Castro. In dying, he has allowed them to indulge in the parody of a popular uprising.

Miami, with its thriving economic growth, is Fidel Castro's greatest urban achievement. It could be argued that the soaring luxury apartment blocks downtown and the opulent condos of Brickell are the flipside of the anti-imperialist struggle, the literacy campaign, and the military intervention in Angola, but they all stem from the same historic flux.

What does not exist in Miami or in Havana—what cannot exist, since it was not a part of Fidel Castro, and these cities are reflections of his personality—is a basic sense of tolerance and democracy. The self-professed freedom of Cubans in Miami is belied by the way they carry on living in a world they supposedly left behind, a society that clings to them like a leech.

Fidel Castro has no greater friend today than the shrill TV channels in Hialeah. Just as those who want to despise him have only to read or watch the eulogies on Cuban state media, so those who want to diminish the status of the dictator have only to listen to the news anchors and the pundits in southern Florida. The genuine pain of Cuban exiles in Miami is all too frequently disparaged and squandered on shrill rhetoric and a lack of journalistic rigor. We find Fidel, for example, being lazily compared to Hitler. The cult of his personality is unstoppable.

Perhaps they could never defeat him, because they devoted their time to defining him as something he was not, wedded to a political agenda that was uninterested in finding out the true nature of their enemy. Maybe they never wanted to completely defeat him, maybe Miami was never anything more than an exclave teeming with State Security agents, all working for Castroism, and the whole so-called fight to the death, the bitter war, was no more than a carefully rehearsed piece of theater intended to confuse ordinary Cubans and the rest of the world, that overwhelming majority who never found a political niche, in or outside Cuba, and became victims of the cross fire.

Miami has not adopted the same political discourse, but it has adopted the same approach, which is worse. Obedience is the norm. In Cuba, to Fidel Castro. In Miami, to the notion of opposing Fidel Castro. The base of Cuban prosperity in Miami is in the non-Cuban part of the city, since it is there that Castroism is most heavily promoted.

=

The carousel shudders and starts to revolve, as though slowly coming to life; its orifices begin to spit suitcases tightly wrapped in plastic, cardboard boxes containing domestic appliances that range from TVs and air conditioners to water heaters and washing machines. After a long wait, the passengers crowd around the luggage belts. This is their business. Once a week, they travel to Mexico or to Panama to buy all kinds of things they can resell, including basic items that are in short supply, like soap, deodorant, and toothpaste.

Currently, during peak hours, Havana Airport Terminal 3 welcomes three times more passengers than it is built to accommodate. The bustle and excitement that now greet arriving luggage—which represents an investment of who knows how much time and money—masks a prosaic indifference to death. It is as though Terminal 3 is not part of the country where the ashes of Fidel Castro have just been buried.

I hand in my customs form, emerge, and change a few dollars at the bureau de change. There is something sickly about the heat today, an almost imperceptible current of cold running through it. You feel sweaty and dirty, your skin is clammy and metallic, but it's not suffocating. It lacks the dazzling brilliance—glorious for some, perilous for others—characteristic of the tropics. In fact, it is a climate of death. The city has the air of an open sarcophagus.

Usually when I come back, I spend the night in Havana. But today I am not going to stop until I get to Cárdenas, Matanzas, a three-hour drive from here, to the apartment where my mother still lives, which I moved out of at the age of fifteen and have visited since only for brief interludes. I am swathed in the orphan's shroud of these events, as though I were just one more package shipped here to be resold. This, in a sense, is what Fidel Castro has done to us: turned us into bargaining chips that could be used to realize his convictions.

Our lives were used to create the sort of elegant linen suit favored by Latin American dictators. We clothed a concept: we were the coats, the trousers, the shirts of an idea. Now that the fabric has been ripped, who will clothe the aged body that is Cuba?

A taxi driver—one of many wearing pale-yellow shirts—approaches me. I tell him I'm going to Boyeros Bus Terminal and he quotes a fare of twenty-five dollars—which is what I used to live on for a month. Reluctantly I agree. He says he is going to fetch the taxi from the parking lot and asks me wait for one minute. One minute becomes five. I wander around the outside of the arrivals hall and no one mentions Fidel. Five victorious minutes seems like brief respite, but anyone who has lived in Cuba knows that, given the circumstances, it is an eternity.

The taxi driver arrives, loads up my suitcase, and we set off. His son, who is sitting in the back seat, is coming with us. He shakes my hand vigorously, as though we've known each other a long time. The taxi driver asks me if the air-conditioning is all right, if I want it lower or higher, asks if the music is all right. I say yes to everything, although I find the music irritating. It is raucous and my body is tired and my eyes are hard as dried cherry stones.

The taxi driver does not say another word nor does the son, and I don't want them to talk. Many taxi drivers think making conversation with the customer is an essential part of the service, reeling off a couple of jokes, commenting on banal, everyday things (and the most important everyday thing is called Fidel Castro). Personally, I believe that, unless the passenger strikes up a conversation, a taxi driver should keep his mouth shut. That's what I would do if I were a taxi driver. And that's what the taxi driver today does.

The taxi is going to take a series of roads that I do not know at all, eventually emerging onto Avenida Boyeros where it runs through Fontanar. As we glide through the city in a straight line, and faced with this journey that I have made a thousand times, my brain will inexplicably bubble with thoughts it has never had before.

In Cuba, spontaneity and constraint are not mutually exclusive. They have learned to coexist, because constraint is totalitarian, but it has been around for so long that it feels like it's not there. Beneath the weight of surveillance, the vertical directives, the paranoia, and the Party discipline, is a society that is more or less spontaneous and adaptable, a society that does things because, at the end of the day, they need to be done.

It's not true that the hundreds of thousands of people who walked past the portrait of Fidel on the Plaza de la Revolución or those who lined the country roads to watch him pass, weeping and grieving at the sight of the urn containing the ashes of el líder, did so because they were forced, or as a pretense. Every last detail was organized and controlled by the highest political echelons, but only because the government is terrified of popular initiative—even those that are positive, not because there was a risk that no one would turn up.

The state can fear the apathy of the people as much as their passion. But a country in mourning, a collective shudder, is not an end in itself. What will come of all this? Nothing. They are outpourings of grief spilled into the sea, like a spoiled sugarcane harvest. What is truly significant is that, in this moment, what has brought the Cuban people out onto the streets is not some rebel marching into Havana, but the theater, the somber atmosphere of the funeral.

The people are burying a part of themselves, bidding farewell to that part of themselves that was Fidel Castro. They are attending their own wake. It is like a final requiem, exorcising something that has lived within us us for more than fifty years.

═══

Let's try to understand the metonymy sold to us by power. Fidel is the Revolution. Fidel is the Motherland. Fidel is the Nation. Look at photos of him from the '60s: fearless, intrepid. Look at photos of him in the '70s: fierce, impulsive, faintly ridiculous. Look at photos of him from the '80s: dour, compact. Look at photos of him from the '90s: superfluous, bullheaded, tiresome. Look at photos of him from the 2000s: long-winded, decrepit, out of touch.

His physical decline mirrors the the spiritual journey of a people.

═══

The taxi driver speeds up, heads right, slows at certain corners, stops at traffic lights, does what you are supposed to do when driving. Cars flow along the Avenida Boyeros like an asphalt river with twin currents. I have always been fascinated by short city journeys, those that last only a few minutes. I never want them to end.

Suddenly, I realize that we have already passed several places where, at another time, I might have gotten out, because at some point in my life I hung out there, or better, because at one stage, those stops were my life. That's where I misspent hours and hours of my time and my youth; now I have no connection to it. No trace of me lingers in those places.

We cross the Avenida de Cien, where I was based for about a month while visiting the largest and most unsanitary landfill in the city where I interviewed a very strange homeless couple.

We cross the Avenida de Santa Catalina, the softball fields of the Fajardo Institute where I was leadoff hitter and center fielder for my university team. The smell of damp grass, the muddy uniform after making a run, the lash of the midday sun, the clichéd scene, played out endlessly in my mind and the mind of every fielder in the world, of the acrobatic catch we would make as soon as the ball came our way. There were more unremarkable catches and throws, but never that long-awaited catch, which is perhaps why we carried on showing up every Saturday to this sweet hell with no boundary fences and no chalk marks.

We pass the Calzada del Cerro, and the last house where my

father lived before he moved to Miami. My father, who grew up in a palm-thatched hut with a dirt floor, who fought in Angola with the internationalist mission, who took a degree in medicine, and who, on the night of July 31, 2006—when a sullen TV news anchor announced that Fidel Castro was critically ill and might die—stubbed out his cigarette in the ashtray, sank back into his seat, and started to sob. The scene was all the more terrible since he was utterly motionless except for these tears. All the tension in his rigid body suddenly spilled out through the tiny delicate openings of his tear ducts.

Next, we passed the Tulipán bus stop, and, on the corner of the *Bohemia* magazine offices, we also passed the Communications Faculty of the University of Havana, where I spent five years studying journalism. Then the taxi, now in the final stretch, stops at the traffic light on Avenida 20 de Mayo, next to the Plaza de la Revolución.

——

The professions that have suffered most in Cuba are those that, in their attempt to adapt to the whims of the government, have had their noble intentions brutally castrated and arbitrarily reversed. Of these, there is no crime greater than the one committed against journalism—the medical equivalent would have been to tell doctors to allow patients to die, or to call cancer the common cold.

In *Archivo*, the most recent novel by Cuban writer Jorge Enrique Lage, there is a very powerful passage. A prisoner, "the best-fed living creature in Cuba," is living on death row. Every day he is asked what he wants to eat, every day the prisoner asks for the finest delicacies, every day they grant the prisoner's wish, and so, every day the prisoner believes they are about to execute him. "I know nobody would believe that they're torturing me, quite the opposite. But look at me. All this rich food and I'm not even putting on weight," the prisoner says. "Tomorrow it's bound to happen. Tomorrow."

In this case, don't think of food as food—something we have never had much of in Cuba. Think of it as the one thing Cubans had far too much of—education. Fidel Castro practiced the most refined form of torture on the Cuban people. He created a society of highly literate professionals, raised educational standards, and then, perversely, refused to allow us to use that knowledge, which has carried on roiling inside our heads until today, when tomorrow has finally come.

=====

From the top of the National Theater they have hung a banner with a photo of Fidel Castro and a quote by him, but the traffic lights turn green and the taxi pulls away before I have time to read it. Finally, we arrive at the bus terminal. I lived near here for a year, in an apartment building on the corner of Pozos Dulces. The white window of what was once my bedroom is closed.

At night, I used to look down at the lights on the Avenida Boyeros, the monuments on the Plaza de la Revolución, the flickering traffic lights, the line of buses, the human hubbub, and the battered old rental cars. In the cafeterias of the bus terminal, I gleefully ate badly, stuffing myself with bars of homemade peanut nougat and the sugary bread pudding called *pan frío*. This fusion gave me a joyous feeling of sophistication, of being at the heart of something, at the epicentre of man's ingenuity.

My life in Havana, I realize, has been spent on the banks of the river that is the Avenida Boyeros, and now the Avenida Boyeros is pulling me along, drifting past the houses where I lived, the places I frequented, as though I were a stranger. But, to some extent, all Cubans are now living in a country that is soon going to emigrate from itself to another country, and we will all feel a little like strangers in the homes, the neighborhoods, the towns where we have always lived, like traveling to the end of Avenida Boyeros without stopping anywhere.

I get out of the taxi, collect my suitcase, and ask about a collective taxi heading for Matanzas, and a *buquenque* (a brownnoser)—that's what they call the people who manage the passengers—leads me to the *colectivo* half a block away. I am the last passenger, and as soon as I get in, we are good to go.

From my seat, before we set off, I watch the driver and the buquenque arguing in the street. The buquenque is demanding his commission for bringing me, and the driver is insisting he's not giving him a peso, since I was already at the terminal and would have found the taxi by myself, so it hardly counts as finding a passenger when all the buquenque did was walk a few meters and pretend he'd just found me.

There is a tense moment as the two glare at each other and I think disaster is imminent, but then nothing much happens. The driver says, "I told you the other day. I warned you not to tout for passengers like that, otherwise I won't pay you."

"Don't talk to me about the other day, buddy," says the buquenque, huffing and puffing. "Don't talk to me about the other day. The other day Fidel was alive and today he's dead."

DEATH IN JESÚS MARÍA

The walls and roof crumble to reveal whole towns, naked, in various poses, most often beseeching mercy. Arms and legs appear from beneath the rubble. The heavens, too, have fallen.

—VICENTE HUIDOBRO, *TEMBLOR DE CIELO*

The little girl, Lisnavy, was arguing with the ice-cream man on a noisy street by the local park. Her ice cream was melting and she wanted him to change it. It is difficult for anyone in Havana to find good ice cream, but when you are eleven years old, you still believe it is possible.

Her mother, sitting on the far side of the park, near the two post office booths on the corner of Vives and Águila, "had just given her some small change to buy plantains and tomatoes for dinner," according to her grandmother, Margarita Rodríguez, who was also on the square at the time.

Lisnavy never got as far as buying anything. Two classmates, Rocío and María Karla, called to her before she reached the opposite pavement, who knows why. It was almost 5:00 p.m. when the unsupported balcony of Building 102, on the corner of Vives and Revillagigedo collapsed. The impoverished neighborhood of Jesús María—the desolate picture postcard of a war that never happened—is afflicted by chronic dereliction, not to mention the greatest housing shortage

273

in a district of Havana old town, which, in turn, is one of the most densely populated areas of the city.

The three girls, aged ten and eleven, were buried beneath the deadly shroud. Iron bars, blunt objects, rubble, lethal shards. One of the slabs, comprising two metal beams set into concrete, crushed the body of María Karla.

"The slab I moved, I don't know how I picked it up, I can't remember how I managed to lift it," says Sergio Gutiérrez, a neighbor from Building 104 and a caretaker at the Quintín Banderas school, which the girls attended. "It must have been about sixty centimeters by sixty, and ten centimeters thick. It weighed a ton."

Sergio ran over from the opposite corner—Revillagigedo and Esperanza—because he thought there was a brawl on the ground floor of the building where he lives with his mother, his son, and his son's girlfriend. He was worried about them. When they hear a booming crash, everyone instantly assumes it relates directly to them. Within minutes, Sergio sees a woman he knows running to the site where the balcony collapsed. "Don't worry, it's not your little girl," he told her. "I know, I know," she said, "but just let me see them."

Señora Ramona, a teacher and a woman well respected at the school and in the neighborhood, tiptoed down the calle Vives, and later went upstairs to her apartment. "She was a ball of nerves, a complete ball of nerves," says Jorge Ortega, a skinny, garrulous man. Days later, Señora Ramona was still in a state of shock.

The scene is a series of splintered fragments, as is the horror. "Lisnavy!" her mother Magdaly screamed from the far side of the park. It was she who dragged her daughter from beneath the rubble and laid her on the opposite pavement. "She was the only one who came out alive, my granddaughter," says Margarita. Cars stopped in the street, the lifeless bodies of the girls were placed inside, and they roared away with their doors still hanging open. Someone remembers seeing a foot, a small, dangling foot being gently placed on the back seat.

Men and women began to wail. Questions shouted into empty air, cell phones switched on. Who are they? Frantic mothers, people taking videos or photos. Screams: "Who are they?" Sobs, their names, whose daughters were they? Voices, more mothers. The whole neighborhood flocked to Building 102, a crowd driven by fear and morbid curiosity, sucked into the vortex of tragedy. Who are they, who were they? People talking about the girls in the past tense, making a dramatic shift in conjugation. "It was so quick," someone explains. "It happened so quickly." Even those who were present knew little about what had happened.

"When you peered through the cloud of dust, you could see the dismembered body of a girl," says Sergio. "The skull was smashed open, the body flattened and badly injured, as though she had been crushed. Their bodies were broken, covered in dust, their faces disfigured. There were huge pieces of rubble."

At this point a rescuer appears without a head. He is imagining a rescuer so that rescue might be possible. Then the swelling thought spills out. Sergio tries to stanch it, but it overflows. "I didn't dream it because I'm not a daydreamer, but the image flashes into my mind at random moments, when I'm talking to someone, when I look over there, when I'm alone." What is it that flashes into his mind, what precisely is this thing that Sergio calls "the image,". what is it? "I prefer not to think about it," he says, "because everyone who was there was pretty fucked in the head by what happened."

They are men aged between forty and sixty. "I'm fifty-seven, I've seen pretty much everything there is to see," says Jorge, "but this case brought me to tears." He pauses. "I'm not someone who cries easily, but this time I did." He has a face as dry and withered as a walnut.

When was the last time Jorge wept? "Pff . . . who remembers stuff like that? The last time was 2010, when, I buried my mother, one of my aunts, and my father in the space of thirty-seven days. You can imagine. What could I do but cry?"

Upset and clearly on the brink of tears, Dayán Poutú communicates in silences. His words, when they come, are little more than the shrill wail of a despair, a grief that expresses itself more forcefully in him than in anyone else. From his face, which looks about to crumble and collapse, hang two desolate eyes, two globes of grief.

Dayán, who is also a security guard at Quintín Banderas school, was on duty, as usual, sitting in the door that opens on to the calle Águila, when he heard the thunderous crash around the corner and thought about his fifteen-year-old daughter. Within minutes he was on the scene, people were lifting away hunks of rubble. Lisnavy was already lying on the opposite pavement, as was Rocío. Sergio lifted the slab and Dayán pulled out María Karla.

He makes a helpless gesture of something breaking, his hands frail, as though María Karla were slipping between his fingers. "Here I am talking to you like this, but I can't sleep anymore," he says. "I'm woken up at two o'clock by the same thing that woke me up at one." Dayán repeats the questions asked of him. "How do you feel? In the moment, you don't feel grief, you don't feel anything. Your whole body is focused on saving a life, this is not a game. You take hold of it and it falls into your hands. This is save and rescue, and I'm not a firefighter."

Rocío and María Karla were killed instantly. In Calixto García hospital, three and a half kilometers away, Lisnavy was still fighting to breathe, as though she no longer knew how, as though she were unlearning, slipping into a state where breathing does not exist.

She was still wearing her primary school uniform, the red skirt and neckerchief. It was January 27, the eve of the anniversary of José Martí's birth, and Lisnavy had just been in the park rehearsing the commemorative ceremony the Pioneers were to give the following day, what they call the Parada Martiana.

Later, the police and officials from the Ministry of the Interior (MININT) arrived on the scene, and did not leave until much later. According to those present, it was too late for the redemption that the government was attempting. If you don't go, you're lazy. If you go, you're an opportunist. "A whole bunch of shameless bastards showed up in funny cars," says Jorge. "I didn't see any of them in a Lada or a UAZ jeep. They were all in silly cars." The officials that Jorge describes with peerless precision as a "bunch of shameless bastards" were the first secretary of the Party and the governor of Havana, or Luis Antonio Torres Iríbar and Reynaldo García Zapata, respectively.

When he saw them, Dayán exploded. "Right there in the street I started screaming about how my kids were out in the streets and look what just happened, and how it was all their fault."

"And there were generals and colonels and police officers," Jorge adds, to highlight the bravery of his friend's words.

"And you can't touch me," Dayán shouted at them. "You can't lay a finger on me." And according to him, they said, "No, this isn't the time for anything like that."

The Building 102 balcony that collapsed overlooked the calle Vives, but there was another in a similar state overlooking Revillagigedo. That evening, a squad from the building company Secons came to shore up the second balcony and take away the remains of the first, while neighbors were holding a vigil for the three girls. There were candles, floral wreaths, letters from schoolfriends, teddy bears and other stuffed animals, an inflatable unicorn.

The apartment at the top of Building 102, now a yawning hole, is where Dayán lived for almost twenty years until Secons set about demolishing the building in November 2019. Eleven people lived in the apartment, most of them children. According to the latest official figures (published in 2017), Cuba has a housing deficit of 883,000 homes, almost of quarter of them in Havana, where, in 2016, 34,400 people were living in properties where their lives are at risk. The figures have only increased since.

First, a beam in the facade collapsed, and Dayán's family were forced to hole up at the back of the building, until they finally had to split up. Some ended up in hostels, others in the homes of other families. These days, Dayán lives—or more exactly, sleeps—in Nuevo Vedado with his two children.

"The counterweight is the embedded part of a beam that holds it in place and stops it falling or collapsing. By removing the upper part of the wall, the beam was left hanging in midair," says Jorge, referring to the girders that support the balconies and are only slightly embedded in the internal structure. "The following morning, I was in the bar on the corner," he continues. "There was a work detail official from MININT, and I saw them tugging on one of the beams of the balcony that was still standing, and it just came away in their hand. They dragged it out into the street and took photos from every angle they possibly could. Coincidentally, this was the section that had collapsed and killed the girls." The balconies were not properly attached.

Shortly after the accident, the official media published a propaganda version of events attributed to a "bystander" that did much to absolve the government of responsibility and shift blame onto passersby. "They were going past one day, and three bricks fell, and they just left them. Then officials cordoned off the street with yellow tape so no one could go past. But people are careless, they ignored the tape, drivers who didn't want to have to make U-turns just drove over it. After that, there was nothing to warn about the risks," according to the witness.

Experience, however, tells us that no one is less careless about the possibility of collapse, or more aware of the situation, than those who know that a building might fall on them at any minute. A nurse standing under a balcony on the corner of Águila and Misión suddenly starts and jumps into the middle of the street, loudly berating herself: How could you forget? You're not supposed to stand there. One of Sergio's friends, a police officer, tells the story of how, up on Monte, a number of cars beeped their horns, shouting, "Officer, get onto the sidewalk," but he doesn't get onto the sidewalk for anyone. Fear hangs over unprotected heads. "Around here, two or three buildings will collapse in the coming days. I think there might even have been one today," Sergio says finally, a little scornfully, as though accustomed to it. The extraordinarily high level of risk puts a stop to the facile notion that these incidents are down to chance.

The official version of the demolition of Building 102 upset the residents of the barrio Jesús María. "There never was any reinforcement on buildings here, never," Alberto Naranjo says angrily. "People from the brigade came, and they never put up anything, they never put up yellow tape like the one they're talking about. Laborers never wear hard hats, but that night they put on hard hats to shore up the other balcony. This is what had to happen for them to do anything. They waited until three girls were dead before they . . . I mean. It's unbelievable."

The last time Alberto saw Rocío, the little girl was sitting on the steps of the building, in her long black skirt, preparing to head off to her Spanish dance class.

"All three of them were pretty, all three of them were pretty, all three of them were pretty," says Dayán over and over, running a hand over his face as though to wipe away a strain. "Sixth grade, all three of them in the same class."

Grieving

For days afterwards, people came and stared at the ruins. There was not a smile left standing. Ghosts passed, covering their eyes and howling, and a deranged man leaped from his head clutching a dagger, seeking a guilty God.

—VICENTE HUIDOBRO, *TEMBLOR DE CIELO*

The three girls lived equidistant from the place where they died, a central point less than 200 meters from their homes. Rocío, on calle Esperanza; Lisnavy, on Águila; María Karla, on the corner of Vives and Factoría.

Near Building 102 is a window where bunches of plantains hang from an open grille. There are also anemic lettuces, green guavas, and ripe guavas piled up in fan covers that have been converted into vegetable crates.

A rare tranquillity hovers over Jesús María. In the park, there are three or four ceiba trees and a statue to someone named Manuel Jesús Doval, "eminent orator and wise teacher to the youth of Havana." The school has a church steeple. Yellow walls, tiled roof, brown cupola. The puddles of fetid water along calle Vives, which has insufficient drainage, are like murky mirrors reflecting this scene that looks like something from another era, but is from this one, vaulted by a dark, leaden sky.

It feels as though all sound has been excised from the place, though it is still marked by a strident gesture. It is the silent tape of a carnival of grief. Two teenagers walk through the park. They don't seem to be listening to anything, or are listening to something only they can hear, but they move like experienced dancers of *reparto*, the most hard-core version of Cuban reggaeton, a frenzied, ear-splitting style with a familiar rhythmic bassline that originated in poor Havana neighborhoods like this one.

Cultural officials despise reparto. They would like to brush it under the carpet, just as political officials would brush the barrio Jesús María under the carpet, this inconvenient neighborhood of poverty and inevitable tragedy. "There's no music allowed," says Sergio. "The barrio has come to a standstill, and this is a neighborhood where there are always loudspeakers out on the street. We take music seriously around here. Rumba practice, people singing hymns."

The neighbors had thought of designing a commemorative plaque to be placed at the site of the accident, but the idea faded. On the Sunday following the collapse, the Iglesia de las Mercedes gave a mass for the girls; people sang children's songs. Dayán attended the mass, just as he did the vigil and the funeral. Talking about these events, his words are charged with a fierce, unconscious irony—they are words with two meanings. "The government showed up at the funeral home. I've got no complaints about the government on that score. At the funeral home, at the cemetery . . . the government behaved really well toward the families and the other mourners. That's one thing we can't complain about." Sergio, for his part, decided not to attend any of the events. Dayán visited the families every day. Sergio could not bring himself to look them in the face.

In the meantime, MININT had launched an investigation to find someone to blame. There was also talk of a cell phone and a chain that were stolen after the accident. The rescuers saw nothing. "It must have happened when the rubble was being cleared," says Sergio. "Who would steal something at a time like that?" He had already been to Picota police station for an interview. That just left Dayán. They came looking for him when he was on guard duty, but Dayán managed to postpone the interview.

"These people came looking for me to ask me whatever questions they want. I don't know why, when I'm the one who rescued a girl only to have her slip through my fingers," he says. "What questions are they going to ask?"

"Don't be afraid," the officers said.

"I'm not afraid," he said.

On Tuesday, February 4, a couple of days after the mass, a spontaneous memorial was organized in the local park. People were going to read poems, and a young reggaeton artist, a local boy into reparto, was going to sing something he had written for the girls, a song that was already being shared on cell phones by neighborhood boys and even some of the grown-ups.

"This is a barrio that, at first glance, might seem like a slum," says Jorge, "the kind of neighborhood where people live in their own little world. It's not. Day to day, people look out for themselves, but when you get a tragedy like this, this place is a single neighborhood, a single world, a single person. It's completely united, this incident proved it. More than proved it."

The police moved the memorial from two o'clock to four, then from four o'clock to six, only to finally cancel it. "They said it was because members of the Ladies in White would infiltrate the event. But there was no one there. It was a lie. The police hung around until 11:30 p.m. and no one showed up," says Alberto, the cook. So no sign of the Ladies in White? "I didn't see anyone, white or black," says Dayán, still seething. "The only people in the park were five patrol officers," says Jorge.

The Ladies in White—*las Damas de Blanco*—are one of the major dissident groups in Cuba. Suggesting that they might be present was a pretext for the government to shut down an event that had been collectively organized since none of the neighbors wanted to politicize the deaths of the girls or, in other words, to reduce a terrible event to a series of slogans.

If it is true that, in Cuba, such incidents often result in tragedy being cheapened at the expense of the ideological struggle, with victims being sidelined and used as crude tools to defend or attack the government with the usual inflammatory language, this particular incident *did* have a political dimension, in the sense that these deaths masked a public responsibility. To refuse to acknowledge this fact is to portray the incident as pure melodrama, and, stripping the girls' deaths of their context (black girls, lower class, derelict neighborhood), demeans the magnitude of the tragedy, distorts the causes, and gives free rein to impunity while employing an abstract idea of grief.

"Let them summon me to appear before President Díaz-Canel, him standing there and me here, and then order me to put a bullet in my brain," says Jorge. "Because I risked my neck for someone else. Because that could have been my granddaughter, my child, my wife. It could have been me."

On the little phone in the palm of his hand, Jorge scrolls through blurry photos, grainy images of local facades and buildings liable to collapse that he has been patiently documenting over the past few months: a sort of collective consciousness, a civic memory that no one heeds. "I went to see the the head of the sector and I said, 'So, you're the head of the sector? Well, you need to deal with this, and this, and this . . .'" He jabs his finger at the pictures.

Immediately afterward, like an expert guide to the ruins, he takes me on a tour of various buildings he has documented. The broken columns of a police warehouse, crumbling balconies, derelict buildings like ominous dead mouths where, at night, people sleep among the rats, people who have migrated from the east of the country, who have no home, who are illegally living in Havana, and also the building on the corner of Cárdenas and Gloria with a slogan on the wall, "Long Live July 26!," which Jorge thinks should be replaced with a poster that reads, "Hopefully still standing on July 26!" Of all these places, none matters more to Jorge than the truly terrifying facade of the bodega on the corner of Vives and Florida.

A deep crack runs from top to bottom, and panes of glass hang precariously from the two upper windows. "I'm sick and tired of talking to Pedro, the head of the government Public Health Service, and I'm sick and tired of talking to Marlén, the head of Housing Works," he says. "Then there's a warehouse that belongs to the ANAP (the National Association of Small Farmers) and, from what I've heard, the manager or the director of the warehouse went to Housing Works, and they sent him to the Institute of Physical Planning, who told him to go back to Housing Works, who sent him back to Physical Planning. They bounced him around the place, and we're talking about an elderly man who can't go running around all over Havana."

Jorge is particularly angered by the fact that, at some point after the balcony of Building 102 collapsed, a Tadano truck with a crane demolished two supporting columns of the house directly opposite the bodega, and then never came back to finish the work. "On the phone, Marlén told me that they're conducting a study," he says angrily, "because they have to shore up the building before they can demolish it. My God, I'm not telling you not to shore it up! But it can't be in 2022. It has to be next week." He takes a breath and continues. "They keep saying that the building hasn't been demolished, a form has to be filled in that needs to be authorized by God knows who. The customers who use the bodega and the butchers are going to wind up as corpses under the rubble of this building. Because sooner or later it's going to collapse, make no mistake. In the end, we get no response. As long as they haven't got the form, there's nothing to be done."

This is not needless intransigence, but evil inefficiency.

Inside the buildings, the situation is no different. Alberto, the cook, lives on one of the upper floors of 918 Águila, between Misión and Esperanza. He has to climb steep stairs and then navigate a series of open spaces, including a narrow concrete bridge, in order to get to his ruined home. They knocked down the building next to his, leaving him with no roof and no side wall.

Alberto blames the government and complains about various city and provincial officials who never listen to what he has to say and who suggest he forget the whole thing. On this particular day, his home is flooded with dirty water, which he shovels out onto the patio so it can drain away. He has been everywhere, including the Council of State, and has spent the night sleeping outside every department—Party, Government, Public Health. Long waits, first sixty days, then three months. His housing file has been dropped, he tells me, "but if I've got $200, they'll give it to me." He is the cook at the local school and he sleeps out in the open, with only some ramshackle corrugated iron sheets for shelter.

Santería does not seem to have helped him much, either, but it is a kind of refuge. His godfather, a babalawo named Angelito, happens to be Rocío's stepfather, having adopted the girl when she was two. Like a dutiful godson, Alberto goes to the house on calle Esperanza whenever he can to talk to Angelito. Right now, the family do not want to talk to anyone else. From the upstairs room, all that can be heard are the wails of Rocío's mother, Gloria, a woman of thirty-five. In the all-consuming atmosphere of grief, mothers are the last stage of language, the point where words fall apart, where everything has been said.

This is probably why María Karla's house is boarded up. Her family have temporarily moved back to where they lived before moving to Havana a few months ago. María Karla had only been at the school since September.

Lisnavy's mother, Magdaly, has moved out to stay at her husband's place, because she and her daughter shared a room and she cannot bring herself to sleep there. She gave Lisnavy's schoolbooks to her teacher so that some other student can use them next year. She also threw out her daughter's half-filled exercise books. Blank pages, half-finished homework brutally interrupted, lessons that no one is ever going to write now.

In a room on the third floor of a building at the rear of Quintín Banderas school, on a table laid with a white tablecloth, the family created a little shrine, a modest, austere expression of grief. There was a picture of Lisnavy in a pink frame, a flat piece of stone on which they set a glass of water containing a crucifix. There was a vase of daisies and sunflowers. The picture frame and the stone were propped against a copy of *Alice in Wonderland*, bright green with pink lettering, perhaps one of Lisnavy's favorite books.

"It's a lie, what people are saying about the government giving us money," Margarita said, hoarse and heartbroken, from her seat on the sofa. "They haven't given us a peso, but they have treated us very well." With her was another daughter, a granddaughter, and another relative. All of them somber, barely present. Some moments later, Margarita returns to the point: "The government did everything they could. They took care of us." Took care of them in what way? "They picked us up and they took us to the vigil and then to the cemetery. They gave us cars, they gave us coffee, they gave us food."

Just as Margarita was explaining that she has been living in Jesús María for sixty-five years, Magdaly came through the door like a raging flood sweeping everything in its wake. Mixed race, not particularly tall, with green eyes and short hair dyed blond. She didn't want anyone in here, she screamed. She screamed a lot of other things, each scream choking back another in her throat. Sometimes two screams would intermingle, and a series of muffled sounds came from her gut in fits and starts, her furious tongue lashing out in a frenzy of invective. When she paused for breath, she seemed to inhale all the air in Jesús María—until she used up the last of those reserves and trailed off, only to start up again.

That same Friday, a little later, in a house in calle Vives between Florida and Alambique, some people were already listening to the catchy reparto song called "Normalmente," performed by the local reggaeton artist Wildey with Yomil and Dany. No one suggested turning the music off, no one said anything. On the cusp of night, in the dim light of a garage with green doors, boys and girls from Jesús María came down onto the floor and they danced and smiled. They were buzzing, brimming with energy. It was a little party among the yellow balloons and the baby buggies.

Eleven days had passed. Something was beginning to be left behind.

BOARDING PASS

The more power you give to power, the harder they'll come and
fuck you.   —MOLOTOV

The immigration officer took my passport and told me to stand aside
and wait. The pandemic era had begun. Inside the face mask, my
breath condensed, misting my glasses. That was an acceptable metaphor for Cuba, a country in a mask, its breath constrained, its gaze
blurred by the breathy fog. Everything that can be simplified stems
from an unfair order. The night before, we had gotten a friend out of
jail. I stayed up into the early hours, drinking too many beers as we
celebrated in a club on 25th Street, while the fingernail of freedom
opened a gash of amazement in the mud of our bodies.

A woman appeared and took my passport. They had been waiting for me. A few weeks earlier, they had called me on my cell phone
to interrogate me. I rejected the call. Later a police officer had been
seen prowling around a friend's house. He asked several of the neighbors about me. They were like the shadow of the medieval wolf.
They slipped behind walls, slithered under a cart, emitting a hoarse
growl. You longed for them to appear so you could finally stop feeling scared.

Fear had settled into us like an icy prosthesis, like a screw buried in flesh. The social body had no voice, subjected as it was to a

medical experiment by the political police. We were accustomed to the dearth of shock, the bureaucratic expression of fear. As a result, a primary way to escape this dictatorship was to embrace it, to go looking for it. When power is forced to show itself, it is invariably weakened.

Some minutes passed. Stretched out by a kind of sadness, the historical sadness of the ultimate absurdity. Why were things as they were? The woman came back with my passport and told me to follow her. An officer in a military uniform, curt, unflustered. She seemed aloof to everything, but I knew that once even she had danced to reggaeton, watched pornography, eaten *frijoles negros.*

We walked past Immigration and Customs. My passport was stamped, they were going to let me leave. Havana was far behind.

Though we had created a future for the city, scrawled on the air with a delirious pencil; though we had moved in lockstep like automata, it was here that the city had finally run aground and been left behind. But behind what? Behind life, perhaps? There was no map of time, no future path, not even in the escape or flight in which Havana once again appeared as it had formerly been: the promise of rescue, of temptation, of personal discovery. Havana had become a city perched precariously between the mists of melancholy and the snare of indifference. Havana still made sense to me only through the salt line of its stifling political situation, one that at any other time would have prompted disgust or contempt. A situation that was contingent, fragile, but now felt like justice deferred.

In an hour and a half, my flight to Mexico City would take off. I desperately wanted to go back. I had spent six months away from that superstition that Lucia Berlin describes as "fatalistic, suicidal, corrupt. A pestilential swamp. Oh, but there is graciousness. There are flashes of such beauty, of kindness and of color, you catch your breath."

The woman led me to one of her superiors. He was a tall, ath-

letic man, with green eyes; he was holding a clipboard of some sort.
I was interested to note his affability—here was a genuinely person-
able man thrust into an arbitrary situation. We said little; I appre-
ciated that. He told me it was just a matter of a few questions; they
would not take up much of my time. He was lying, of necessity. No
man in his official position, who had no opportunity to resign his
post, could possibly be my ally when the entire country had made
itself my enemy. A good man in a bad situation becomes a bad man
who pretends.

I walked past the toilets and the trinket shops of Terminal 3, the
tacky theme park of symbols of the Revolution: the boxes of Cohíba
cigars, the bottles of Havana Club, the faces of Che Guevara. A pop-
art patchwork of tattered ideology, a tapestry of dreams so often
patched with terror that the patches had become the whole tapestry.

I passed another checkpoint and the official left me in a cramped,
soulless office. Two men were seated at a desk. I had to sit facing
them. Finally. I wanted to see who they were. I stared at them. Their
faces were half-hidden by green masks, that sinister dark green of the
public hospitals. So, this was who they were. I had seen them so often
before, I ran into them on every street, every day of my life in Cuba.

Any Cuban prepared to stare into a crowd, to look along a line
of people waiting outside a bodega, to watch the popular national
video clips of ragged, boisterous crowds would instantly recognize
these two men. Any Cuban had only to look in the mirror, and, if he
did not put his fist through the glass, did not gash his hand, did not
take a hammer to the mirror, he would see them there too.

They were not the classic good cop/bad cop partnership. One,
the senior officer, was short, squat, and spouted drivel. The other
was broad, powerful, almost too big for his chair, and did not seem
to have any particular role in this scenario. Perhaps, as Barbara
Demick describes in her book *Nothing to Envy: Ordinary Lives in
North Korea*, they were assigned in pairs for the same reason that

foreign journalists in North Korea are assigned two guides, so that each can monitor the other, thereby ensuring neither strays from the official script. All things considered, as far as these two officers were concerned, I was a foreign journalist, from the specific subspecies of foreigner composed of Cubans who have renounced the native soil of Castroism.

I suspected the second officer was here in order to observe and learn. A rookie officer supporting a veteran officer thereby rounding out the inquisitorial process to the totalitarian machine whose cruelty stems not from intelligence but from stupidity.

I asked their names. They were called something like Carlos or Alejandro or Jorge. Fake names, the same old names, the names of dead kings. They didn't have the names Yasmany or Yasiel, real names, the names of real people who sweated real sweat. I felt sure that they answered to Maikel or Yandro when they stepped out into the street, and people could see them struggling to get by, enduring the same harsh sun as everyone else.

They always used aliases, and nothing betrays a person more than an alias. A number of other journalists who wrote for the magazine I edited were also interrogated during this period, in the midst of the global pandemic. Since the word belonged to history, it was the oppressor who was forced to hide. It was the oppressor who could not reveal his name, who had to move like a phantom through this room of the last judgment, an unassuming yet decisive room where we were gambling with the value of that curious creature, freedom.

From whom is the oppressor hiding, since it is he who oppresses? He is hiding from some future moment, from a time that some of us had launched ourselves into, which was precisely why we were being interrogated. Beneath the mask of some present guilt, what the oppressors were really asking was how it would work, this moment of ours, this moment they could not comprehend. It's fragile, we would have told them, it is not a closed time like the one in which you live.

But those who ask lots of question have no wish to listen, only to defeat the other.

In this country I was fleeing, people died at the age of eighty and existed only from Wednesday to Thursday, constantly tiring themselves out over short distances. One day at a time for a whole lifetime, this was all that had been allocated to us. What was devastating about totalitarianism was this oppressive, unchanging, endlessly recurring moment.

The senior officer had a Havana accent, gruff and more prosodic; the other had an accent from somewhere in the east, softer and more cadenced. The junior officer did not say much, but in what little time he was granted succeeded in highlighting his particular gifts. I had met a lot of men like him during military service. Over the years, most of them ended up pickled by booze, smelling of gasoline, desperately waiting for August so they could grab life by the balls, spend a weekend in a ramshackle campsite on the northern coast.

His boss spat words, while he felt uncomfortable in the mask that shifted and stifled him. Every time he tried to say something, the words, like flecks of spittle, caught in this fabric muzzle. There they died, unintelligible, a series of flattened sounds that neither I nor his boss could untangle. Extracting any sense from his babble was like picking up grains of rice. The chief looked on patiently, never reproaching him. The junior officer pushed the mask away and spoke out of the side of his mouth.

When his words finally reached me, the gist and tone of the question was one that his boss had already asked. I've already answered that, I said repeatedly. Maybe he too was being assessed. He had to ask a question and couldn't think of one. He was like a student who joins the last class of a particular course without having had an oral assessment and feels they have to say something just to avoid being failed.

If he didn't have any ideas, his superior had one. An idea that was fixed, absolute, and reserved for him alone. It is something we've all see once. The notion of a boorish man in a position of power who believes he is right. "How much do you get paid for your Facebook posts?" he asked. "Who pays you?" "How do you know the people that you know?" And so on. Ad infinitum. The rhetorical snail of his questions spiraled in on itself. They believed that everyone acted as they did. According to orders, for a meager pittance, governed by obscure hierarchies.

They made my head spin. The official who brought me here suddenly burst into the room and said that the flight would be taking off soon. Then he left, cordially complicit. I could not think of a way to respond to this hilarious outburst with a minimum of honesty, a shred of dignity, or even mild sarcasm, which was how I had somewhat condescendingly imagined I would react when the situation first arose. They had ensnared me in their sluglike logic. We could use a phrase from Robert Walser: "There are limits in life to any attempt to rise above vulgarity."

They questioned me about my friends, about my family. They showed me photos of people I didn't know, or had briefly encountered. What kind of connections and conspiracies had they dreamed up in their schizophrenic minds? I thought. If all of this sounds vague, that's because it is. They were looking for something that wasn't there. Something about which I knew nothing and they knew even less, something that existed in the past only inasmuch as they who had put it there. They dredged the memory of the crime in the bread crumbs of nonsense, smearing everything with sticky logic, making me dirty.

I tried as hard as I could to drive out the thought that they were producing in me, the thought of the answers, and every time it happened, I realized what I was actually trying to do was not betray anyone. Not that I could, of course, since there was no one to betray, but my interrogators were not interested in such details, because they did not want me to betray people, they wanted me to *try not* to betray anyone. To them, it was proof there existed someone behind the scenes who *could* be betrayed.

But the crime *did* exist; it was Cuba itself. The only way these two officers could save themselves was by pretending to investigate me. Late totalitarianism, as I experienced it, could not be seen as a metaphor for the total destruction of the individual, but, on the contrary, as a process by which the individual acquired antibodies in order to deceive Big Brother. He did not love Big Brother, he cuckolded him, but he served Big Brother, because not only did he realize that he was being deceived, he wanted to be deceived, thereby eventually creating the sort of dishonest, dissembling individual who was unfaithful to himself, and whose antibodies were just another symptom of the disease.

At the end of the day, in totalitarianism there can be no infidelity that did not already exist within the marriage, but if my interrogators did not stick to this marriage contract, and carried on investigating those who had set about destroying Cuba, all that awaited them was exile or civil death, the fate suffered by almost all those before them who had unraveled this simple crime.

In Leonardo Sciascia's novel *The Knight and Death*, the unnamed vice chief of police known only as *il Vice* is investigating the death of a famous lawyer, an investigation that leads him to none other than the president of United Industries, another temporary placeholder for power. Meanwhile, newspapers are persuaded to write stories pinning the blame on an anarchoterrorist group of dissatisfied youths called the Children of Eighty-Nine, the same year I was born. Il Vice only pretends to investigate this purported group of anarchists to keep his boss happy, but, despite the plausible new stories, he is not convinced. When he persists, and begins to get close to the truth, he is shot dead, in one of the most beautiful final scenes ever written.

It is not as though the political corruption and general frustration in Sicily described in *The Knight and Death* could not have prompted a group like the Children of Eighty-Nine to rise up. After all, I had risen up, together with many others. It was the fact that power had committed a specific crime, one they deemed manageable, necessary, and unavoidable for other reasons, and then pinned the blame on a predetermined enemy, an enemy seemingly rooted in domestic terrorism. This was one of the greatest historical successes of Castroism. We had to deal with the exhausting task of not becoming a credible enemy, one that fitted the only story they knew how to write, and instead commit our own crime.

On page 64 of my edition of *The Knight and Death* is the following bitter exchange:

"Have you noticed? It is impossible to be bored in this country: we are all Children of Eighty-nine now."

"Indeed, Children of Eighty-nine." With irony, with malice.

"What do you make of it?"

"I think it is all so much hot air, pure fantasy. And you?"

"So do I."

"I am glad you agree. I read in the papers that your office is taking the whole thing seriously."

"Yes, of course, Do you expect them to miss out on such a splendid invention?"

"That's it exactly. It seems to me something invented round a coffee-table, as a game, as a calculation . . . what is going to become of these poor devils, these poor idiots who want to continue believing in something after Khrushchev, after Mao, after Fidel Castro and now with Gorbachev? They must be thrown some kind of sop, something which can be tossed back in the oven after two hundred years, something soft and scented with celebrations, rediscoveries and re-assessments: and inside the same hard stone to break the teeth."

The cake reheated after two hundred years is the French Revolution, and one slice of that cake is the notion and the structure of the Republic. In a free interpretation of *The Knight and Death* as non-fiction novel, maybe the ominous "Children of Eighty-Nine" could bite into the cake and avoid the stone.

The officers asked me about Luis Manuel Otero, an artist friend of mine they had arrested on trumped-up charges and been forced to release the night before. They asked how long we had known each other, what had brought us together. This had all been written already. It was they who had brought us together, obviously, though I'm not sure I told them that.

The third officer reappeared. Ten minutes to takeoff. At this point, they adopted a clumsy tactic. They suggested we could have coffee when I came back to Cuba. Just something informal, they didn't want to issue a summons. For an instant, I freaked out, as though I'd already agreed. I remembered that while doing military service, a counterintelligence officer had called me into his office to ask me to rat out other soldiers if they absconded or slept during sentry duty. Such offers triggered in me a particular kind of revulsion.

I said no. The only way we're going to talk is if you get a summons, I blurted out. They asked what date I was coming back. I didn't know. They told me they would see me when I got back. I told them to do whatever they had to. Then they resorted to a little sophistry. My decision not to come in for an interview after they called me on my cell phone demonstrated a defiance that was unlike me, they said. I told them they had no idea what I was like. In all honesty, I had no idea either, but it was a phrase that, however clichéd, came in useful at that moment—it might slow them down and it sounded good.

They spoke as if it was they who had called my cell phone. They were right. Although we were in Havana and the call had come from Matanzas, a completely different province, I was dealing with a single creature that, according to time or place, could manifest itself in particular individuals without being fragmented. There was nothing to differentiate between them.

The interrogation had gone on for more than an hour. It is tempting to see such encounters as Kafkaesque. They're not, they are unworthy of the term. There had been too much talk. In Kafka, officers don't ask questions, they have no need to uncover anything. Their actions are brutal; their speech is terse and peremptory and has the dual effect of closing one door only to open up a dizzying network of pathways, and it is in this labyrinth, rather than behind the closed door, that the miserable prisoner is trapped.

By the time the interrogators tried to pressure me, it was already too late, they had run out of time. The third officer reappeared to say that he could no longer hold the flight. Before I left, there was a panicked pause in which they explained that that was why I should report to them as soon as they called my cell phone, allowing us to have a relaxed conversation and avoiding the need for them to send a patrol car to pick me up. This wasn't a conversation, I said, it was an interrogation. An interrogation, they informed me, was something much worse. They spluttered something else, but by now I was no longer listening, we were all completely numbed.

The whole encounter seemed utterly anachronistic. This was March 14, 2020, a time when Stalinist aesthetics could be seen only as folklore. Outside, the news was all about the pandemic. Before long, tens of thousands would be dying all over the world. Three days earlier, Cuba had identified its first cases of coronavirus.

I rushed onto the plane and looked for my seat. The passengers looked at me disapprovingly. They probably assumed I had left everything until the last minute. In my seat, with my seatbelt buckled, with no battery on my cell phone, I collapsed. It was as though I had sat down twice, or as though I had left a part of me behind. But this was not the only part of me that had lagged behind. Over the following days in Mexico City, various parts that had been lingering in the interrogation came back to me.

It was understandable. There had been a rift in reality, such that you arrived at a place as you were leaving it. The flight took off. I closed my eyes and allowed myself to glide into the lofty darkness of nowhere in particular. What had been was outweighed by what was yet to come.

CARLOS MANUEL ÁLVAREZ is a journalist and author. He is the director of the Cuban online magazine *El Estornudo*. He regularly contributes to the *New York Times*, *El País*, and the *Washington Post*. In December 2016 he was selected among the best twenty Latin American writers born in the 1980s at the Guadalajara Book Fair in Mexico; in May 2017 he was included in the Bogotá39 list of the best Latin American writers under 40; and in April 2021 he was chosen by a panel of judges for inclusion in *Granta*'s second Best Young Spanish-Language Novelists issue. In April 2021 he also received the Don Quijote Prize from the King of Spain International Journalism awards for his article "Tres niñas cubanas," published in *El Estornudo*. In addition to *The Tribe*, he is the author of the novel *The Fallen*.

FRANK WYNNE has translated works by authors including Michel Houellebecq, Patrick Modiano, Virginie Despentes, Jean-Baptiste Del Amo, Javier Cercas, and Almudena Grandes. His work has earned various awards, including the IMPAC Prize (2002), the Independent Foreign Fiction Prize (2005), the Scott Moncrieff Prize (2008, 2016), and the Premio Valle Inclán (2011, 2013).

RAHUL BERY translates from Spanish and Portuguese and is based in Cardiff, Wales. His full-length translations include *Kokoschka's Doll*, by Afonso Cruz, and *Rolling Fields*, by David Trueba.

The text of *The Tribe* is set in Adobe Garamond Pro.
Book design by Rachel Holscher.
Composition by Bookmobile Design and Digital
Publisher Services, Minneapolis, Minnesota.
Manufactured by McNaughton & Gunn on acid-free,
100 percent postconsumer wastepaper.